INTERNATIONAL
ECONOMIC INSTABILITY

ECONOMICS HANDBOOK SERIES

SEYMOUR E. HARRIS, *Editor*

ADVISORY COMMITTEE: Edward H. Chamberlain, Gottfried Haberler, Alvin H. Hansen, Edward S. Mason, and John H. Williams. *All of Harvard University.*

International Economic Instability

The Experience after World War II

Joseph D. Coppock

Professor of Economics, Earlham College

McGRAW-HILL BOOK COMPANY, INC.

New York   San Francisco   Toronto   London

INTERNATIONAL ECONOMIC INSTABILITY

To Esther McKenzie Coppock

PREFACE

This study is an outgrowth of my academic interest and governmental involvement in the problem of international economic instability. In studying and teaching courses in international economics and economic fluctuations, I have found the international aspects of the instability problem intriguing—and not very satisfactorily described and analyzed. From 1945 to 1953 and again in 1961–62 I dealt with this problem from the vantage point of the United States Department of State in connection with a variety of policy proposals.

The opportunity to undertake intensive research in this field came in 1959–60 as a result of my receiving a sabbatical leave from Earlham College and a National Research Professorship from the Brookings Institution. The research work was done at Stanford University through the courtesy of the Food Research Institute.

This study is largely descriptive and analytical. There is very little abstract theorizing in it. Policy considerations are in the background except in the final chapter. I believe that the description and analysis do, however, expose the inadequacies of simple theories and throw some new light on policies in this field.

Fortunately, most of the statistical series carry through the year 1958, which in many ways can be considered the last year of the post-World War II economic reconstruction period. Inflation had been brought under control in many countries, balances of payments in the principal countries were fairly close to equilibrium, international monetary reserves of the principal countries had been substantially restored, and the currencies of the principal trading countries were generally convertible. Thus this study treats a rather well-defined historical period, 1946 to 1958.

Lothar H. Huhne, Patricia E. Rogow, Joseph Bornstein, and Margaret P. Apgar provided competent statistical and clerical assistance. Professor Frank W. Fetter of Northwestern University read the manuscript and made many useful suggestions. My principal acknowledgment is to my wife, Esther McKenzie Coppock, to whom this book is dedicated. She graciously arranged to move the family across the country, and she encouraged completion of the manuscript in every possible way.

Joseph D. Coppock

CONTENTS

TABLES

For list of Appendix tables, see first page of the Appendix.

FIGURES

Chapter I

THE PROBLEM OF INTERNATIONAL ECONOMIC INSTABILITY

Instability in the trade and financial relations among nations has frequently been an important problem for many countries. Indeed, with the increasing number of national states during this century, and with no prospect of a decline in the opportunities for advantageous international trade and investment, the problem may well be of greater importance in the future than it has been in the past.

Concern with the problem of international economic instability had three peaks during the first half of the twentieth century. The first was during the aftermath of World War I, the second was in connection with the Great Depression of the early 1930s, and the third was around the end of World War II, when it was widely expected that the process of reconverting the war economies to a peacetime pattern would spread economic depression and political confusion over much of the world. During World War II an almost neurotic conviction developed on the part of many articulate persons concerned with public affairs that the United States would not be able to make the transition from war to peace without a major depression, and that other countries economically close to the United States would be dragged into the economic abyss.

These anticipations were not realized during the 15 years after World War II. International trade of the world increased in value and volume nearly every year. The United States experienced minor contractions that reached their low points in 1949, 1954, and 1958, but no major depressions or extreme inflations interrupted the overall functioning of the economy. The foreign trade and financial relations of the United States contributed to, rather than detracted from, the orderly economic reconstruction and development of other countries. Only in 1949 was there some basis for the view that the United States was exerting a depressive influence on other economies, but even in that instance Marshall Plan and other aid was at its highest postwar level ($5.2 billion). Moreover, adjustments were overdue in many countries because of inflation, over-

1

valued currencies at the official rates of exchange, and distorted production structures held over from the war years.

This book is an inquiry into the international economic relations of the post-World War II period (in particular, 1946 to 1958), with a view to (1) discovering the different degrees of instability in various kinds of international economic relations and (2) explaining them in some rational fashion. It should provide one basis for appraising and devising policies for reducing international economic instability.

Factors Underlying Postwar International Economy

Before getting into the details of post-World War II international economic instabilities, it seems desirable to point to some of the broad influences which contributed to the existence of *more* orderly international economic relations over most of the world during this period than were expected by many observers at the close of World War II. One powerful influence was the political determination, particularly in the industrial countries, to take whatever measures were necessary to avoid a depression like the one of the early 1930s. The political drive for "full employment" was strong enough after 1945 to support government policies which would keep employment reasonably close to the goal, even in the most laissez-faire countries.

A second influence was the determination in many countries to avoid extreme inflation. The determination stemmed from the experience of many countries with inflation of their currencies, particularly in connection with World War I and World War II. Inflation characterized the world economy from 1945 to 1959—and some countries experienced extreme inflation—but the inflation was not so great, nor so disproportionate, in the countries carrying on the bulk of the international trade of the world that it disrupted economic relations among nations very seriously. The median cost of living index for the 10 largest trading countries stood at 125 in 1958 (1950 = 100), and for 64 countries at 141.

Another major force which appears to have helped indirectly to reduce instabilities in international economic relations has been the expansionist military-political pressure of the Soviet Union and Communist China. This pressure gave rise to large military and foreign economic expenditures, especially by the United States, and thus contributed to the relief of the "dollar shortage," and probably raised the level of employment. The United States provided net foreign grants and credits of $67 billion from July 1, 1945, through December 31, 1958.[1]

The other major force that should be cited in this connection was the

---

[1] Of this total, $55 billion were grants; nearly $24 billion of the $67 billion were military, almost entirely grants. U.S. Department of Commerce, "Foreign Grants and Credits by the United States Government," December, 1958, Quarter.

large and fairly steady volume of *domestic* capital outlays, private and governmental, in many countries. These helped to keep employment and production at fairly high and steady levels in the segments of the economies which are most generative of instability.

In addition to these major forces which were apparently contributing to stability in the international economy, there were some forces which received much attention during the period but which do not appear to have been very important quantitatively. One was the strong political and vocal drive of the numerous underdeveloped countries for economic development. The share of these countries in world exports fell from 38.4 per cent in 1948 to 30.7 per cent in 1957.

Another factor that could have been disturbing but does not seem to have been so was the functioning of capitalist economic systems. The potentiality of large and sudden changes in demand, especially for durable goods, is at least as great in the capitalist economies now as in the past, so that severe depressions or booms *could* occur before the presumably adequate Keynesian remedies could be brought into action. Despite the improvements in money systems and various built-in compensatory arrangements, the relative stability of the principal capitalist economies during the post-World War II period, as compared with the period between World War I and World War II, would seem to be attributable more to a fortunate combination of circumstances than to a change in basic economic structure or to the application of anticyclical and full-employment policies.

The third factor which might appear as a powerful force making for international economic stability in the post-World War II period was the group of international economic policies and institutions which were created during and shortly after the war. These are represented mainly by the International Monetary Fund, the International Bank for Reconstruction and Development, and the as yet unformalized organization composed of the Contracting Parties to the General Agreement on Tariffs and Trade (created in 1947 in anticipation of the International Trade Organization, which was not established). These three institutions embody the efforts of governments to work jointly to have a satisfactory international monetary system, to have a greater flow of investment funds across national borders than would occur otherwise, and to negotiate generally low and nondiscriminatory barriers to trade among nations. The direction of the influence of these organizations and the national policies coordinate with the policies of these organizations was clearly toward a better-functioning international economy, including a reduction of international economic instability. The magnitude of their influence has been small, however, compared with the other forces at work.[2]

[2] Gross "drawings" of member countries from the International Monetary Fund

Significance of the Problem

International economic instability is important because of its effects on the level of living, on internal economic stability, on the rate of economic growth, and on the distribution of income and wealth. It is also important because of its effects on the internal and external politics of many countries. In the present and prospective configuration of international politics, the importance of international economic instability is most apparent in the context of the rivalry between the Communist countries, led by the Soviet Union, and the countries of the Free World, led by or potentially defended by the United States.

Effective resistance by the Free World to the Soviet-Communist expansionist thrust depends in considerable measure on the ability of the countries of the Free World to participate in a mutually advantageous international economic system. The need for such a system is crucial for small countries, since it offers the principal route to economic improvement and a firm basis for political cooperation. In order to put the problem of international economic instability in proper perspective, the principal elements of such an international economic system may be indicated:

A satisfactory international monetary mechanism

Low enough tariffs and other trade barriers to permit most economically advantageous trade to occur

Political and legal arrangements which facilitate international investment and enterprise

Institutional facilities to promote the interchange of persons and ideas

Special arrangements for dealing with international economic instability

A system with these elements, functioning reasonably well, would make a significant contribution to economic well-being, including economic growth.

The present study has to do with the last-mentioned of the elements of such an international economic system, namely, the arrangements for dealing with the international economic instability. The rather fragile international economy can be seriously disrupted by the lack of arrangements for dealing with the international spread of major fluctuations. The consequent internal economic distress provides one basis for political

---

($3.244 billion) amounted to ⅓ of 1 per cent (0.36 per cent) of world exports for the 12 years 1947 to 1958. Total loan disbursements by the IBRD for the same years ($3.088 billion) were about the same fraction (0.345 per cent) of world exports. If United States tariff duties as a per cent of the value of dutiable imports may be used as an index of changes in trade barriers, it may be noted that this percentage dropped from 13.87 in 1948 (the first year for the rates negotiated under GATT in 1947) to 11.15 in 1958.

disturbances. Political disturbances create opportunities for Soviet-Communist penetration and the weakening of the relative power position of the Free World. Although there are many possible sources of political disturbance and many pretexts for Soviet-Communist intervention, an economic fluctuation which emanates, or appears to emanate, from capitalist industrial countries provides an unusually good opportunity for intervention—political, propagandistic, economic, or military, in whatever combination seems effective. Moreover, quite aside from Communist pressure, many countries of the world, highly industrialized or not, are politically sensitive to external economic disturbances. The possibility of widespread and substantial international economic instability is particularly unattractive politically for the United States as the keystone of resistance to Soviet-Communist expansion, and for its close allies, since such instability would tend to disturb the alliance.

Position of the United States

There is a widely held view over the world that international economic instability is caused by the United States. This view stems in part from the natural tendency of people to blame their troubles on others, especially powerful foreign countries, but there are some more plausible reasons for this view. One is that the United States is a large factor in the world economy, with one-third or more of the "gross world product," and with one-half or so of the "gross Free World product."

A second reason is that the United States is a large factor in the international trade of the world. It had 17 per cent of total world exports and imports (combined) in 1957, for example.

Another is that the United States is an even more important source of international investment funds; it furnished, directly or indirectly, during the 1950s, approximately three-fourths of the world total. International grants come in even larger proportion from the United States.

Still another reason is that the length and severity of the Great Depression of the 1930s in the United States has been widely and repeatedly publicized over the world. Marxist and other critics depict the United States economy as continually on the brink of deep depression.

Also, foreign economic relations, though important to the United States, are not as important as they are to most other countries. Hence, changes in various imports or exports are relatively minor for the United States, but they are relatively large for other countries. They do not usually elicit corrective action by the United States government.

Another reason the United States is considered a source of international economic disturbance is that its foreign economic relations are highly political, from the point of view of domestic politics. This is illustrated vividly by congressional and public debates on the tariff throughout American history, and more recently by controversies concerning foreign aid, agricultural protection, and surplus disposal arrangements. Thus United States foreign economic connections are subject to disruption for strictly internal political reasons. By and large, the United States has not felt compelled to adapt its foreign economic policies, nor its internal economic life, to external circumstances to a very great extent. This freedom of action has had many comfortable aspects, but it has meant that other countries, because of the importance of American foreign relations to them, have generally had to do the adapting when adaptation was required.

It is small wonder, therefore, that other countries tend to look upon the United States as the major source of international economic instability and also as the major source of curative or ameliorative measures. Even allowing for some exaggeration in this viewpoint, it remains true that the size, international connections, and potential volatility of the United States economy make it a major possible source of dislocation.[3] Equally important is the fact that the United States has the economic power and international connections to play a major role in dealing with the problem of international economic instability.

In the political structure of the contemporary world it is in the interest of the United States—as well as in the interest of other countries of the Free World—to have ready for use the measures and institutional arrangements for dealing with the problem of substantial international economic instability, if and when it arises. The primary motivation, from the point of view of the United States, is undoubtedly its national security interest, but there are economic benefits also from the reduction of international economic instability, for the United States as well as for other countries. Other countries also have national security interests in its reduction, but their concern with the economic benefits is relatively greater than that of the United States. Economic instability—beyond the minimum inevitably involved in accomplishing shifts in the use patterns of resources in response to changes in tastes, resources, and technology—involves sheer economic waste, unnecessary human denial or misery, and a slowing down of the pace of economic development.

The problem would exist quite aside from the Soviet-Communist expansionist pressure. If the Soviet Union—already the sixth largest factor in international trade in 1957—would not try to thwart or sabotage cooperative efforts to deal with this and related problems, its participation in intergovernmental consultations and actions would obviously be desirable. There is little about Soviet behavior, either before or after World War II, however, to support the view that the Soviet Union would be interested in effec-

---

[3] Chapter 4 provides measures of the relative importance of individual countries as contributors of international economic instability.

tive measures to reduce international economic instability. It is good sense, of course, to leave the door open for Soviet participation, but not to fail to undertake appropriate action because of Soviet objections or absence. Large expansion of trade between the members of the Communist bloc and the countries of the Free World would tend to impede effective international action in this field, if the Soviet Union retains its traditional views.

International Consideration of the Problem—Prewar

Intergovernmental consideration of the problem of international economic instability first became important in the early 1930s, under the aegis of the League of Nations. Probably the high point during that decade was the preparation for and calling of the London Economic Conference of 1933, which was to deal with a broad range of questions of common interest. The withdrawal of the United States from the conference shortly after it had convened effectively thwarted any positive action, whether or not anything useful could have been achieved had the United States stayed. The League of Nations continued to publish valuable statistical reports and analytical studies on the problem.[4]

Although a limited international gold bullion standard was established for major currencies by 1936, and although the United States Trade Agreements Program for the reciprocal reduction of trade barriers was launched in 1934, these measures of intergovernmental cooperation represented only modest steps toward the restoration of the international economy. Nothing constructive was done to restore or improve the international capital market. The problem of instability was widely viewed as a matter to be dealt with on an individual industry or commodity basis, by means of cartels or other commodity control schemes. Despite the failure of some of these arrangements, others were initiated in the 1930s. These trade-control arrangements obviously constituted a very limited approach to the problem of international economic instability. By and large, national governments had despaired of doing much internationally. Domestic recovery programs and military measures were of necessity the dominant government concerns of the major trading countries in the late 1930s.

International Consideration of the Problem during the War

During World War II the international spread of inflationary boom conditions was not considered to be a problem of sufficient importance or

[4] Particularly noteworthy is *Economic Stability in the Post-war World,* by the League of Nations Delegation on Depressions, chaired by W. W. Riefler. The report, not published until 1945, contains probably the best comprehensive discussion of the international aspects of the problem of economic instability.

tractability to warrant international action. The economic control measures considered appropriate for war economies were handled by national governments. These included monetary and fiscal policy, foreign exchange and trade controls, price, wage, and credit controls, allocation systems, subsidies, etc. The various "combined boards," managed mainly by the United Kingdom and the United States, were concerned primarily with the adequacy of essential supplies and their allocation to uses considered most contributive to an Allied victory. Destabilizing effects on other warring or nonwarring countries did not have a high priority.[5]

It is less understandable why wartime planning for peacetime international relations did not give the problem of international economic instability a more prominent place. The real answer lies in the details of the history of the efforts to plan for the peace, mainly in Washington, but to some extent in London. The main reasons seem to be these. There was far from complete agreement, even among experts in international economics, as to *what* should be done in detail about long-run international economic cooperation in its various aspects—trade barriers, currencies, investment, cartels, commodity problems, development, stability, etc. There was even less agreement about *how* cooperative activities might be organized.[6]

In planning for the United Nations, a decision was made fairly early to emphasize the international security arrangements and to leave economic, social, and related activities mainly to loosely affiliated organizations. The idea of a coordinating Economic and Social Council eventually emerged. The United Nations Charter was brief and general in this field.[7] The con-

---

[5] S. E. Harris (ed.), *A Manual of Price Control,* U.S. Government Printing Office, 1943; Eric Roll, *The Combined Food Board: A Study of Wartime International Planning,* Stanford University Press, Stanford, Calif., 1956.

[6] This interesting topic cannot be pursued here. Three major studies which throw light on this subject are: Ruth B. Russell and J. E. Muther, *A History of the United Nations Charter,* The Brookings Institution, Washington, 1958; R. E. Asher et al., *The United Nations and the Promotion of the General Welfare,* The Brookings Institution, Washington, 1957; E. F. Penrose, *Economic Planning for the Peace,* Princeton University Press, Princeton, N.J., 1953. In a paper presented at the Midwest Economics Association meeting in April, 1954, on "Why the International Trade Organization Did Not Come into Existence," the present author traced some of the history. Apparently, nobody closely acquainted with the wartime details in Washington has undertaken to write a detailed history. An official study is U.S. Department of State, *Postwar Foreign Policy Preparation, 1939–1945,* 1950.

[7] The United Nations Charter, Article 55, states: " . . . the United Nations shall promote: *a.* higher standards of living, full employment, and conditions of economic and social progress and development. . . . " Article 57 provides that "specialized agencies . . . shall be brought into relationship with the United Nations. . . . " Article 60 states that "responsibility [for this coordination lies] in the General Assembly, and, under the authority of the General Assembly in the Economic and Social Council. . . . " Article 61 provides that the Economic and Social Council shall consist of 18 members, and Article 62 that it "may make or

ception was that of quasi-independent organizations—"specialized agencies"—subject to some degree of coordination by the Economic and Social Council. This Council was also to have subordinate commissions and subcommissions.

As plans developed during the war, it became apparent that five specialized agencies and one commission would be concerned in part with the problem of international economic instability; it was expected that the Economic and Social Council would be able to pull the various threads of the problem together. The commission, under ECOSOC, was first conceived of as a general economic commission, but it was given the name of "Economic and Employment Commission" in January, 1946, in order to emphasize UN responsibility in the stability field, as a result of the pressure of various small countries, led by Australia, that feared a United States depression and the collapse of international demand. Thus it was the intention of the early organizers of the United Nations that one United Nations body should have a continuing concern with this problem.

The five specialized agencies which, according to their planners, would have direct interest in international economic instability were the International Monetary Fund (IMF), the International Bank for Reconstruction and Development (IBRD), the International Trade Organization (ITO), the Food and Agricultural Organization of the United Nations (FAO), and the International Labor Organization (ILO). Except for the ILO, these organizations were conceived out of the experience of the 1930s, in the expectation that the postwar years would need permanent specialized international agencies, in addition to normal intergovernmental contacts and the United Nations forums, in order to deal with international economic problems. The International Monetary Fund was to provide a pool of international short-term capital as a supplement to national monetary reserves, a minimum code of behavior in the international monetary realm, and a forum for negotiating changes in exchange rates and related matters which were manifestly of international import. The resources of the Fund were expected to be sufficient to meet emergency short-term balance-of-payments deficits. Hence, the Fund represented one of the main elements in the international program for reducing the international impact of economic change.

The International Bank was devised to increase the volume of and incidentally reduce the volatility of international investment, compared with the interwar period. It was given a substantial capital and broad powers to borrow, and authority to lend and guarantee loans to governments or

---

initiate studies and reports . . . and make recommendations to the General Assembly, to the Members, and to the Security Council." Article 68 states that the "Economic and Social Council shall set up commissions. . . . "

economic units within member countries. Although the emphasis in the planning was on "productive" loans, less instability in the international flow of long-term capital was expected to result from the Bank's operations. Hence, the International Bank for Reconstruction and Development represents a second intergovernmental institution which can contribute to the reduction of international economic instability.

The International Trade Organization was to provide countries with a set of rules to govern international trading relations and an organization through which mutually beneficial negotiations with respect to trade barriers would be carried on and disputes settled. The conception of the ITO was first laid out systematically in the United States *Proposals for Expansion of World Trade and Employment* in November, 1945, after prolonged interdepartmental discussions and arguments and after intermittent discussions with the British, dating back to mid-1941. The final form of the ITO Charter, known as the "Havana Charter for an International Trade Organization," was not reached until March, 1948, at the United Nations Conference on Trade and Employment. The organization did not come into existence, mainly because of the failure of the United States to ratify the Charter, but the central parts of the Charter, the commercial policy provisions, were in effect as an international agreement after 1947, under the General Agreement on Tariffs and Trade.[8]

The relation of the ITO Charter to international economic instability was indirect rather than direct. It is plausible, but not rigorously demonstrable, that if nations lowered their trade barriers and applied the remaining trade barriers on a nondiscriminatory basis the larger volume of trade that would result, with multilateral balancing rather than bilateral balancing of international accounts, would be conducive to less instability in international trade. This was the main contribution the ITO could have been expected to make to international economic stability. There was, in addition, a pledge by members to "take action designed to achieve and maintain full and productive employment" (Article 3), "with due regard to the desirability of employing methods which expand rather than contract international trade" (Article 4). Also, members should "seek to avoid measures which would have the effect of creating balance-of-payments difficulties for other countries" (Article 3).

In the course of the prolonged negotiations, provisions were added which relieved countries of their obligations to pursue nondiscriminatory trade

[8] Much of the background of the ITO is provided in *The United States and the Restoration of World Trade,* by W. A. Brown, Jr., The Brookings Institution, Washington, 1950. Chapter VII of Asher et al., *op. cit.,* provides a summary. See also Penrose, *op. cit.,* passim; and W. Diebold, *The End of ITO,* Princeton University Press, Princeton, N.J., 1951; C. Wilcox, *A Charter for World Trade,* The Macmillan Company, New York, 1948.

policies if they had declining or low monetary reserves (Article 21). During these negotiations the United States was almost universally viewed as the major source of decline in demand and the potential victim of these retaliatory trade barriers.

The ITO Charter had two other chapters which bore indirectly on the problem of international economic instability, the one on restrictive business practices (V), and the one on international commodity agreements (VI). Restrictive business practices were disapproved of, in general, and provision was made for filing complaints, investigating them, and recommending remedial action. International (intergovernmental) commodity agreements for primary commodities were not disapproved of, but they were expected to conform to certain standards and they were to come into existence only after certain formal procedures had been followed. There is no simple or clear connection between international control arrangements, of either the cartel or commodity agreement type, and international economic instability, but since the view is so widely held by various economic interest groups that the route to international economic stability is the "stabilization" of the individual international markets for particular types of goods, it may be observed that the ITO Charter represented pressure against such arrangements, compared with previously existing international pressures. Even though the ITO Charter was not ratified and the organization did not come into existence, the points of view expressed and procedures provided for in the ITO Charter have continued to characterize international policy in these spheres.[9]

While the planning for postwar organizations was proceeding with reference to the Fund, the International Bank, and the ITO, a crosscurrent developed in the form of the Food and Agriculture Organization of the United Nations, which was able to enlist strong political support from farming, welfare, and humanitarian groups. The 1943 conference, which gave birth to the FAO, sought unsuccessfully the authority to devise and administer commodity control arrangements with respect to foods and other agricultural materials. An attempt, similar to that of the FAO, to create an international minerals organization, presumably with similar trade-control powers, was abortive. The International Labor Organization, another specialized agency under the United Nations, which had occupied

---

[9] In March, 1947, the Economic and Social Council passed a resolution (30-IV) which recommended that governments follow the provisions of the commodity agreements chapter of the draft ITO Charter as a guide in dealing with international commodity problems. An Interim Coordinating Committee for International Commodity Arrangements was established to follow these matters. The committee was still functioning in 1961. A parallel attempt to have the chapter on restrictive business practices, with some modifications, endorsed by the United Nations has been before the ECOSOC various times since 1951, but as of 1961 nothing conclusive had happened.

a special position in the League of Nations structure, continued its interest in the problem of economic instability, with particular reference to the employment effects, but it did not try to acquire a major responsibility for the problem.

International Consideration of the Problem—Postwar

This has been a brief review of the wartime planning for international economic agencies which were to be concerned, among other things, with the problem of international economic instability. All of these organizations except the ITO have functioned during the postwar period. The key portions of the ITO Charter, dealing with tariffs and international trade barriers generally, have been in operation since 1947 under the General Agreement on Tariffs and Trade (GATT), and the governments which are "Contracting Parties" to it meet regularly to negotiate changes in tariffs and to settle disputes. The various organizations with an interest in the problem of international economic instability have not, however, been put to the test of a major depression or a major inflationary boom. The most severe depression of the period was that of 1949–50, and the main boom, so far as international repercussions are concerned, was in 1950–51 in connection with the Korean crisis. The International Bank and the International Monetary Fund decided to conserve their resources during the period of greatest reconstruction needs immediately after World War II, when various aid programs, particularly the Marshall Plan, were in operation. The FAO proposed two elaborate schemes for expanding the international movement of food and raw materials (the World Food Board in 1946 and the International Commodity Clearinghouse in 1949). The Economic and Employment Commission held inconclusive sessions from 1946 to 1953, when it was reorganized. An International Materials Conference set up machinery in 1951 for dealing with shortage problems in connection with the Korean crisis, but it was not extensively used.

By far the most serious consideration governments gave the problem of international economic instability during the postwar period was at the meeting of the Economic and Social Council in 1950.[10] The resolution passed by the Council in August, 1950, was the result of a lengthy and careful examination of the problem. Council deliberations were greatly facilitated by the report entitled *National and International Measures for Full Employment,* prepared by a group of experts in response to a 1949 resolution of the Council.[11]

[10] See Asher et al., *op. cit.,* chap. 9, for a similar judgment.

[11] Under the leadership of N. Kaldor. A subsequent report, *Measures for International Economic Stability* (1951), also prepared by an expert group, led by J. W. Angell, was given less attention because the Korean conflict was in full swing. Three

The documents and discussions connected with the 1950 ECOSOC resolution represented the most enlightened thinking on the subject of international economic instability at the time, and in neither governmental nor academic circles were there developments during the 1950s which represented significantly different conceptions of or approaches to the problem.

International Economic Instability a Neglected Problem

The problem of international economic instability did not receive very much attention during the 1950s by governments, international organizations, or economists. Such attention as it did have was principally in connection with the "low" and unstable export earnings of some underdeveloped countries.[12] Studies of the "terms of trade" for various countries, or groups of countries, or commodity groups, reflected a similar interest.

One of the main reasons international economic instability did not receive much attention during the 1950s is that it was not a major problem of the countries which conduct most of the international trade of the world. Neither the mild depressions of 1949–50, 1953–54, and 1957–58 nor the inflationary surges shortly after World War II and in connection with the Korean crisis were sufficient to elicit major international political attention. Economic and Social Council resolutions "noted" developments and "urged" governments to take "appropriate" actions.[13]

Despite the occasional warnings by economists and others, there is much evidence that public opinion in the industrialized countries increasingly views a fairly high and stable level of employment and economic activity as normal. Memories of the Great Depression have been fading and confidence in antidepression measures has been increasing—even though the measures have not been put to a severe test. The belief is widespread that, barring a major war, there is an excellent prospect for reasonable economic stability, accompanied by economic growth, for many countries. Governments have been able to concentrate major attention on such economic ills as gradual inflation rather than on those of stagnation and unemployment.

---

other reports of experts should be mentioned: *Commodity Trade and Economic Development* (1954), chairman, J. Goudriaan; *Trends in International Trade* (1958), prepared under GATT auspices, chairman, G. Haberler; and *International Compensation for Fluctuations in Commodity Trade* (1961), chairman, J. G. Crawford. Regular and special reports of the United Nations Secretariat contributed much to the discussions of the problem.

[12] For example, *Instability in Export Markets of Under-developed Countries,* United Nations Secretariat, 1952, as well as the reports by experts cited earlier.

[13] The United Nations *Yearbook* provides good annual summaries of issues discussed and resolutions passed by the various UN bodies.

Another aspect of this attitude of neglect is the prominence that has been given to the problem of economic development or economic growth in the postwar period. One of the major results of World War II, not fully anticipated, was the strong political drive for economic advancement in the relatively backward countries. "The revolution of rising expectations" became a force to be reckoned with. The international organizations, more numerous than ever and with representatives of the many old and new underdeveloped countries, increasingly became forums for demands upon the relatively few advanced countries for economic assistance. The rivalry between the democracies and the Communist bloc abetted the political drive of the underdeveloped countries. The representatives of underdeveloped countries frequently talked about instability in their international economic relations, but in nearly all instances they sought not a stable flow of economic resources from other countries but a flow that would increase as rapidly as possible and have no downturns. Many frankly sought an international version of the United States farm price-support system or the institutionalizing of a flow of foreign aid. Concern with instability was only incidental to their interest in the problem of economic development.

Many economists sought a conceptual framework and correlative policies which would have economic growth swallow up the problem of economic instability. Answers were sought to the question, "What are the conditions of stable economic growth?" It was hoped that the very process of maintaining a fairly high average rate of growth would in itself—by keeping capital investment progressively higher—subordinate the instability problem.[14]

The problem of disequilibrium in balances of international payments bothered many countries during the postwar period. It was widely characterized by the invidious term, "the dollar shortage," with its implication that the United States restricted the supply of dollars unduly. The problem of disequilibrium is fairly closely related to the problem of international economic instability, but they should be distinguished. First, there can be large fluctuations in international economic relations that need not involve balance-of-payments disequilibrium. Second, balance-of-payments disequilibrium can arise from domestic causes (e.g., inflationary policies) or from foreign causes (e.g., a negative shift in demand for a country's sales products), but such disequilibrium might or might not give rise to appreciable instabilities in other countries. There is a tendency, however, for relatively large disequilibria in balances of payments—or sudden corrective measures—to give rise to international economic instability, and for

[14] See, for example, E. D. Domar, *Essays in the Theory of Economic Growth,* Oxford University Press, New York, 1957, and W. J. Fellner, *Trends and Cycles in Economic Activity,* Holt, Rinehart and Winston, Inc., New York, 1956.

relatively large instabilities to give rise to balance-of-payments disequilibria. During the postwar period the many countries with balance-of-payments disequilibria were fortunate, by and large, in not having to cope with large instabilities emanating from other countries. The problems of establishing realistic exchange rates and fairly general convertibility of currencies, with a gradual reduction of exchange controls and other trade barriers, would have been far less tractable than they actually were if there had been large fluctuations in economic activity generally, and particularly in the international sector.

One more plausible reason why governments have not done much about the problem of international economic instability is that economists have not studied the problem with the same intensity with which they have studied several others, and hence have not publicized systematic measures for coping with the problem. The problem of international economic instability has been studied mostly as one aspect of the general problem of instability, particularly cyclical instability, and as one aspect of international economics. It has been touched lightly by many investigators. Nothing like the time or energy has been devoted to it that has been devoted to the problem of achieving and maintaining equilibrium in a country's balance of international payments. Nor has it received even a tiny fraction of the amount of professional talent that has gone into the study of the domestic aspects of the problem of economic instability, particularly since the early 1930s, when Keynes's *General Theory of Employment, Interest, and Money* (1936) was being written. The Keynesian analysis, as usually translated into policy, emphasizes the domestic or national, rather than the international, aspects of the problems of unemployment and instability.[15]

Plan of Book

Chapter 2 deals with definitional and technical questions of measurement. In Chapters 3 and 4 are set forth what appear to be the principal relevant facts regarding international economic instability since World War II. Chapters 5 and 6 attempt to explain this instability, mainly by statistical analysis. Chapter 7 provides the summary and some reflections on policies for mitigating international economic instability.

---

[15] This comparative neglect of the international aspects of the instability problem is also noted in O. Morgenstern's *International Financial Transactions and Business Cycles,* National Bureau of Economic Research, 1959, and by J. J. Polak in *The Business Cycle in the Post-war World,* International Economic Association, 1955.

Chapter 2

MEASUREMENT OF INTERNATIONAL ECONOMIC INSTABILITY

The purpose of this chapter is to describe and compare ways of measuring the phenomenon with which we are concerned—international economic instability. A preliminary step, however, is a clear statement of the concept of international economic instability.

Meaning of International Economic Instability

Although it is possible to talk about international economic instability in general terms, as was done in Chapter 1, attempts to measure it, theorize about it, and develop policies for dealing with it require greater precision. The first point is that the phenomenon under investigation falls in the broad category of the *economic* relations among *nations*. Economic relations are distinguished from political, military, social, cultural, scientific, and other relations among nations. Nations are distinguished from other associations of people. We have accepted the contemporary practice of considering a group of people a nation when it has substantial self-determination of its affairs, domestic and international.

In selecting *international* economic relations for attention, we thereby put into a subordinate place the *market* analysis which so often takes first place in economic analysis. Market forces, in our framework, become one of the sets of factors affecting the international economic relations, particularly the instability with which we are concerned. It is possible, of course, to analyze economic behavior for the world basically from the point of view of markets of similar commodities, and to treat the national or international forces as factors affecting market behavior. We have selected the former approach, however, because of the general policy orientation of this study, with its focus on the relations of national states.

International economic relations may be classified into (1) trade in goods and services, (2) financial relations, (3) permanent or temporary migration of people, and (4) interchange of knowledge that is connected

16

with economic activities. Financial relations include exchange rates, capital movements, foreign investment holdings, gifts, indemnities, etc. All four of these variables, whether precisely measurable or not, change through time. Since our inquiry has to do with instability of international economic relations it is concerned with fluctuations in these variables.

We are delimiting the field, however. We are not going to deal directly with migration or with the interchange of knowledge. These are obviously important international economic relations and they obviously fluctuate through time, but we are simply choosing to exclude them from explicit inquiry. These two types of relations are indirectly reflected in the trade and financial relations, however. Movements of people are partly reflected in the tourist and other travel outlays described in the customary balances of international payments of countries, and transmission of knowledge is reflected in trade, investment changes, and other transactions that are covered in balances of payments. Another reason for not dealing with permanent migration and interchange of knowledge is that they do not seem to be the kind of variables which can be controlled in such a way as to mitigate short-run international economic instability, though both have, of course, been subject to government restriction and facilitation. There is every reason to believe, however, that they will continue to be of great importance to the development of the world economy.

Our attention is focused, therefore, on those international economic relations embraced by the notions of trade and finance. Which variables under these headings are most relevant? To answer this question, let us envisage the network of international trade and finance. Goods and services are transferred, in a legal sense, from economic units of each country to economic units of some or all other countries. The economic units may be natural persons, business firms, governments, or other organizations. Sometimes the transfer involves the physical movement of goods between countries, sometimes it does not. The transfers are described in terms of the physical units appropriate to particular items; they are also described in terms of economic value, measured or measurable in terms of monetary units. The value measure is, in this context, the price per unit multiplied by the physical quantity of the particular good or service. Alongside these "real" international exchanges of goods and services is the "financial overlay," which by and large facilitates the exchanges of goods and services.

In order to keep our inquiry within manageable bounds it is necessary to delimit the field again. We have decided, therefore, to concentrate our attention, in the first instance, on one major composite variable. This variable is the *export proceeds* from the sale of goods and services by a country to other countries. We have selected this variable rather than, for example, "foreign exchange availabilities," a more inclusive concept, in order to emphasize the foreign earning performance of any particular country. Foreign exchange availabilities of a country for a period include, in principle, (1) a country's stock of foreign exchange, gold and other other assets readily convertible into foreign exchange and (2), in addition to export proceeds, net capital imports and net donations received. If there are net capital exports or net outward donations, foreign exchange availabilities for other uses are correspondingly reduced. If capital imports involve future capital exports, as repayment or repatriation of advances, they are essentially claims on future export proceeds. Hence, export proceeds remain the fundamental variable. To the extent that capital movements or donations do not give rise to future claims against export proceeds, export proceeds do not satisfactorily summarize the forces at work. For example, foreign exchange availabilities, and hence imports, could be increased by unilateral-transfer receipts that would have no direct or close connection with exports. Such transfers, whether in the form of international grants, war indemnities, or one-way capital transfers, have not been large for many countries and have been confined to short periods for countries for which they have been large. We shall take them into account when it seems useful.

It might be contended that the value of imports of goods and services should be the variable which we should treat as most important. This is a completely valid contention from the point of view of the principal economic benefits which a country derives from its foreign financial and trade relations. There are some points against it, however. Imports of goods and services can reflect capital imports and donations received, as well as earnings from exports, and thus include some of the compensatory actions undertaken to counteract inadequacies of export earnings. Also, the degree of fluctuation of imports may reflect choices of buyers or governments rather than externally imposed necessity.

It might also be contended that the *net* trade balance for foreign transactions in goods and services (which is also *net* capital movements, including unilateral transfers, in theory though not in statistical practice) should be the variable on which we should concentrate.[1] This variable is very important from the point of view of equilibrium in a country's balance of payments, but even if it were constant it could disguise large parallel fluctuations in exports and imports for a country. Such fluctuations obviously have important ramifications for an economy, even though the balance-of-payments relation is satisfactory.

Another variable which might be considered is the "terms of trade" of a country. This variable has received much attention in recent years. It

---

[1] Padraic P. Frucht obtained a correlation coefficient of .89 between the net trade balance and net capital exports for the United States for the years 1946 to 1959. U.S. Congress, Joint Economic Committee, *Staff Report on Employment, Growth, and Price Levels,* Dec. 24, 1959, p. 448.

is the ratio of a country's export price index to its import price index, or, in more fundamental terms, the quantum of import goods and services a country can obtain for a given quantum of exports. Like its counterpart in United States agricultural economics, the farm "parity ratio," it is a measure of relative price changes. Terms of trade express, of course, a reciprocal relation, so favorable terms of trade for one country are, *ipso facto,* unfavorable terms of trade for one or more other countries. A country's export proceeds, however, depend upon price *and* quantity of exports; the imports it receives by spending its export proceeds depend on the export proceeds *and* the price of imports, as well as the decisions and ability to import more or less, by value, than current export proceeds. Thus, although the ratio of export prices to import prices is of interest, it is just one element in the situation. Moreover, to direct attention to the terms of trade would, from a policy point of view, lead toward policies which would attempt to achieve or maintain some particular pattern or range for terms of trade. The implication would be that price relations should conform to some predetermined pattern rather than perform the normally expected function of responding to and influencing demand and supply conditions in the various markets. We do not wish to overstate the point about terms of trade, for it might be sensible policy, in the light of sharply fluctuating terms of trade and other conditions, to take some actions which would have the effect of moderating them.

Hence we come back to export proceeds as the best single variable upon which to focus our attention. Export proceeds can be broken down on a commodity basis, and the values for particular commodities can, in many cases, be further divided into quantity and price components. Proceeds can also be divided by country of destination. Moreover, export proceeds can be related to gross national product or similar aggregates for a national economy. When we attempt to explain fluctuations in a country's export proceeds, we should find it illuminating to examine the markets for particular types of goods and services and to see what demand and supply changes lie behind the changes in quantity and price.

In deciding to focus on export proceeds from the sale of goods and services to foreigners as the prime variable in considering the problem of international economic instability, we do not mean to deny the possible relevance or validity of other approaches. A thorough inquiry should eventually deal with the same cluster of variables, whatever the starting point.

Domestic and International Aspects of Economic Instability

Another element in the concept of international economic instability has to do with the distinction between domestic and international, or internal and external, economic activities. Exports "come out" of the economy of a country and imports "go into" it. Exactly the same pattern exists among the regions of a particular national economy. The "real" gross national product includes exports; the "real" national income includes imports. We are taking for granted here the necessary condition of different relative scarcities of goods and services in various countries, and nonprohibitive transfer costs, as the basis for trade. The question is whether, when examining fluctuations in certain international economic relations, it is necessary to try to trace out the origin and the impact of these fluctuations in the various national economies, or, in still more general terms, throughout the entire world economy (if this concept has a counterpart in reality). The issue has been treated on a theoretical basis and in very general terms under the heading of the "foreign trade multiplier," as an amplification of the Keynesian system. The "input-output" or "network-of-international-trade" analysis also provides a frame of reference for tracing out the ramifications of changes.

The tendency of this kind of "general equilibrium" thinking, intellectually appealing though it be, is to discourage concentration of analytical efforts on the smaller number of variables which seem to be most closely related to the one under direct inquiry. In this study we are choosing to follow the less comprehensive approach. "Internal" or domestic variables will be examined only if they seem to have a close connection with the definitely international or "external" variables. It is probable that the specific internal variables which have a close association with the external variables are different from country to country and from time to time.

Measurement of Export Proceeds

The preceding discussion should have made clear the reasons for choosing export proceeds as the "primary dependent variable" in connection with the problem of international economic instability. We now turn to the specific problems involved in measuring variations in export proceeds through time.

The first question is the unit of measurement. Export proceeds are in terms of monetary values. What currency should they be expressed in? This question would not arise if all currencies were interchangeable at set ratios, or if international transactions were all conducted in one currency, or in a few currencies which were convertible into each other at fixed rates of exchange. But such is not the case. Use of each national currency does not affect comparisons of rates of change, but it precludes some international comparisons. Therefore, conversion of values into a common currency unit is necessary. During the post-World War II period most statistical collections have expressed monetary values in terms of United

States dollars when international comparisons were desired. We shall follow this practice, but the implicit errors should be noted. The appropriate rate of exchange between any given currency and the United States dollar is sometimes difficult to determine.[2] Official rates and free rates frequently diverge widely. Exchange controls and other controls blur the meaning of the rate. Also, it is misleading to express export proceeds of a country in terms of United States dollars when it actually uses the proceeds to purchase its imports, say, in Europe. Also, exchange rates used may not correspond to the appropriate "purchasing power parities," that is, to the relative internal price levels. Even so, we shall express export proceeds in terms of United States dollars, generally in accordance with International Monetary Fund practice.

Another question about measurement is whether export proceeds should be adjusted for changes in the value of money. A case could be made for such adjustment if there were available a good index of the price of internationally traded goods and services. Even if there were such an index, it would hardly be applicable to all countries, because of the different collections of goods they import and export. Conceivably the export proceeds of any particular country could be adjusted according to changes in the prices of the goods and services it ordinarily bought. One would wonder, however, about the comparability of the results. We choose not to make such corrections. As will come out presently, the measure of instability we shall use implicitly corrects for secular inflationary or deflationary influences. In general, the influences in the postwar period were inflationary.

The third observation about measurement has to do with the time period. We are using annual data. One of the main reasons we are using annual data is that quarterly or monthly data are not available for many countries, and we consider comprehensive country coverage to be a very important aspect of this study. It would obviously be desirable to have quarterly or monthly data in order to show more precisely the timing of fluctuations and in order to reveal more accurately the amplitude of fluctuations, even though laborious corrections would have to be made for seasonal variations. The annual data—on a calendar year basis in nearly all cases—clearly understate the actual fluctuations. There is another reason for not being too much concerned about the use of annual data. The reason is that this study, though mainly descriptive and analytical, is oriented toward policies for mitigating international economic instability, and in the present and prospective state of international relations, instability has to be quite severe before much international action can be expected. It should be fully recognized, however, that the "instability in-

[2] See, for example, the discussion in *International Financial Statistics*, March, 1960, p. iv.

dexes" which will be presented later will understate the actual extent of instability because of the use of annual data.

The Instability to Be Measured

Another point of importance in delineating the field of inquiry is that not all changes in the relevant variables constitute instability which should be considered undesirable. Seasonal variations are an important type of fluctuation, and there is much to be said in favor of reducing some kinds of seasonal variation, but it is our tentative opinion that seasonal variations in international trade do not constitute enough of a problem to warrant major intergovernmental consideration. There are other changes in international economic dealings, which are the result of changes in consumer tastes, in production technology, and in supplies of factors of production. In general, these changes are to be considered desirable because they reflect changes in consumer choices and in cost conditions. Changes consequent upon them are considered desirable adaptations of production conditions to changes in demand or supply conditions. The purpose of economic activity is assumed to be the most efficient use of changing resources to meet changing wants, not the rigid stabilization of certain flows or relations. Also, the economic changes associated with war or natural disasters involve adjustments many of which cannot be adjudged undesirable instabilities, once given the originating disturbances.

Beyond all of these changes, however, there seems to be a residuum of instability which serves no useful purpose and which can be considered wasteful or unjust in its effects. It is difficult, to be sure, to distinguish the wasteful or inequitable kind of instability from the changes which are unavoidable or desirable. The recognition of the "problem" of instability, whether domestic or international, implies the possibility of identifying the undesirable changes and doing something about them, or mitigating their effects. Of course the extent of instability considered undesirable varies among people or groups of people and over time. And the willingness to do something about the international aspects of the problem varies through time, although there has undoubtedly been an increase in the willingness to take action, national or international, for this purpose since, say, the 1920s.[3]

Recognition of some fluctuations as undesirable clearly involves an ethical value-judgment, just as does the recognition of an unsatisfactory

[3] J. M. Clark, in his "Separate Concurring Statement" to the United Nations experts' report in 1950 on *National and International Measures for Full Employment,* pp. 103–104, suggests that "the world situation . . . imposes an obligation on countries that rank as industrial leaders, and makes it to their interest to demand a higher performance from themselves than they might be inclined to do on domestic considerations alone."

rate of growth of the national income, or an undesirable distribution of income, or an unjust tax system. It does not follow necessarily, however, that recognition of an evil calls for attempts to cure or even alleviate it, for the real costs of curing or alleviating the evil might be greater than the evil itself.

The empirical part of the present study will enable us to see where the principal instabilities lie, so far as the international economic relations among countries are concerned. It will be possible to show the relative instabilities of important variables and to provide some basis for judging whether action is needed or worth considering. Although the facts about the problem and the analysis of it can be objective and scientific, the judgment as to whether something should or should not be done about it is a political-ethical one, to be made in the light of the facts and the political-ethical values involved.

An Index of Instability

We now arrive at the point of describing the principal statistical measure of instability we shall use. What we seek is a measure that will show typical year-to-year relative changes corrected for trend influences. The reasons for using annual figures were explained above. The reason for using relative changes is in order to make country-to-country, commodity-to-commodity, or similar comparisons. Trend influences were so strong in the postwar period that they must be removed in order to isolate the fluctuations.

One may think of the matter graphically by supposing that the annual figures for export proceeds of Country A for the years 1946 through 1958 are plotted; then a smooth trend line (of whatever shape) drawn for the series; then "relatives," corrected for trend, obtained by expressing the actual value for each year as a percentage of the corresponding trend value; then the difference between the relatives for Year 1 and Year 2 expressed as a percentage of the relative for Year 1, and likewise for the other successive pairs of years; then the resulting year-to-year percentage changes averaged. The result would be the average year-to-year percentage change, adjusted for trend. Seasonal influences would be eliminated by using annual figures.

Although the method of obtaining an average measure of instability just described seems most satisfactory, we adopted a system which was less laborious and lent itself to machine methods.[4] The process was as follows:

[4] H. S. Houthakker of the Stanford University Department of Economics and Holbrook Working of the Stanford Food Research Institute helped develop the method.

1. Logarithms were obtained for each annual value of a variable, for example, total exports for Year 1, Year 2, etc.

2. The logarithm of the value for Year 2 was subtracted from the logarithm of the value for Year 1, etc., in order to get the first differences of the logarithms. (The antilog of this difference is the ratio of the value for Year 2 to the value for Year 1.)

3. The arithmetic mean of the logarithmic first differences was then obtained. (The algebraic sum of the differences is used in the numerator.)

4. This logarithmic mean was then subtracted from each year-to-year logarithmic first difference in order to obtain the logarithmic difference between the actual and the average (or trend) year-to-year logarithmic differences.

5. These logarithmic differences from the trend—some positive and some negative—were then squared, summed up, and divided by the number of years minus one. The resulting number was referred to as the "log variance."

6. The next step was to take the square root of the log variance and obtain the antilog of the square-root value. Unity was subtracted from the antilog and the decimal moved two places to the right. The resulting "instability index" is a close approximation of the average year-to-year percentage variation, adjusted for trend.[5]

Since the empirical parts of this study rely so heavily on the measure of instability, it was decided to compare this "log variance" method with two other methods. The first of these other methods involves obtaining the average of percentage deviations from the least-squares trend line through the actual annual values. By steps, first the least-squares trend line was obtained; second, the absolute deviation between the actual annual value and the trend value was obtained for each year; third, this absolute value was expressed as a percentage of the trend value for each year; fourth, these percentage deviations from trend were then summed up and divided by the number of years.

The second of these additional methods was that used by the United Nations Secretariat in its 1952 study, *Instability in Export Markets of Under-developed Countries*. This method involves no formal adjustment for trend. It consists of obtaining the absolute difference in values from

---

[5] In algebraic terms the process is as follows: Let X_t equal the value of a country's exports in year t; N, the number of years minus 1; m, the arithmetic mean of the differences between the logs of X_t and X_{t+1}, X_{t+1} and X_{t+2}, etc.; and $V_{\log}$, the logarithmic variance of the series. The formula is

$$V_{\log} = \frac{\sum \left(\log \frac{X_{t+1}}{X_t} - m \right)^2}{N}$$

The instability index (I-I) = antilog $\sqrt{V_{\log}}$.

year to year, expressing this difference as a percentage of the *larger* of the two annual values, and then averaging these percentages. "In this report a rise is measured as a percentage of the terminal high point, rather than of the lower starting point, of an increase. Thus, a rise from 100 to 150 was not considered an increase of 50 per cent . . . but an increase of 33⅓ per cent . . . The conventional method of measuring decreases was retained . . ." (p. 77).

This method has some deficiencies. For example, a steady increase of 10 per cent per year in the values of a series, such as 100, 110, 121, etc., would, according to the United Nations system, yield fractions like $10/110$, $11/121$, etc., which, when averaged, would be less than the conventional 10 per cent, but the resulting percentage would indicate considerable instability when in reality there would be none at all! There would be perfectly steady percentage or logarithmic growth. The authors of the United Nations study apparently were deliberate in choosing this method, for they say that their "measure has the advantage of simplicity, since it avoids complicated logarithmic scales or the relation of changes to hypothetical average figures" (p. 79). The "hypothetical average figures" are presumably trend lines, calculated on some mathematical or freehand basis. Although there is nearly always a problem of what is a proper trend, it seems appropriate, when there is obviously a trend, to allow for it according to some rational system. It should be noted that the United Nations system does provide some allowance for trend influences, since it uses the actual values for each pair of years in the general manner of chain relatives. These year-to-year changes, expressed as percentages according to the United Nations system or the conventional system, give larger percentage figures for instability than do the measures which calculate the deviations around a trend line, whatever the slope or shape of the trend line.

Comparison of the Three Measures of Instability

In order to understand more fully the relation between the three measures, correlation analyses were made for export proceeds for the 83 countries used in this study. The correlation coefficient r between the instability indexes by the log variance method and those by the average-percentage-deviation-from-trend method is $+.89$. The correlation coefficient between those by the log variance method and those by the United Nations method is $+.91$. It is reassuring to discover that these three methods show such similar results.

Each of these three measures corrects for trend. The log variance method involves a constant percentage trend—a straight line on semilog paper. The average-percentage-deviation method involves a constant absolute change from year to year—a straight line on regular graph paper. The United Nations method involves a rather haphazard correction for trend.

Of course any summary statistical measure fails to represent all differences in the collection of data it summarizes. In the present study the best way to determine whether the instability indexes reflect fairly well the instabilities of the various series is to compare them with the corresponding graphs of the series. Such comparisons are provided in several instances in later chapters.

The *relative* position of various countries or commodities with respect to instability is more important, so far as the use of the statistical measure is concerned, than the value obtained with a particular measure. Differences in the instability index must always be treated with caution, however, because of the large influence of one or two years of relatively large change and because of the statistically small samples in some instances.

Conclusion

The principal indicator we shall use for measuring international economic instability is export proceeds. The principal measure we shall use for measuring the degree of instability is the log variance measure described in detail above. This measure of instability will also be used for several other variables which seem to bear on instability of export proceeds.

We now turn to the actual measurement of international economic instability for the period after World War II.

Chapter 3

INSTABILITY OF INTERNATIONAL TRADE SINCE WORLD WAR II

This chapter presents a broad picture, in statistical terms, of instability of world international trade for the dozen or so years after World War II. It also provides some breakdowns of the world aggregates on a commodity basis and some comparisons with other variables.

World Exports, 1947 to 1958

A backdrop against which to see the fluctuations in international trade is the total value of exports (or imports) from year to year. Table 3-1 shows total exports of goods, expressed in current United States dollars, of the non-Communist countries for the years 1947 to 1958. The most striking thing about this series is the doubling over the period. Also, this increase in value is almost matched by the increase in volume of trade, as shown by the quantum index numbers in the table. Figure 3-1 shows the index numbers for the value, quantum, and unit value of world exports.

The instability index (I-I) for value of exports is 9.1, as compared with 4.2 for quantum of exports and 7.6 for unit value of exports.[1] It

[1] See Chap. 2 for a description of this instability index, which corrects for trend influences. It is convenient to use "I-I" as a symbol for this index. For comparative purposes the United Nations instability index, described in the same section above, was calculated for these variables. For value of exports, the index was 7.4; for quantum, it was 6.0; for unit value, it was 5.0. Just as with the logarithmic variance method, the export value index by the United Nations method showed more instability than the quantum and unit value indexes. It may be noted, though, that the quantum and unit value indexes were in a different order, the quantum index smaller with the logarithmic variance method and the unit value index smaller with the United Nations method.

27

is evident that the fluctuations in physical volume of exports were quite small, since an I-I of zero would mean no deviations around the trend line with a constant relative change from year to year. The fact that the I-I for value exceeded that for quantum and unit value means that changes in quantities and prices tended not to offset each other, but to move together. This is most clearly seen in the changes from 1950 to 1951, when the quantum index jumped from 85 to 95 and the unit value (or price) index from 89 to 108. Even with the adjustment for trend influences, these changes are sizable and in the same direction.

Table 3-1
World Exports, 1947–1958

Year	Total value* (in millions of current U.S. $)	Total value index (1953 = 100)	Quantum index† (1953 = 100)	Unit value index† (1953 = 100)
	(1)	(2)	(3)	(4)
1947	48,567	65	68	95
1948	54,075	72	70	103
1949	55,131	73	76	97
1950	57,222	76	85	89
1951	77,247	103	95	108
1952	74,376	99	94	105
1953	75,252	100	100	100
1954	78,032	104	105	99
1955	84,799	113	114	99
1956	94,130	125	124	101
1957	101,063	134	131	103
1958	96,078	128	129	100
Instability index....	9.1	9.1	4.2	7.6

* Goods only; excluding Communist countries. Source: *International Financial Statistics*, December, 1951, and February, 1960.

† Source: UN *Statistical Yearbook*, 1955, p. 395; 1958, p. 377. There are some minor discrepancies among these indexes.

According to the logarithmic variance method of measuring instability around the trend, price fluctuations (I-I = 7.6) were a more important source of instability in export receipts than quantity fluctuations (I-I = 4.2).[2] In a formal sense, the fluctuations in the value of exports can be fully accounted for by the fluctuations in quantity and price, since price multiplied by quantity per year for each kind of commodity necessarily gives the annual value figures, but the relation of the instability indexes for the three variables cannot be defined so neatly. In the limiting case of

[2] Interestingly, the United Nations method of measuring instability shows price (I-I = 5.0) less important than quantity (I-I = 6.0). For the reasons given in Chap. 2, we have more confidence in the logarithmic variance method.

I-I$_q$ = 0, then clearly I-I$_v$ = I-I$_p$, if the statistical data for the three series are internally consistent; likewise, in the limiting case of I-I$_p$ = 0, then I-I$_v$ = I-I$_q$. For values above zero for all three instability indexes, the relation among them is uncertain, because I-I$_p$ and I-I$_q$ may be compensating or reinforcing. The business cycle generally shows reinforcing rather than compensatory patterns. In ordinary competitive demand-sup-

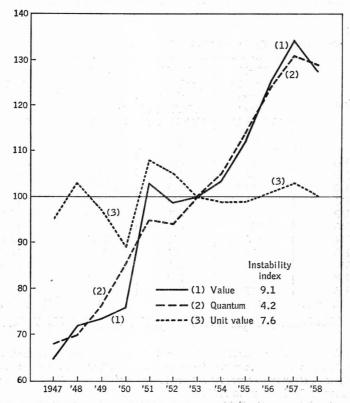

Figure 3-1. World exports, 1947–1958. Indexes of value, quantum, and unit value (1953 = 100). Source: Table 3-1.

ply analysis, the relation is most easily explained by shifting demand curves against stable positively-sloping supply curves. Total receipts would then vary according to the elasticity of the supply curves and the size of the shifts in the demand curves. Shifts in supply curves and market imperfections would have to be allowed for in order to make this analysis realistic.

Several types of demand-supply situations are consistent with the resulting instability indexes. The main fact is that I-I$_v$ exceeds I-I$_p$ and I-I$_q$, which shows that the changes in demand-supply conditions serve to increase the instability of export proceeds (import outlays) rather than to reduce them.[3]

World Exports and World Production

Another backdrop against which to view the fluctuations in total international trade is world production. The first striking fact is that total

Table 3-2
World Production and Trade, 1948–1958

Year	World production volume index* (1953 = 100)	World production value† (in billions of 1953 U.S. $)	World exports value‡ (in billions of 1953 U.S. $)	World exports as % of world production, Col. (3) as % of Col. (2)
	(1)	(2)	(3)	(4)
1948	73	456	52.5	11.5
1949	74	462	56.8	12.3
1950	84	525	64.3	12.2
1951	91	569	71.5	12.6
1952	93	581	70.8	12.2
1953	100	625	75.3	12.0
1954	100	625	78.8	12.6
1955	111	694	85.7	12.3
1956	116	725	93.2	12.9
1957	120	750	98.1	13.1
1958	117	731	96.1	13.1
Instability index...	4.7	4.7	4.2	(Average 12.4%)

* Source: UN *Monthly Bulletin of Statistics*, August, 1959, p. x. Excludes Communist countries.

† The index numbers in Column (1), divided by 100, were multiplied by $625 billion (for 1953) to obtain the value of world production. The UN *Statistical Yearbook*, 1958, p. 54, note, estimates aggregate national income of the non-Communist countries at $600 billion to $650 billion in 1953.

‡ Figures in Column (1), Table 3-1, corrected by unit value index numbers in Column (4) to obtain value of exports adjusted for price changes. This adjustment was necessary because there are no estimates of world production in current prices.

(non-Communist) world exports amounted to about 12 per cent of total (non-Communist) world production for nearly every year from 1948 to 1958 (Table 3-2). The average of the 11 annual percentages was 12.4,

[3] The United Nations study found the same relation for a different period. "All types of fluctuations in proceeds . . . were in each case higher than those in volume or in price alone. This indicates that changes in price and in quantity had a destabilizing effect on each other." United Nations, *Instability in Export Markets of Under-developed Countries*, 1952, p. 7.

and the dispersion around this average percentage was only from 11.5 to 13.1. The 1:8 ratio between trade and production held despite the large changes in the value, volume, composition, and direction of trade, as well as in production, during this period.[4]

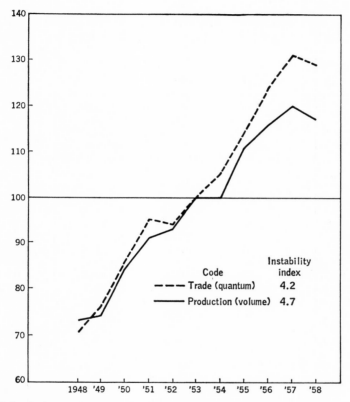

Figure 3-2a. Indexes of volume of world production and international trade, 1948–1958. Source: World production index: Table 3-2, Column (1); world international trade index: Table 3-1, Column (3).

It should be noted that United States production and trade, especially production, weigh very heavily in these figures, since the United States produced during this period about half of the output of the Free World and supplied about one-fifth of the exports. Inclusion of the Communist

---

[4] *International Trade 1957–1958,* by the Secretariat of the Contracting Parties to the General Agreement on Tariffs and Trade (Geneva, 1959), shows (p. 9) *goods* exports as about 20 per cent of *goods* output. The *Statistical Yearbook,* United Nations Secretariat, 1958, p. 54, note, considers goods output as 60 per cent of total output, so our 12 per cent is consistent with the GATT 20 per cent.

countries in the total—not possible to do for most years because of lack of reliable data—would raise the world production total for 1957 from $750 billion to perhaps $1,100 billion or $1,150 billion and the world goods export total from $101 billion to perhaps $107 billion. Addition of exports of *services,* for the whole world, might add another $10 billion

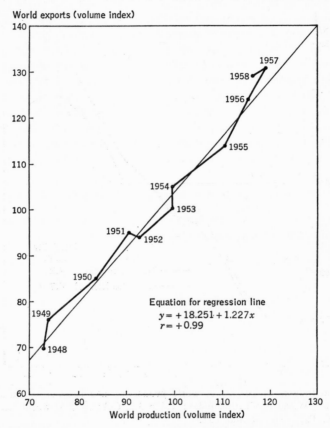

World exports (volume index)

Equation for regression line
$$y = +18.251 + 1.227x$$
$$r = +0.99$$

World production (volume index)

Figure 3-2b. Correlation of indexes of volume of world production and exports, 1948–1958 (1953 = 100). Source: World production: Table 3-2, Column (1); exports: Table 3-1, Column (3).

to $15 billion. Hence, for the whole world, goods and services exports amount to about 10 per cent of total production of goods and services. The United States and the U.S.S.R., which together produced about half of the world's output, exported less than five per cent of their output, while the other countries of the world, as a group, exported more than 20 per cent of their output. This figure was about 30 per cent of *goods* (without services) in 1957 for the Free World countries other than the United States.[5]

The instability index (I-I) for world production (quantum) for the years 1948 to 1958 is 4.7, compared with I-I for quantum of world exports of 4.2. This similarity is consistent with the small deviations in the ratio of exports to production. Figure 3-2*a* shows the close relation of postwar exports and production.[6] Figure 3-2*b* presents the same information in the form of a correlation chart. The correlation coefficient between the quantum of world output and the quantum of world trade is +.99.[7] In only one of the 10 pairs of years was the movement of trade and production in opposite directions: this is 1951 to 1952, when trade fell back after the Korean conflict boom. From 1953 to 1954 trade increased, production remained the same; from 1957 to 1958, both decreased. Otherwise, the two series moved up together. This high positive correlation of the two series is associated with strong upward trends in both series; it would probably not hold in the absence of such secular trends.

Instability of World Exports of Primary and Manufactured Goods

We now compare the instability indexes for the two broadest commodity groups—manufactured goods and primary goods:

	Instability indexes	
	Primary goods	Manufactured goods
Exports:		
Total value.........	3.8	6.8
Quantum...........	4.7	7.1
Unit value.........	8.4	7.6

[5] GATT, *International Trade 1957–58*, p. 9.

[6] Using League of Nations figures, the I-I for world exports for 1925 to 1938 was 7.8 and for world production was 5.8. (By the United Nations method the instability values were 6.7 and 5.7, respectively.) Thus, instability was greater before the war for both series. Also, before the war the export instability index exceeded the output instability index (7.8 to 5.8), whereas after the war the output instability index exceeded the export instability index (4.7 to 4.2). This opposite relation reflects, on the one hand, the severe shrinkage of international trade in the early 1930s and, on the other hand, the maintenance of world trade, especially by means of United States aid and other financial measures, during the post-World War II decade or so. These very low instability index values, in both periods, contrast sharply with the much higher values for individual countries given in Chap. 4.

[7] This nearly perfect correlation is surprising. However, there is evidence of a close relation for the years 1881 to 1938 in W. A. Lewis, "World Production, Prices and Trade, 1870–1960," *Manchester School,* vol. 20, 1952.

Table 3-3
World Exports and World Production of Primary Goods and Manufactured Goods, 1948–1958
(Index numbers—1953 = 100)

Year	Primary goods				Manufactured goods				Terms of trade
	Exports, total value	Exports, quantum	Exports, unit value	Production, quantum	Exports, total value	Exports, quantum	Exports, unit value	Production, quantum	Col. (3) as % of Col. (7)
	(1)	(2)	(3)	(4)	(5)	(6)	(7)	(8)	(9)
1948	76	75	101	86	64	64	102	73	99.0
1949	81	77	93	86	68	78	97	74	95.9
1950	92	91	97	89	78	78	86	83	112.8
1951	97	96	117	93	93	93	103	92	113.6
1952	94	95	104	97	93	93	104	93	100.0
1953	100	100	100	100	100	100	100	100	100.0
1954	104	105	103	101	105	105	98	100	105.1
1955	113	114	99	105	115	113	99	111	100.0
1956	122	124	100	109	126	125	103	116	97.1
1957	128	129	100	109	133	133	107	120	95.3
1958	119	126	97	108	130	130	107	117	90.7
Instability index....	3.8	4.7	8.4	1.9	6.8	7.1	7.7	4.8	7.4

Contrary to widely held views, *export proceeds were decidedly more stable for primary goods than for manufactured goods.* Quantum of exports showed about the same relative instability as value. The I-I for unit value is greater for primary goods than for manufactured goods, however, which accords with customary views. The low I-I for the value

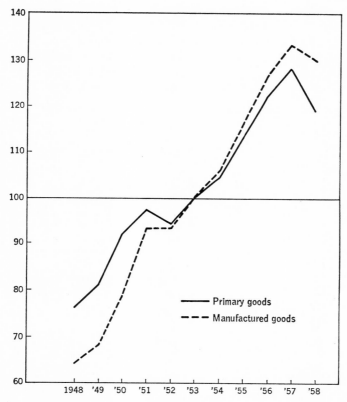

Figure 3-3a. Total value of world exports of primary goods and manufactured goods, 1948–1958. Source: Table 3-3, Columns (1) and (5).

of primary goods exports is clearly the result of compensatory relations between price and quantity changes: higher prices were partly offset by lower quantities and lower prices were partly offset by higher quantities. As noted earlier, a complete offsetting would put the instability index for value at zero. Table 3-3 shows the index numbers from which the instability indexes were calculated.

In Figure 3-3a are shown the time series of index numbers of export value for primary goods and manufactured goods. The most noticeable fact is that the two series generally moved together, although manufactured exports rose more steeply than did exports of primary goods. Table 3-4 shows the value of world exports of primary and manufactured goods, 1948 to 1958. The increasing share of manufactured goods in world trade between 1950 and 1958—43.7 to 51.8 per cent—is the largest change in many decades.[8] Although the export instability index for primary goods (3.8) is lower than that for manufactured goods (6.8), both are quite low, so too much should not be inferred from their relations, despite the fact that the opposite relation would generally be expected.

Figure 3-3*b* depicts the variations in unit value for exports of primary goods and manufactured goods. It is apparent from the graph, as well as

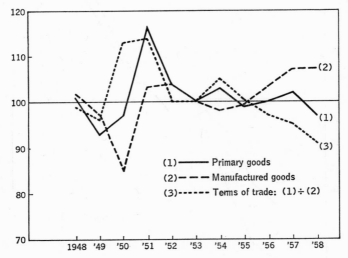

Figure 3-3b. Unit value of world exports of primary goods and manufactured goods, 1948–1958. Source: Table 3-3, Columns (3) and (7).

from the comparative instability indexes, that primary-goods prices were only slightly more unstable than manufactured-goods prices. The terms of trade between primary goods and manufactured goods, as measured by the ratio of the unit values of exports [Table 3-3, Column (9), and Figure 3-3*b*] have an I-I of 7.4, which is slightly smaller than the I-I for export prices and import prices alone. It is quite conceivable that the terms of trade should be much more stable than either export prices or import prices, since the two price series could move together; alternatively,

[8] *Ibid.*, pp. 106–107. Although commodities are classified somewhat differently, this percentage ranged from 33.9 to 39.2 during 1881–1913, and from 35.9 to 41.5 during 1921–1938.

the terms of trade could be less stable than the other series. There seems to be no way of deducing or predicting this relation.

Table 3-4
World Exports of Primary Goods and
Manufactured Goods, 1948–1958

Year	Primary goods		Manufactured goods		Total*	
	Billions U.S. $	Per cent	Billions U.S. $	Per cent	Billions U.S. $	Per cent
1948	29.4	55.5	23.6	44.5	53.0	100.0
1949	30.6	55.5	24.5	44.5	55.1	100.0
1950	31.2	56.3	24.2	43.7	55.4	100.0
1951	40.5	54.1	34.4	45.9	74.9	100.0
1952	37.5	51.9	34.8	48.1	72.3	100.0
1953	37.4	51.0	35.9	49.0	73.3	100.0
1954	39.1	51.4	37.0	48.6	76.1	100.0
1955	41.9	50.6	40.9	49.4	82.8	100.0
1956	45.4	49.3	46.6	50.7	92.0	100.0
1957	48.8	48.6	50.8	51.4	98.8	100.0
1958	46.6	48.2	48.0	51.8	94.6	100.0
Instability index...	3.8		6.8		9.8	

* These figures differ somewhat from the International Monetary Fund figures used in Table 3-1. The reconciliation is provided in *Direction of International Trade*, e.g., vol. IX, no. 10, p. 6, 1958. It is not surprising, therefore, that the instability index (9.8) differs from the one calculated with the International Monetary Fund figures (9.1).

Instability of World Production of Primary and Manufactured Goods

World production of manufactured goods was much more unstable than world production of primary goods during the period 1948 to 1958. The instability index for physical volume (quantum) of manufactured goods was 4.8 and for primary goods 1.9. This relation accords with customary views, though it should be noted that the instability around the trend was quite low for each group. The two time series may be compared in Figure 3-4 and Table 3-3 [Columns (4) and (8)].

It is also informative to compare the quantum of exports and of production for primary goods and for manufactured goods. The time series are shown in Figure 3-4 and Table 3-3. Primary-goods exports are more unstable (I-I = 3.8) than primary-goods production (I-I = 1.9). The same relative condition holds for manufactured goods, though in smaller degree, since I-I for exports is 6.8 and I-I for production 4.8.

Index numbers

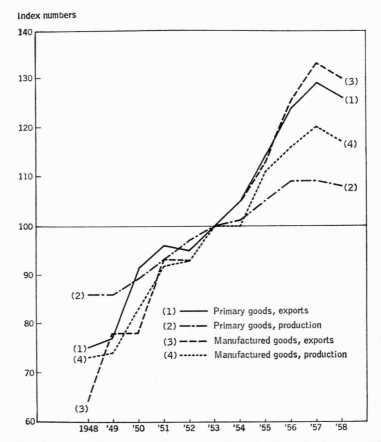

Figure 3-4. Quantum of exports and quantum of production of primary goods and manufactured goods, for world, 1948–1958 (1953 = 100). Source: Quantum of exports: Table 3-3, Columns (2) and (6); quantum of production: Table 3-3, Columns (4) and (8).

Attention should be called to the fact that, although the instability index for a component of an aggregate is usually greater than the index for the aggregate, such is not the case in several instances with primary and manufactured goods:

For total value of exports:
  I-I for primary goods (3.8) > I-I for total world exports (9.1).
  I-I for manufactured goods (6.8) > I-I for total world exports (9.1).
For unit value of exports:
  I-I for primary goods (8.4) > I-I for total world exports (7.6).
  I-I for manufactured goods (7.6) = I-I for total world exports (7.6).

For quantum of exports:

I-I for primary goods (4.7) > I-I for total world exports (4.2).

I-I for manufactured goods (7.1) > I-I for total world exports (4.2).

For quantum of world production:

I-I for primary goods (1.9) < I-I for total world production (4.9).

I-I for manufactured goods (4.8) < I-I for total world production (4.9).

In only three of the eight instances is the expected relation present. This may be explained in part by the deficiencies in the time series used to calculate the instability indexes; a close examination of the value, quantum, and unit value indexes reveals inconsistencies. The observed relation may also be explained by the series themselves, since it is possible for the aggregation of the components, especially if they have different weights, to make the aggregate more volatile than the components. The measure of instability may also contribute to this result.

Instability of Exports for SITC Groups

The Standard International Trade Classification (SITC), in effect for a gradually increasing number of countries since the early 1950s, provides the basis for a systematic comparison of the behavior of many individual commodities moving internationally and diverse combinations of them. The next appropriate breakdown for our analysis of the instability of exports is by groupings of commodities according to SITC classes. Unfortunately, the United Nations does not present the data in a form which shows total exports (or imports) by these classes, even for the countries and for the years available. The figures are shown by country of destination and by country of provenance, for each SITC class, as well as for a finer breakdown, with 150 groups.[9] The deficiencies in the data, arising from the fact that only about 30 countries are using the SITC system, make the aggregation task questionable, at least for some commodities. The Food and Agriculture Organization shows in its annual publication[10] compilations of trade figures, but the number of countries covered is far from complete and the number varies from year to year.

The Secretariat of the Contracting Parties to the GATT is apparently the only agency that has attempted to overcome this serious deficiency

[9] For example, United Nations, *Commodity Trade Statistics,* Statistical Papers, ser. D, vol. VIII, no. 4, January–December, 1958.

[10] For example, *Trade Yearbook 1958* (FAO, 1959), Table 1, shows three classes of agricultural products for 1951 to 1957, but the number of countries varies from 29 to 68.

in international trade statistics. Table 3-5 and Figure 3-5 show world exports, excluding the Communist countries, for eight commodity classes, as drawn from the GATT annual publications.[11] Data are available for only six years, 1952 through 1957. Figure 3-6 shows graphically the differences in the instability index numbers for these broad commodity classes. It is indeed notable that *export proceeds for food and agricultural raw materials*

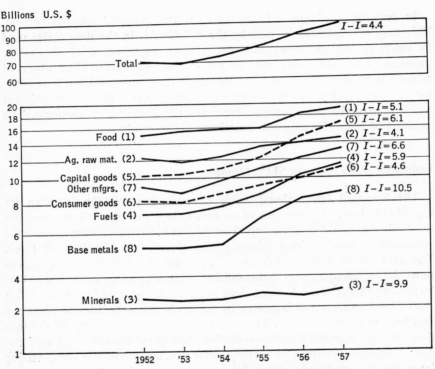

Figure 3-5. Value of exports, 1952–1957, by commodity classes. Source: Table 3-5.

show such low instability index values (5.1 and 4.1), as compared with base materials (10.5) and minerals (9.9). Both the logarithmic variance and UN methods of measuring instability were employed in order to provide a double check on the results. Figure 3-6 shows how the instability indexes vary for the two measures, but the ranking is not seriously upset. If the two measures are averaged for each group, the ranking is the same

[11] GATT, *International Trade 1952* through *International Trade 1957–58.*

Table 3-5
World Exports, by Broad Commodity Classes, by Years,
1952–1957, with Instability Indexes
(In millions of United States dollars)

Commodity classes	1952	1953	1954	1955	1956	1957
1. Food (I-I = 5.1*)..................	15,060	15,740	15,970	16,040	18,520	19,150
2. Agricultural raw materials (I-I = 4.1)	12,230	11,830	12,450	13,620	14,220	14,720
3. Minerals (I-I = 9.9)...............	2,520	2,400	2,440	2,860	2,680	3,100
4. Fuels (I-I = 5.9)..................	7,170	7,210	7,720	8,650	10,350	11,560
5. Capital goods (I-I = 6.1)..........:...	10,310	10,460	11,050	12,330	14,800	16,890
6. Consumer goods (I-I = 4.6).........	8,160	7,940	8,640	9,390	10,100	11,090
7. Other manufactures (I-I = 6.6)......	9,300	8,790	9,790	11,070	12,260	13,270
8. Base metals (I-I = 10.5)............	5,300	5,250	5,410	7,040	8,320	8,810
9. Total (I-I = 4.4).................	70,050	69,620	73,470	81,000	91,250	98,590

* Instability index, logarithmic variance method. By UN method, results were as follows: (1) 4.6; (2) 4.9; (3) 8.2; (4) 9.0; (5) 9.2; (6) 6.9; (7) 8.9; (8) 9.6; (9) 6.7.

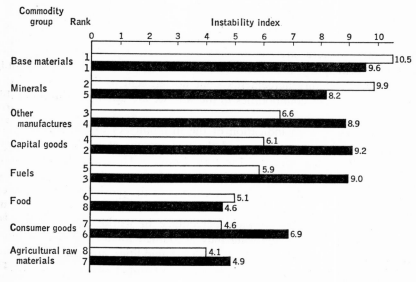

Figure 3-6. Instability index numbers for value of world exports, 1952–1957, by commodity groups. The upper bar for each commodity group shows the instability index calculated by the logarithmic variance method, the lower bar by the UN method. See Chapter 2 for description of methods. Source: Table 3-5.

as for the logarithmic variance method except for food moving from sixth to seventh place (exchanging places with consumer goods).

From these calculations it is clear that some primary goods yield the most stable export receipts while others yield the most unstable. Generalization about primary commodities is thus invalid in this respect. A reminder should be given here that these comparisons are based on trade for only the years 1952 through 1957. Some of the large fluctuations of the post-World War II period occurred before 1952.

Instability of Value of Exports of Individual Commodities

In moving toward finer and finer detail in discussing the instability of the value of exports for the world as a whole, we are now ready for individual commodities or relatively small groups of particular commodities. Unfortunately, the statistical basis for our calculations of instability indexes becomes progressively less satisfactory. Although the SITC classification provides for 150 subgroups, and many more particular commodities within these subgroups, the figures are not aggregated by these subgroups or for particular commodities. No government, intergovernmental organization, or private body publishes figures purporting to show international trade, on a global basis, for the various individual commodities or fine classes of commodities. There are some time series for a few individual commodities—principally those few for which there are international study groups or commodity agreements—but not enough to make comparisons for various types of commodities in the way we are attempting to do in this study.

In order to have an indication of the instability of export proceeds for a few commodities, we have used the percentages of world exports provided by the International Monetary Fund.[12] These percentages were applied to the Fund's figure for total world exports for the appropriate year in order to get dollar totals for exports of the particular commodities. Table 3-6 shows the results for 29 commodities, for the years 1950 to 1958, ranked according to their percentage in world exports (1954 to 1957 average). In the aggregate they accounted for 30 per cent of international trade in goods.[13] All of these commodities are "primary" commodities and are thus *not* a representative sample of the goods traded

---

[12] For example, *International Financial Statistics*, February, 1960, p. 28.

[13] These commodities accounted for a similar percentage for the years 1935 to 1938. Cf. M. K. Bennett and associates, *International Commodity Stockpiling*, The Stanford University Press, Stanford, Calif., 1949, p. 174. The 21 commodities which are on both his list and ours accounted for 30.02 per cent of world trade in 1935 to 1938, but only 26.48 per cent in 1954 to 1957.

Table 3-6
Value of World Exports of Various Primary Commodities, 1950–1958*
(In millions of United States dollars)

Commodity† (instability index)	1950	1951	1952	1953	1954	1955	1956	1957	1958
1. Petroleum (11.7)	3,992	3,215	3,468	3,588	4,148	4,754	5,085	5,485	5,195
2. Coffee (18.6)	1,228	1,946	2,021	2,190	2,302	2,087	2,309	2,111	1,924
3. Pulp and paper (41.4)	1,251	2,888	1,778	1,599	1,775	1,918	2,099	2,131	1,924
4. Cotton (19.7)	2,196	2,730	2,125	1,674	2,076	1,764	1,967	2,111	2,011
5. Wool (24.9)	1,590	2,169	1,416	1,741	1,465	1,455	1,534	1,777	1,539
6. Wheat (24.5)	1,228	1,946	1,955	1,786	1,350	1,374	1,807	1,626	1,520
7. Timber, lumber (16.2)	759	1,130	1,224	1,188	1,318	1,540	2,099	2,131	2,020
8. Sugar (15.3)	827	969	1,047	1,083	968	1,060	1,082	1,394	1,106
9. Copper (21.9)	459	608	826	807	822	1,051	1,318	990	914
10. Rubber (40.3)	1,188	1,899	1,114	777	765	1,272	1,092	1,070	1,000
11. Coal (10.6)	730	908	922	852	867	874	1,035	1,050	962
12. Tobacco (12.6)	544	641	536	647	640	712	687	687	625
13. Rice (15.2)	452	579	736	692	585	543	565	596	557
14. Tea (17.2)	355	440	364	436	577	543	565	526	480
15. Cocoa (23.5)	383	463	402	459	687	534	424	404	384
16. Iron ore (34.0)	103	139	350	361	351	475	565	657	625
17. Fish (6.5)	343	371	387	391	429	449	537	546	519
18. Jute bagging (39.6)	538	811	354	406	421	458	395	384	346
19. Butter (8.2)	395	379	394	406	390	407	395	323	288
20. Tin (16.5)	303	433	424	361	320	322	329	303	269
21. Bananas (9.3)	240	263	312	331	320	305	301	283	250
22. Hides and skins (10.7)	292	294	245	293	289	271	292	313	298
23. Coconuts and products (26.2)	320	425	245	293	289	263	282	263	240
24. Wine (12.7)	235	216	231	203	234	263	254	323	308
25. Lead (16.6)	223	270	290	211	234	263	292	273	250
26. Corn (19.6)	200	247	260	309	250	195	245	293	279
27. Citrus fruits (16.8)	137	193	186	188	195	220	188	243	231
28. Barley (38.8)	103	209	238	263	211	161	198	131	125
29. Zinc (36.9)	132	209	253	128	125	153	179	162	154

* The dollar values were calculated by applying the percentages provided in *International Financial Statistics*, various issues, e.g., February, 1960, p. 28, to the world totals of exports for various years, e.g., February, 1960, p. 24.

† Ranked by value, 1954–1957.

internationally. It is not certain that the export proceeds of these commodities are more unstable than the proceeds of a group of manufactured commodities. The presumption is to the contrary, on the basis of the instability index values for the groups of commodities discussed in the preceding sections of this chapter, but clear evidence is lacking. Figure 3-7

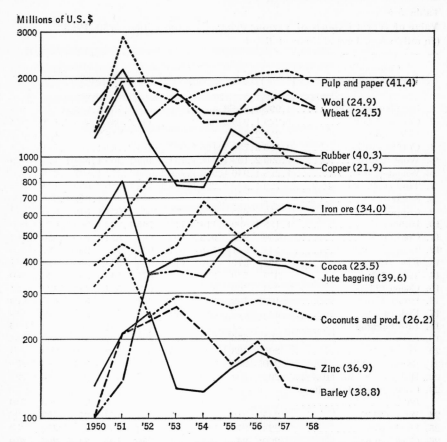

Figure 3-7. Value of world exports, 1950–1958, of primary commodities having high instability indexes (ratio scale). Source: Table 3-6.

shows graphically the fluctuation in the value of exports for the most unstable commodities.

Figure 3-8 shows the export instability indexes for the 29 commodities, from highest to lowest. The range, from 41.4 for pulp and paper to 6.5 for fish, is impressive. The median I-I for the 29 commodities is 17.2, the unweighted average, 20.9, and the weighted average (weighted by relative export values), 20.4.[14] Table 3-7 provides the instability index of export prices for 22 of the 29 commodities and the percentage shares of the 29 commodities in international trade.

[14] Interestingly, these are close to the typical figures for the 83 countries. See p. 50.

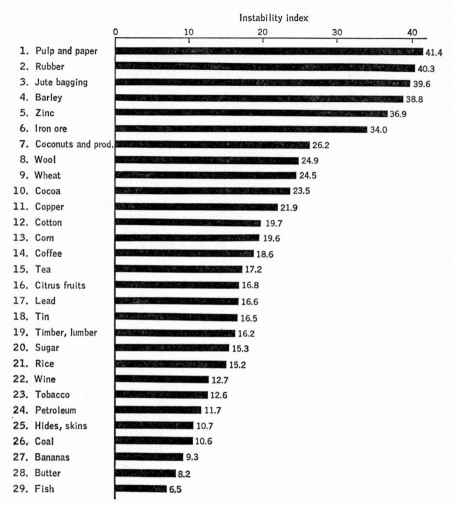

Figure 3-8. Instability index numbers for value of world exports of various primary commodities, 1950–1958. Source: Table 3-7.

For the 22 commodities for which there are instability indexes for both export value and prices (in international trade) there is a relatively high positive correlation between these two variables ($r = +.72$). The scatter diagram (Figure 3-9) illustrates the relation. The median instability index for export prices was 23.2, compared with 17.2 for export value. Usable quantity figures were not available. The correlation between the value of exports and the export instability index for these individual commodities is insignificantly small.

Table 3-7
Instability Indexes of Export Proceeds and Prices
for Various Individual Commodities, 1950–1958

Commodity	Instability index			Exports as % world exports, 1954–1957		Col. (1) × Col. (4)
	Value of exports		Prices			
	I-I	Rank	I-I	Per cent	Rank	
	(1)	(2)	(3)	(4)	(5)	(6)
Pulp and paper.......	41.4	1	36.3	2.23	3	92.32
Rubber..............	40.3	2	46.2	1.18	10	47.55
Jute, etc............	39.6	3	28.6	0.47	18	18.61
Barley..............	38.8	4	—	0.20	28	7.76
Zinc................	36.9	5	32.6	0.17	29	6.27
Iron ore.............	34.0	6	—	0.57	16	19.38
Coconuts, etc........	26.2	7	33.4	0.31	23	8.12
Wool...............	24.9	8	32.8	1.75	5	43.58
Wheat..............	24.5	9	16.2	1.72	6	42.14
Cocoa, etc...........	23.5	10	49.4	0.59	15	13.87
Copper..............	21.9	11	27.6	1.21	9	26.50
Cotton..............	19.7	12	8.5	2.23	4	43.93
Corn................	19.6	13	—	0.28	26	5.48
Coffee..............	18.6	14	25.3	2.51	2	46.69
Tea.................	17.2	15	21.4	0.63	14	10.83
Citrus fruits.........	16.8	16	—	0.24	27	4.03
Lead................	16.6	17	25.1	0.30	25	4.98
Tin.................	16.5	18	19.6	0.36	20	5.94
Timber, etc..........	16.2	19	—	1.64	7	26.56
Sugar...............	15.3	20	25.0	1.23	8	18.82
Rice................	15.2	21	19.1	0.65	13	9.88
Wine...............	12.7	22	—	0.30	24	3.81
Tobacco.............	12.6	23	3.5	0.77	12	9.70
Petroleum...........	11.7	24	18.3	5.47	1	64.00
Hides and skins.......	10.7	25	—	0.33	22	3.53
Coal................	10.6	26	8.0	1.07	11	11.34
Bananas.............	9.3	27	2.3	0.34	21	3.16
Butter..............	8.2	28	15.8	0.43	19	3.53
Fish................	6.5	29	11.6	0.55	17	3.58
	Md = 17.2		Md = 23.2	Σ29.73%		Σ605.89

Unweighted average export I-I = 20.9; weighted average export I-I = $\dfrac{605.89}{29.73}$ = 20.4

This brief dip into commodity analysis, limited though it is, illustrates how the instability index of any particular country will tend to vary according to the instability of the proceeds from the commodities it exports and the relative importance of these commodities among its exports. Compensatory movements modify this tendency, of course. We shall have

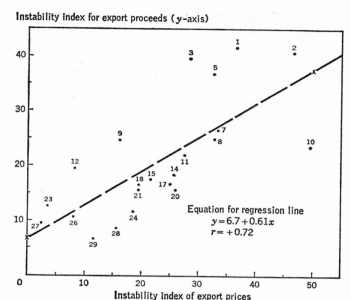

Figure 3-9. Correlation chart showing relation between export proceeds and export prices for 22 commodities. Source: Table 3-7; numbers from Column (2) identify the commodities.

occasion to refer to the instability of particular commodities in connection with our investigation of individual countries.

Conclusion of Chapter

A comparison of instability indexes can well summarize the main points of this chapter:

	Instability index
Series	
World exports of all goods, value, 1947–1958	9.1
World exports of all goods, volume, 1947–1958	4.2
World production, volume, 1948–1958	4.7
World production, volume, 1925–1938	5.8
World exports of all goods, volume, 1925–1938	7.8
World exports, primary goods, value, 1948–1958	3.8
World exports, manufactured goods, value, 1948–1958	6.8
World exports, primary goods, volume, 1948–1958	4.7
World exports, manufactured goods, volume, 1948–1958	7.1
World production, primary goods, volume, 1948–1958	1.9
World production, manufactured goods, volume, 1948–1958	4.8
Terms of trade, primary and manufactured goods, 1948–1958	7.4

World exports, value, 1952–1957	*Instability* *index*
Base metals......................	10.5
Minerals........................	9.9
Other manufactures...............	6.6
Capital goods....................	6.1
Fuels...........................	5.9
Food...........................	5.1
Consumer goods..................	4.6
Agricultural raw materials..........	4.1

For 29 important primary products, comprising 30 per cent of world exports in the mid-1950s, the instability indexes ranged from 41.4 down to 6.5. Statistics are not available to compare these instability indexes with those for individual manufactured commodities.

Chapter 4

INSTABILITY OF FOREIGN TRADE
OF INDIVIDUAL COUNTRIES

This chapter is devoted largely to a quantitative description of the principal phenomenon we are seeking to measure and explain—instability of export proceeds of individual countries.

Two criteria were employed in selecting the 83 countries which are covered in this analysis. The first was political autonomy, or a close approximation of it. The second criterion was availability of sufficient information on the balance of payments, foreign trade, and internal economic activity to permit of useful analysis. The countries included accounted for about 97 per cent of the international trade of the world in 1957.

Export Instability Indexes for 83 Countries

Figure 4-1 presents the instability index numbers for the value of exports of goods and services, 1946 to 1958, for 83 countries. This figure shows graphically the variations in instability with which we are concerned. The instability index (I-I) is the logarithmic variance measure described in Chapter 2.[1]

At one extreme are Iran and Indonesia, with 73.8 and 57.2, and at the other extreme are Switzerland and Ireland, with 6.2 and 6.3. This is a wide spread. One-fourth of the countries are below 14.2 and one-fourth above 26.6. The median I-I is 19.4 and the simple average I-I is 21.8. If the country instability indexes are weighted by the value of their exports in 1957, the weighted average I-I is 20.0. Figure 4-2a provides a frequency distribution of the countries according to I-I values. The distribution is skewed slightly to the right.

In interpreting these indexes of instability it must be borne in mind

[1] Appendix Table A-2 shows the rankings and values according to the average deviation method [Column (15)] and the United Nations chain-relative method [Column (29)].

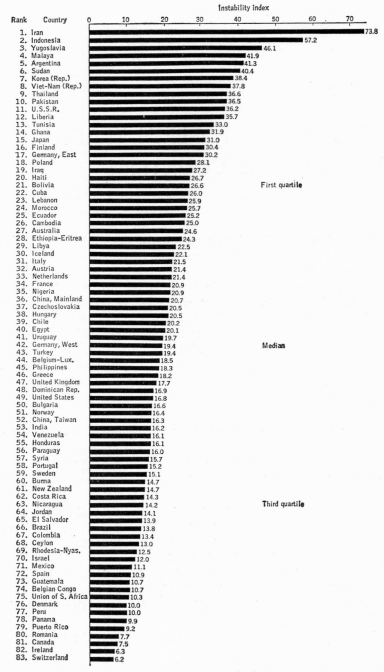

Figure 4-1. Instability index numbers for exports of 83 countries, 1946–1958. Source: Calculations from export figures shown in Appendix Table A-1.

50

that there are no standards by which to judge how much instability in export proceeds is "too much." Perhaps even the typical I-I of about 20 is too high and could be lowered advantageously and fairly easily, but as a first approximation we shall consider that the 21 countries in the highest fourth have "high" instability of exports. We shall examine the year-to-year export pattern of these high-instability countries individually later in this chapter.[2]

Instability of Exports by Geographic Region

There are sizable differences in the typical export instability indexes for the five continental groupings of countries. The median instability index for Asia is 24.8, while that for North America is 14.0. Medians and ranges for countries grouped by continents are shown in Table 4-1.

Table 4-1
Export Instability of Countries, by Continent
(Ranked by median instability index)

Continent	Median I-I	Range of I-I	Number of countries
(1)	(2)	(3)	(4)
Asia*......................	24.8	12.0–73.8	22
Africa.....................	23.4	10.3–40.4	12
Europe†...................	19.4	6.2–46.1	26
South America..............	16.1	10.1–41.3	13
North America..............	14.0	7.5–26.7	10
World..................	19.4	6.2–73.8	83

* Including Oceania.
† U.S.S.R. and Turkey included in Europe, not in Asia.
Source: Figure 4-1.

Export instability tends to be greater in Asia and Africa than in other continents, though the ranges reveal much dispersion within each continent.

Dispersion of instability indexes within continents is brought out more clearly in Figure 4-2*b*. The continents are ranked there according to

[2] Six of these twenty-one countries in the highest quarter, according to the logarithmic variance measure of instability, were not in the highest quarter by the average deviation method of measuring instability, but none fell below the 65th percentile. Only 2 of these 21 countries fell below the highest quarter by the United Nations chain-relative measure—Bolivia at the 58th percentile and Poland at the 37th percentile. The high correlation of the three measures was discussed in Chap. 2. Appendix Table A-2 shows the instability indexes for each country by all three measures [Columns (1), (15), and (29)].

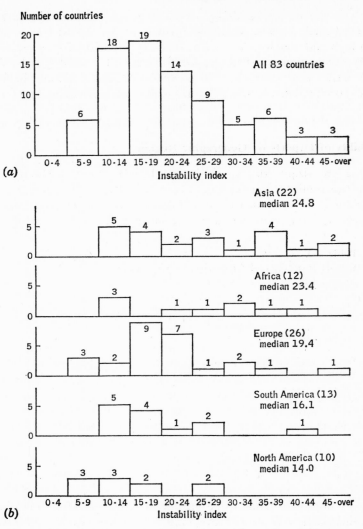

Figure 4-2. Frequency distributions of countries, total and by continent, according to index of instability of export proceeds. Source: Figure 4-1.

the median export instability indexes in Table 4-1. Only in the case of Europe is there a significant tendency toward concentration. Great variation in instability indexes among countries within each continent is the most apparent characteristic of these frequency distributions. It should be noted, however, that 9 of the 12 countries with I-I values of 35-over were in Asia and Africa, while all 6 of the countries with I-I values under 10 were in Europe and North America.

Instability of Exports by Monetary Group

The International Monetary Fund classifies countries for statistical purposes with reference to their principal monetary and economic connections: United States and Canada, Latin America, Continental European Fund (formerly European Payments Union), Sterling Area, and Rest of World. Table 4-2 shows the instability indexes for countries grouped

Table 4-2
Export Instability of Countries, by Monetary Group
(Ranked by median instability index)

Group	Median I-I	Range of I-I	Number of countries
(1)	(2)	(3)	(4)
Rest of World..................	27.2	7.7–73.8	29
Continental European Fund....	18.5	6.2–25.7	15
Sterling Area..................	17.0	6.3–41.9	16
Western Hemisphere...........	16.0	7.5–41.3	23
World......................	19.4	6.2–73.8	83

Source: Figure 4-1.

in this way (with all Western Hemisphere countries together). The striking result is that export instability tends to be much higher in the Rest of World than in the other groups: a median I-I of 27.2, compared with medians for the other groups of from 16.0 to 18.5. The countries in the Rest of World are those of Eastern Europe, Asia, and Africa, but excluding the members of the Sterling Area. The differences among the medians for the other three groups are probably not significant. If, however, the Western Hemisphere countries are divided into "dollar" and "other" countries, following the occasional practice of the International Monetary Fund, the "other" countries have a median instability index of 17.4 and a range of 10.0 to 41.3, while the "dollar" countries have a median I-I of 14.3 and a range of 7.5 to 26.7. The "other" countries are Argentina, Brazil, Chile, Paraguay, Peru, and Uruguay. Thus the Latin American countries closely associated with the United States, according to the Fund's criteria, tend to have lower instability indexes than do those in other groups.

Figure 4-3 brings out the dispersions of export instability indexes among the IMF groups. The Continental European Monetary Fund group has the least dispersion and Rest of World the most. Nine of the twelve countries with instability indexes of 35-over are in Rest of World; seven of these nine are located in Asia and Africa.

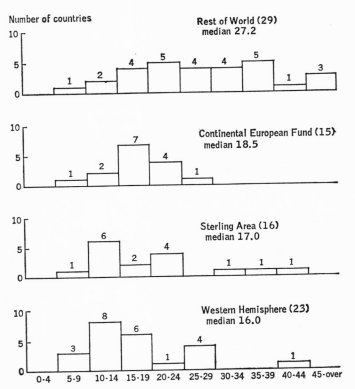

Figure 4-3. Frequency distributions of countries, by monetary groups, according to index of instability of export proceeds. Source: Figure 4-1.

Instability of Exports by Political Group

The distribution of export instability according to political grouping of countries also reveals interesting variations (Table 4-3 and Figure 4-4). Five groups of countries are used: members of the North Atlantic Treaty Organization (NATO), other allies of the NATO countries outside the Western Hemisphere, Latin America, countries uncommitted in the political rivalry between democracy and Communism, and the Communist bloc.

The median I-I for the Communist countries is 20.6 and for all other countries as a group, 18.5. The same is true with other measures of concentration. The simple average I-I for the Communist countries is 22.6, compared with 21.8 for all countries, including the Communist countries. The weighted average I-I (with 1957 exports as weights) for the Communist countries is 27.7, compared with 20.0 for all countries. The difference reflects mainly the instability of the Soviet Union's exports.

The dispersion of the instability indexes around the typical values for each political group is brought out in Figure 4-4. The uncommitted countries have the greatest spread, while the NATO group has the least. Only in the NATO group is there a heavy concentration, this in the 15 to 19 class. Of the 12 countries with I-I values of 35-over, all but 2, the U.S.S.R. and Argentina, are in the Asian-African group of uncommitted countries and other Free World allies. Three of the four countries with I-I values of 30 to 34 are also in this same group. In the next lower bracket—I-I of 25 to 29—Latin America matches this group in supplying four countries each.

Table 4-3
Export Instability of Countries, by Political Group
(Ranked by median instability index)

Political group	Median I-I	Range of I-I	Number of countries
(1)	(2)	(3)	(4)
Other allies...................	25.2	10.9–73.8	12
Uncommitted countries.........	22.5	6.2–57.2	27
Communist countries..........	20.6	7.7–36.2	8
NATO countries..............	18.2	7.5–22.1	15
Latin American countries.......	16.0	9.2–41.3	21
World.....................	19.4	6.2–73.8	83
Non-Communist countries....	18.5	6.2–73.8	75

Distribution of Export Instability in World International Trade

The next step in this general view of instability of exports, by country, is to measure the distribution of export instability throughout the world. The problem is approached as follows: With a given percentage distribution of exports among countries, and with the same instability index of exports for all countries, then the percentage distribution of export instability over the world would be exactly the same as the percentage distribution of exports. With different export instability indexes for the various countries, however, the distribution of instability would not be the same as the distribution of exports. What is needed, therefore, is the percentage distribution of exports weighted by the instability index numbers of the various countries. This is shown in Column (2) of Table 4-4 for the 25 countries, each of which contributed 1 per cent or more of the world export instability. The unweighted percentage distribution of exports is

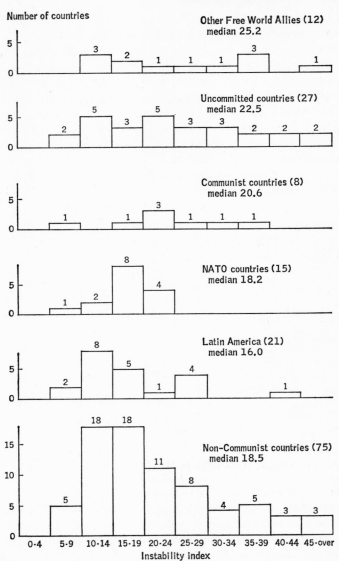

Figure 4-4. Frequency distributions of countries, by political group, according to index of instability of export proceeds. Source: Figure 4-1.

given in Column (4). Ranking is according to the weighted distribution, which shows the relative contribution of each country to export instability in the world. Figure 4-5 shows graphically the 25 countries which contributed 1.0 per cent or more apiece to the export instability of the world. (The percentages for all countries are shown in Appendix Table A-3.)

Table 4-4
Percentage Distribution of Export Instability among Countries

Country [ranked by value in Col. (2)]	Percentage of world export instability*		Percentage of world exports		Rank, by value in Col. (4)
	By country	Cumulative	By country	Cumulative	
(1)	(2)	(3)	(4)	(5)	(6)
1. United States..........	16.6	16.6	20.0	20.0	1
2. United Kingdom.......	8.1	24.7	9.3	29.3	2
3. Germany, West........	7.9	32.6	8.1	37.4	3
4. U.S.S.R...............	7.5	40.1	4.2	41.6	6
5. France...............	5.1	45.2	4.8	46.4	5
6. Japan.................	4.2	49.4	2.7	49.1	9
7. Netherlands...........	3.1	52.5	2.9	52.0	8
8. Belgium-Luxembourg...	2.8	55.3	3.0	55.0	7
9. Australia.............	2.6	57.9	2.1	57.1	13
10. Indonesia.............	2.6	60.5	0.9	58.0	20
11. Germany, East........	2.6	63.1	1.7	59.7	15
12. Italy.................	2.6	65.7	2.4	62.1	10
13. China, mainland.......	2.3	68.0	2.2	64.3	12
14. Canada...............	1.9	69.9	5.2	69.5	4
15. Argentina............	1.9	71.8	0.9	70.4	18
16. Iran†.................	1.8	73.6	0.5	70.9	25
17. Venezuela............	1.8	75.4	2.2	73.1	11
18. Sweden...............	1.5	76.9	2.0	75.1	14
19. Malaya†..............	1.4	78.3	0.7	75.8	24
20. Czechoslovakia†.......	1.3	79.6	1.3	77.1	16
21. Poland...............	1.3	80.9	0.9	78.0	21
22. Finland.....	1.2	82.1	0.8	78.8	23
23. India................	1.1	83.2	1.3	80.1	17
24. Austria...............	1.0	84.2	0.9	81.0	19
25. Cuba†...............	1.0	85.2	0.8	81.8	22
25 countries‡............	85.2	—	81.8	—	
58 other countries........	14.8	—	18.2	—	
83 countries...........	100.0	100.0	100.0	100.0	

* Percentages obtained as follows: Dollar value of 1957 exports (*International Financial Statistics*, February, 1960, pp. 24, 26) for a country is multiplied by its instability index for exports; these products summed, and the product for each country expressed as a per cent of the sum.

† Not among top 25 in distribution of *import* instability.

‡ Three other countries had 1.0 per cent or more of world exports, but contributed less than 1.0 per cent to export instability: Brazil, 1.3 (sixteenth in rank) and 0.9; Union of South Africa, 1.2 (nineteenth) and 0.6; Denmark, 1.1 (twentieth) and 0.6. Column (6) shows the ranking of countries, by value of exports in 1957, for the countries with more than 1 per cent of world exports.

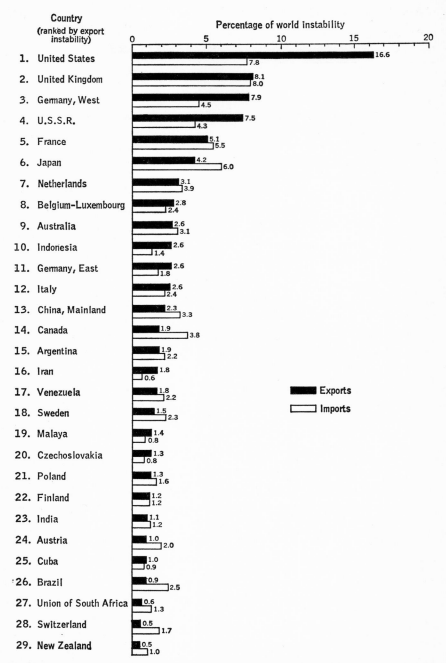

Figure 4-5. Distribution of export instability and import instability among countries accounting for 1 per cent or more of world export or import instability. Source: Appendix Table A-3, Columns (1) and (2).

58

The United States contributed most to export instability (16.6 per cent), despite its below-average instability index, because of its large share (one-fifth) of world exports. Six countries—the United States, United Kingdom, West Germany, the U.S.S.R., France, and Japan—as a group contributed 49.4 per cent of the instability and 49.1 per cent of the exports. The 25 countries provided 85.2 per cent of the export instability and 81.8 per cent of the exports. The fairly close relation be-

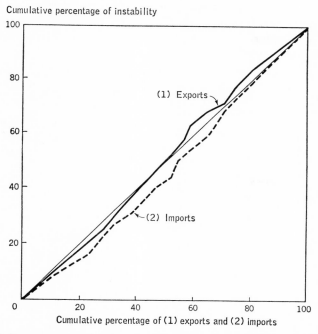

Figure 4-6. Lorenz curves showing, for 83 countries: (1) relation between shares of world export instability and shares of world exports and (2) relation between shares of world import instability and shares of world imports. Source: (1) export curve: Table 4-4, Columns (3) and (5); (2) import curve: Table 4-5, Columns (3) and (5).

tween the percentage distribution of export instability and exports is illustrated by the Lorenz curve in Figure 4-6. Looked at another way, the 12 countries with the most exports (66.7 per cent) supplied 63.9 per cent of the export instability.

The overall pattern, which shows that export instability is distributed in fairly close conformity with the value of exports, covers up some notable divergences. Canada, which provided 5.2 per cent of the world's exports, accounted for only 2.0 per cent of the export instability. Japan, with 2.7 per cent of the exports, contributed 4.2 per cent of the instability.

We have used the terms "contributed" and "supplied," to describe a country's share in world export instability. A different interpretation might be placed on these percentages by observing that a particular country "suffered" or "endured" a certain percentage of the world's export instability. Expressed this way, 6 leading exporting countries bore the burden of half of the export instability in the postwar world, while 77 others shared the rest. This statement tells nothing, of course, about the ability of the various countries to bear the burden.

It is interesting to pick out the countries which are in the highest fourth, as measured by their export instability indexes, and which are also in the highest fourth, as measured by their relative contributions to world export instability. There are eight such.

Table 4-5
Countries with High Export Instability Indexes and Making High Contributions to World Export Instability

Country	Export instability index	Percentage of world export instability	Percentage of world exports
(1)	(2)	(3)	(4)
Iran	73.8	1.8	0.5
Indonesia*	57.2	2.6	0.9
Malaya	41.9	1.4	0.7
Argentina*	41.3	1.9	0.9
U.S.S.R.	36.2	7.3	4.2
Japan*	31.0	4.2	2.7
Germany, East	30.2	2.6	1.7
Poland	28.1	1.3	0.9
		23.1%	12.5%

* Also on corresponding list for imports, Table 4-7.

Table 4-5 demonstrates that there is considerable overlap—8 out of 21—among the countries when they are classified according to both high export instability and high contribution to world export instability. It is notable that none of these eight countries is in the North Atlantic group.

Distribution of Import Instability in World International Trade

Although this chapter is approaching international trade instability mainly from the point of view of exports, it is informative to look at the distribution of import instability among the countries of the world in the same way we have just looked at exports. Imports of a country are exports of other countries, of course, but the instability pattern can differ greatly. Table 4-6 and Figure 4-5 provide the information for the countries which

Table 4-6

Percentage Distribution of Import Instability among Countries Accounting for 1 Per Cent or More of World Import Instability

Country [Ranked by value in Col. (2)]	Percentage of world import instability*		Percentage of world imports		Rank by value in Col. (4)
	By country	Cumulative	By country	Cumulative	
(1)	(2)	(3)	(4)	(5)	(6)
1. United Kingdom.......	8.0	8.0	10.2	10.2	2
2. United States.........	7.8	15.8	12.8	23.0	1
3. Japan................	6.0	21.8	3.8	26.8	6
4. France...............	5.5	27.3	5.5	32.3	5
5. Germany, West........	4.5	31.8	6.7	39.0	3
6. U.S.S.R..............	4.3	36.1	3.5	42.5	8
7. Netherlands..........	3.9	40.0	3.7	46.2	7
8. Canada..............	3.8	43.8	5.7	51.9	4
9. China, mainland.......	3.3	47.1	1.9	53.8	13
10. Australia............	3.1	50.2	1.7	55.5	15
11. Brazil†..............	2.5	52.7	1.3	56.8	19
12. Italy................	2.4+	55.1	3.3	60.1	9
13. Belgium-Luxembourg...	2.4−	57.5	3.0	63.1	10
14. Sweden..............	2.3	59.8	2.2	65.3	11
15. Venezuela............	2.2	62.0	1.7	67.0	16
16. Argentina............	2.2	64.2	1.2	68.2	20
17. Austria..............	2.0	66.2	1.0	69.2	22
18. Germany, East........	1.8	68.0	1.4	70.6	18
19. Switzerland†..........	1.7	69.7	1.8	72.4	14
20. Poland..............	1.6	71.3	1.1	73.5	21
21. Indonesia............	1.4	72.7	0.7	74.2	24
22. Union of South Africa†.	1.3	74.0	1.5	75.7	17
23. Finland..............	1.2	75.2	0.8	76.5	23
24. India................	1.2	76.4	2.0	78.5	12
25. New Zealand†........	1.0	77.4	0.7	79.2	25
25 countries‡............	77.4	—	79.2	—	
58 other countries........	22.6	—	20.8	—	
83 countries..........	100.0%	100.0%	100.0%	100.0%	

* Percentages obtained as follows: dollar value of 1957 imports (*International Financial Statistics*, February, 1960, pp. 25, 27) for a country multiplied by its instability index for imports (Figure 4-7, below); these products summed and the product for each country expressed as a per cent of the sum.

† Not among top 25 in distribution of *export* instability.

‡ Four other countries had 1.0 per cent or more of world imports, but contributed less than 1.0 per cent to import instability: Czechoslovakia, 1.24 per cent of total imports (twenty-first in rank), 0.83 per cent of total import instability; Denmark 1.21 (twenty-second), 0.67; Mexico, 1.03 (twenty-sixth), 0.78; Norway, 1.14 (twenty-fourth), 0.94. Column (6) shows ranking of countries, by value of imports in 1957, for countries with 1 per cent or more of world imports.

accounted for 1 per cent or more of the import instability during the period. (Appendix Table A-3 contains the figures for all 83 countries. The sources and methods are the same as for exports.)

The most notable thing in Table 4-6 is that *the United Kingdom made a slightly greater contribution to import instability in the world than the United States.* The United States accounted for only 7.8 per cent of the instability of imports and, obversely, of the instability of exports for other countries.

The next noteworthy point is that 10 countries supplied half (50.2 per cent of the world's import instability, as compared with 6 countries (with 49.4 per cent) in the case of exports. This same tendency toward greater diffusion of import instability than of export instability holds for the 25 countries with the highest percentage contributions. By coincidence the same number of countries, 25, had 1.0 per cent or more of the world totals in both distributions, although only 21 were the same countries. The top 25 countries in the case of imports contributed 77.4 per cent of the instability, compared with 85.2 per cent in the case of exports. The 21 countries appearing on both lists accounted for 79.7 per cent of the export instability and 70.9 per cent of the import instability.

Table 4-6 also permits comparison of the relation between a country's proportionate share of world imports [Column (4)] and its proportionate share of world import instability [Column (2)]. Although the United States and the United Kingdom together took nearly a fourth of the world's imports, they contributed less than a sixth of the total import instability. The other 8 of the first 10 importers took 32.5 per cent of the imports but provided 34.4 per cent of the instability. All 25 of the leading importers bought 79.2 per cent of the total imports and provided 77.4 per cent of the instability. The other 58 countries bought 20.8 per cent of the imports and contributed 22.6 per cent of the import instability. Figure 4-6 shows, by means of a Lorenz curve, the extent to which the percentages of import instability and of imports deviate from equal percentage distributions (as represented by the 45-degree line). It is visually evident that imports deviate more than exports; the average percentage deviation around the 45-degree import line is nearly twice as large as around the 45-degree export line.[3]

Import Instability Indexes for 83 Countries

The individual country indexes of import instability are presented in Figure 4-7. This chart parallels Figure 4-1, which shows export instability.

---

[3] It is 4.33 for imports and 2.31 for exports. They were obtained by getting 9 vertical differences between the ogive and the 45-degree line at 10, 20, . . . , 90 per cent of exports (or imports), summing the differences without reference to sign, and dividing by 9.

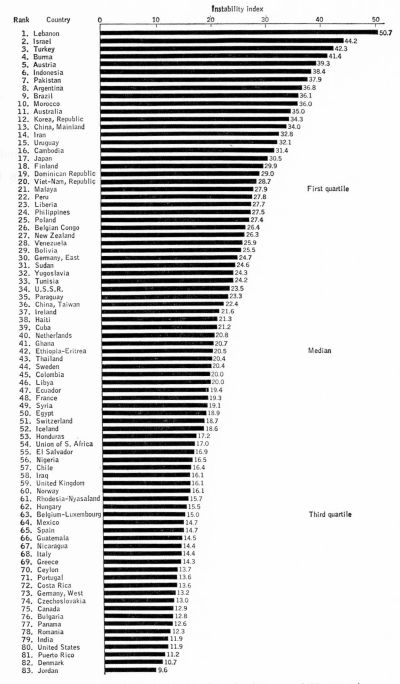

Figure 4-7. Instability index numbers for imports of 83 countries.

63

The range for import instability is from 50.7 for Lebanon to 9.6 for Jordan; the median is 20.5. Figure 4-8 is the frequency distribution of countries according to their import instability indexes.

Although there is no necessary systematic connection between the instability of exports and the instability of imports, because of the almost

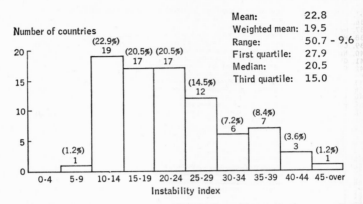

Figure 4-8. Frequency distribution of 83 countries according to index of instability of imports. The weighted mean is by value of imports in 1957.

infinite variety of possible patterns of trading relations among 83 countries over 13 years, it is intriguing to discover the similarities of the frequency distributions of countries according to these two variables. The following tabulation shows the close relation:

Measure	Export instability	Import instability
Range..........................	73.8–6.2	50.7–9.6
First quartile..................	26.6	27.9
Median........................	19.4	20.5
Third quartile.................	14.2	15.0
Interquartile range............	12.4	12.9
Simple mean...................	21.8	22.8
Weighted mean................	20.0	19.5
Standard deviation............	11.5	9.1
Coefficient of variation........	52.9	40.1

The correlation coefficient r between export instability and import instability is $+.43$. This is one of the highest correlation coefficients found in measuring the relation between export instability and other single variables.

Table 4-7 shows the seven countries in the top quarter, according to the import instability index, and also in the top quarter when the countries are ranked according to their contribution to world import instability.

Table 4-7
Countries with High Import Instability Indexes and
Making High Contributions to World Import Instability

Country	Import instability index	Percentage of world import instability	Percentage of world imports
(1)	(2)	(3)	(4)
Austria...............	39.3	2.0	1.0
Indonesia*.............	38.4	1.4	0.7
Argentina*.............	36.8	2.2	1.2
Brazil.................	36.1	2.5	1.3
Australia..............	35.0	3.1	1.7
China, mainland.........	34.0	3.3	1.9
Japan*................	30.5	6.0	3.8
		20.5%	11.6%

* Also on corresponding list for exports, Table 4-5.

These seven countries with high import instability indexes accounted for 20.5 per cent of world import instability. Three of these countries—Indonesia, Argentina, and Japan—were also on the parallel list of eight countries compiled for exports. These three countries, which had only 5.1 per cent of world trade (exports plus imports), provided 9.2 per cent of the world's instability of exports and imports. The 12 countries in the top quarter for either exports or imports, according to these two measures, provided 22.3 per cent of the instability of international trade (both exports and imports) while they had only 12.1 per cent of it. In citing these countries, it should be noted that some other countries had higher instability indexes for exports and/or imports, but accounted for a smaller share of world trade instability because of their small trade volume; while still other countries accounted for larger shares of world trade instability but had relatively low instability indexes.

Instability of Imports of Countries, by Geographic Region

Table 4-8 brings out the fact that imports are much more unstable in Asia, South America, and Africa than in Europe and North America. The median instability index for Asia (29.6) is twice as large as that for North America (14.5).

There is one pronounced difference in the relative positions of the continents in this table, as compared with the corresponding table for exports (Table 4-1): South America has a median import instability index of 25.9, second highest, compared with a median export instability

Table 4-8
Import Instability of Countries, by Continent
(Ranked by median instability index)

Continent	Median I-I	Range of I-I	Number of countries
(1)	(2)	(3)	(4)
Asia..........................	29.6	9.6–50.7	22
South America................	25.9	13.6–36.8	13
Africa.......................	20.6	15.7–36.0	12
Europe.......................	17.4	10.7–42.3	26
North America................	14.5	11.2–21.3	10
World.......................	20.5	9.6–50.7	83

index of 16.1, fourth highest. The other continents have their same relative positions with Asia highest and North America lowest.

Instability of Imports of Countries, by Monetary Group

Table 4-9 brings out one difference in typical import instability indexes. When the countries are grouped according to the classification used by the

Table 4-9
Import Instability of Countries, by Monetary Group
(Ranked by median instability index)

Group	Median I-I	Range of I-I	Number of countries
(1)	(2)	(3)	(4)
Rest of World................	24.6	12.3–50.7	29
Western Hemisphere...........	19.4	11.2–36.8	23
Sterling Area................	19.3	9.6–41.4	16
Continental European Fund.....	18.7	10.7–42.3	15
World.......................	20.5	9.6–50.7	83

International Monetary Fund, with minor consolidations, Rest of World has a higher median instability index for imports (24.6) than the Western Hemisphere (19.4), the Sterling Area (19.3) and the Continental members of the European Fund (18.7).

Instability of Imports of Countries, by Political Group

Table 4-10 shows instability of imports for countries classified into political groups as of the 1950s. There are two main observations here. Members of the North Atlantic Treaty Organization had a below-average median instability index. "Other Allies" of the United States had a median I-I of 31.2; only one of these 12 countries had below-average instability of imports. The Communist countries, Latin America, and "Uncom-

Table 4-10
Import Instability of Countries, by Political Group
(Ranked by median instability index)

Group	Median I-I	Range of I-I	Number of countries
(1)	(2)	(3)	(4)
NATO countries..............	15.0	10.7–42.3	15
Communist countries...........	19.5	12.3–34.0	8
Latin America.................	20.0	11.2–36.8	21
Uncommitted countries........	20.7	9.6–51.0	27
Other allies..................	31.2	14.7–50.7	12
World.....................	20.5	9.6–50.7	83
Non-Communist countries....	20.5	9.6–50.7	75

mitted" countries had about typical median instability indexes. Other Allies also had the highest median instability index for exports (Table 4-3).

Exports of Countries with Highest Instability Indexes

The instability index provides a summary measure of the instability of a particular time series, with adjustment for trend, but it does not disclose the pattern of variation around the trend. Figure 4-9 portrays the year-to-year pattern. It shows graphically the exports of each of the 21 countries with the highest export instability indexes, generally for the years 1946 to 1958. Appendix Table A-1 gives the figures for all 83 countries. The logarithmic scale is used on the y-axis in order to facilitate comparison of relative changes.

Although this chapter is intentionally largely statistical, it seems appropriate to call attention to some of the main events in the "annals" of these individual countries which contributed significantly to their export instability. The very high instability index of Iran (73.8) is principally the result of the struggle over the ownership and operation of the petroleum industry in that country in the early 1950s. Indonesia's high I-I (57.2) is largely attributable to the low state of exports after the

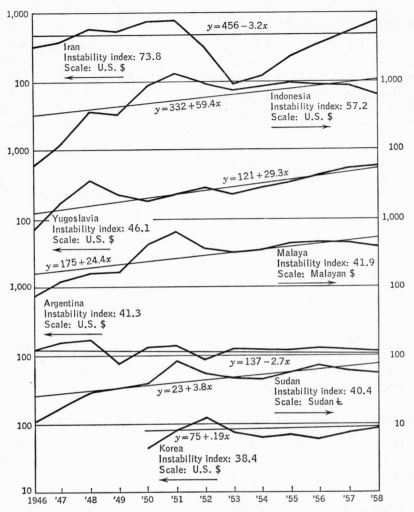

Figure 4-9. Exports, 1946–1958, of countries with the highest export instability indexes. (Ratio scale in millions of currency units as noted.) Source: Appendix Table A-1.

Japanese occupation and during the political struggle with the Dutch, though the 1951 peak must be attributed to the Korean crisis. (Part of this instability, as measured, must be credited to the use of the straight, logarithmic trend line, since it is apparent from the graph that there are two phases in the trend 1946 to 1951 and 1952 to 1958. Separate instability indexes for these subperiods would be much lower.) Yugoslavia's instability is concentrated in the early postwar period, much of it attrib-

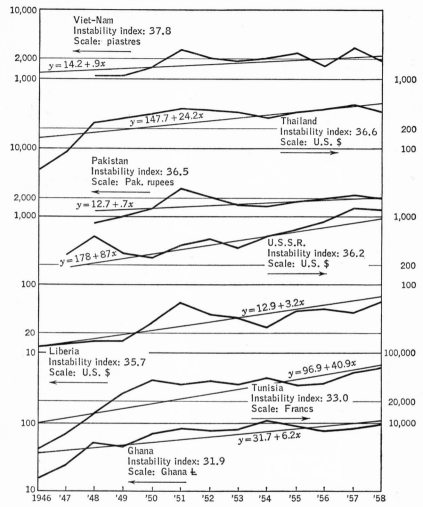

Figure 4-9, Part 2. For descriptive legend see opposite page.

utable to the Soviet attempt to dominate Marshal Tito by economic pressure. Malayan instability is largely the result of the immediate post-war confusion and the Korean crisis. Argentina's instability index of 41.3 is linked in part with Peron's economic adventures. Sudan's high rank is linked particularly with cotton and the expansion associated with the Korean crisis. Korea's 38.4 is connected with the exodus of the Japanese and the confusion which accompanied the hostilities which began in June, 1950. Vietnam's export instability is also closely linked with its political troubles—with the Japanese, the French, and the Chinese

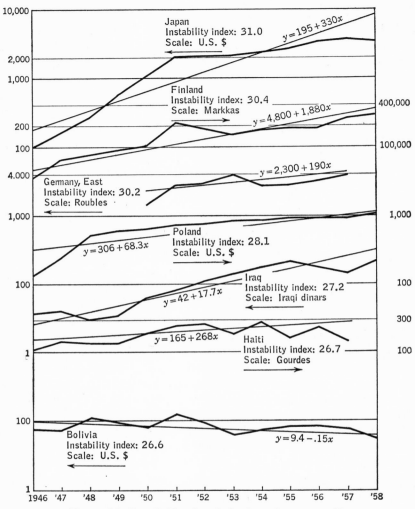

Figure 4-9, Part 3. For descriptive legend see page 68.

Communists. Thailand's relatively high index stems from the immediate postwar years; after 1948 the exports were fairly stable. Pakistan's instability index of 36.5 arises mainly from the upsurge of demand for raw materials associated with the Korean conflict.

The time series for the U.S.S.R. requires more comment. The figures are for Soviet exports to the non-Communist countries of the world; figures on total Soviet trade are not available for years before 1955.[4]

[4] U.S. Department of State, *Statistical Review of East-West Trade 1956–57*, July,

Soviet exports to the Free World, as a per cent of total Soviet exports, gradually increased from 18.5 per cent in 1955 to 24.1 per cent in 1958. The information is lacking to show the degree of instability of Soviet trade with its Eastern European satellites and Communist China. Part of the instability of Soviet exports to the Free World can be attributed to the strategic trade controls maintained in varying degrees by the NATO countries and Japan during much of the period; part must also be attributed to Soviet availabilities and trade policy. Whatever the explanation, the facts, as they are available, show the Soviet Union to be the most unstable exporter among the major trading countries.

Liberia's ups and downs in export proceeds arise mainly from rubber production and prices. Tunisia's high instability figure appears to be more "statistical" than real, since the path for 1946 to 1950 is smooth, and the bobbles are not large for 1950 to 1958. Ghana's instability index of 31.9 is largely the story of cocoa during this period. Japan's inclusion may also be viewed as partly a statistical result, arising from the very different trends from 1946 to 1951 and 1951 to 1958. The large cycle in prices of lumber and lumber products, 1950 to 1953, explains much of Finland's export instability. The instability index for East Germany (30.2) is derived from data for the years 1950 to 1958, so it almost certainly understates the actual instability. If the reconstruction years of 1946 and 1947 were excluded, Poland would have a much lower instability index. Iraq's relatively high figure is largely explained by oil prices and internal politics. Haiti's exports were unstable mainly because of the gyrations of the coffee market. Boliva's fluctuations in export proceeds are closely associated with prices and trade in nonferrous metals, particularly tin.

This enumeration of the events which affected the stability of exports of these 21 countries with the highest instability indexes reveals that there were specific influences in nearly every case. It would be a mistake to attribute the instability of exports of these countries simply to these specific influences, however, since many other countries were subjected to these or similar influences but had much lower instability indexes. Our discussion in Chapters 5 and 6 attempts to sort out the characteristics of countries which tend to be associated with high or low export insta-bility. "Explanation" of an historical sequence for an area is always in terms of a combination of influences, some of which are present in other areas as well as in the particular area, and some of which are

---

1958, p. 2. With the ruble at four to the dollar, and using the figures on the Soviet Union's total exports on p. 571 of the United Nations *Yearbook of International Trade Statistics,* 1957, the exports of the Soviet Union to non-Communist countries as a per cent of its total exports were: 1955, 18.5 per cent; 1956, 22.6 per cent: 1957, 23.8 per cent. With GATT and IMF data, the 1958 per cent is 24.1.

unique to the area. Some of the classifications used in this essentially descriptive chapter anticipate the later attempts at explanation.

Instability of Exports of Principal Exporting Countries

In 1957, six countries—the United States, the United Kingdom, Western Germany, Canada, France, and the U.S.S.R.—accounted for 51.6 per cent of world exports. It is of particular interest, therefore, to look at their exports for each of the years 1946 to 1958. Figure 4-10 provides graphs of export proceeds of the six countries. The ratio scale is used on the y-axis to facilitate comparisons. These countries accounted for 47.1 per cent of the world instability of exports [Table 4-4, Column (2)]. It is visually clear that the instability indexes reflect quite well the relative instability of exports of these major traders. Canada is the most stable and the U.S.S.R. the most unstable. Germany calls for comment. If there were usable figures for West Germany for 1946 and 1947, they would be relatively small, and the straight-line logarithmic trend line would be even less appropriate than it is for the German series, so the instability index would be considerably larger than 19.4.

Distribution of Instability of International Trade among Countries

In this section we bring together the instability measures of exports *and* imports, for the various countries, in order to provide a panoramic view of instability in international trade.

A country's instability index for exports and its instability index for imports are both elements in international economic instability. Although we hide some of the variability in the process, in this section we average each country's export instability index number and import instability index number in order to obtain its "foreign trade instability" index number. In a like manner we average, for each country, its percentage share of instability of world exports and its percentage share of instability of world imports. It will be recalled from the discussion earlier in this chapter that these percentage shares are the percentage shares of world exports (or imports), adjusted for each country's export (or import) instability index. The result is each country's "percentage share of instability of world international trade." For convenience this percentage is called "S" and the trade instability index is called "X_t" in this discussion and in Table 4-11, which provides the basic compilation.

Table 4-11 shows countries grouped into thirds according to each of the variables, S and X_t. It enables us to see at a glance which countries were the low, medium, and high contributors to the world total of international trade instability (across), and which countries had the low,

Billions of U.S. $

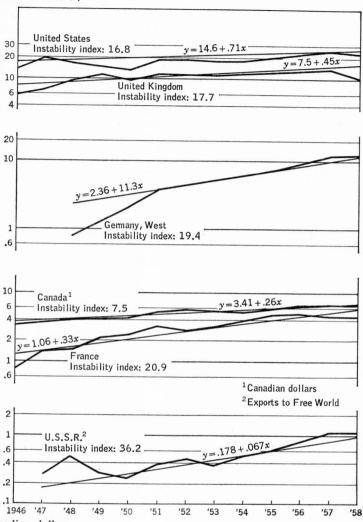

¹ Canadian dollars.
² Exports to Free World.

Figure 4-10. Exports of leading exporting countries, 1946–1958 (ratio scale).

Table 4-11

Eighty-three Countries Classified According to (S) Percentage Share of Instability of World International Trade and (X_t) Index of Instability of Foreign Trade

Index of instability of foreign trade (X_t)	Percentage share of instability of world international trade (S)									Total
	Lowest third by (S)			Middle third by (S)			Highest third by (S)			
	Country	(X_t)	(S)	Country	(X_t)	(S)	Country	(X_t)	(S)	
Lowest third of countries by (X_t)	Romania	10.0	0.185	Puerto Rico	10.1	0.290	Canada	10.1	2.850	No. of countries = 28
	Panama	11.3	0.045	Denmark	10.4	0.615	Switzerland	12.5	1.075	Median X_t = 14.5
	Jordan	11.9	0.025	Spain	12.8	0.415	Union of South Africa	13.7	0.975	Range X_t = 10.0–16.8
	Guatemala	12.6	0.080	Mexico	12.9	0.580	India	14.1	1.140	Median S = 0.320
	Ceylon	13.4	0.230	Ireland	14.0	0.310	United States	14.4	12.200	Range S = 0.025–12.200
	Costa Rica	14.0	0.060	Rhodesia-Nyasaland	14.1	0.330	Germany, West	16.3	6.200	ΣS = 33.385
	Nicaragua	14.3	0.045	Norway	16.3	0.790	Czechoslovakia	16.7	1.075	
	Portugal	14.4	0.260	Colombia	16.7	0.380	Belgium-Luxembourg	16.8	2.575	
	El Salvador	15.4	0.090							
	Bulgaria	15.8	0.245							
	Greece	16.3	0.265							
	Honduras	16.7	0.055							
			ΣS = 1.585			ΣS = 3.710			ΣS = 28.090	
	N = 12			N = 8			N = 8			
	Md_{X_t} = 14.2; Range X_t = 10.0–16.7			Md_{X_t} = 13.5; Range X_t = 10.1–16.7			Md_{X_t} = 14.3; Range X_t = 10.1–16.8			
	Md_S = 0.085; Range S = 0.025–0.265			Md_S = 0.398; Range S = 0.290–0.790			Md_S = 1.858; Range S = 0.975–12.200			
	Country	(X_t)	(S)	Country	(X_t)	(S)	Country	(X_t)	(S)	Total
Middle third of countries by (X_t)	Syria	17.4	0.135	Hungary	18.0	0.475	United Kingdom	16.9	8.270	No. of countries = 27
	China, Taiwan	19.4	0.165	Chile	18.3	0.380	Sweden	17.8	1.900	Median X_t = 20.4
	Paraguay	19.7	0.025	Belgian Congo	18.6	0.385	Italy	18.0	2.510	Range X_t = 16.9–25.9
	Iceland	20.4	0.065	Nigeria	18.8	0.335	France	20.1	5.260	Median S = 0.380

74

Country	(X_t)	(S)	Country	(X_t)	(S)	Country	(X_t)	(S)	Total
Libya	21.3	0.045	Egypt	19.5	0.475	Venezuela	21.0	2.010	Range S = 0.025-8.270
Ecuador	22.3	0.130	Peru	19.9	0.330	Netherlands	21.1	3.530	ΣS = 31.340
Ethiopia	22.4	0.080	New Zealand	20.5	0.770	Cuba	23.6	0.955	
Dominican Republic	23.0	0.155	Iraq	21.7	0.355	Brazil	24.9	1.690	
Haiti	24.0	0.040	Philippines	23.9	0.645				
Uruguay	25.9	0.225							
N = 10		ΣS = 1.065	N = 9		ΣS = 4.150	N = 8		ΣS = 26.125	
Md_{x_t} = 21.8; Range X_t = 17.4-25.9			Md_{x_t} = 19.5; Range X_t = 18.0-23.9			Md_{x_t} = 20.6; Range X_t = 16.9-24.9			
Md_S = 0.105; Range S = 0.025-0.225			Md_S = 0.385; Range X = 0.330-0.770			Md_S = 2.260; Range S = 0.955-8.270			

	Country	(X_t)	(S)	Country	(X_t)	(S)	Country	(X_t)	(S)	Total
Highest third of countries by (X_t)	Bolivia	26.1	0.100	Ghana	26.3	0.305	China, mainland	27.4	2.815	No. of countries = 28
	Cambodia	28.2	0.071	Burma	28.1	0.360	Germany, East	27.5	2.210	Median X_t = 30.6
	Tunisia	28.6	0.215	Israel	28.1	0.480	Poland	27.8	1.445	Range X_t = 26.1-53.3
	Liberia	31.7	0.075	Thailand	28.5	0.505	Australia	29.8	2.845	Median S = 0.620
	Sudan	32.5	0.250	Morocco	30.9	0.540	U.S.S.R.	29.8	5.875	Range S = 0.070-5.875
	Vietnam	33.3	0.260	Turkey	30.9	0.545	Finland	30.2	1.225	ΣS = 35.275
				Yugoslavia	35.2	0.800	Austria	30.4	1.515	
				Korea, Republic	36.4	0.370	Japan	30.8	5.105	
				Pakistan	37.2	0.695	Malaya	34.9	1.085	
				Lebanon	38.4	0.315	Argentina	39.1	2.055	
							Indonesia	47.8	2.020	
							Iran	53.3	1.195	
	N = 6		ΣS = 0.970	N = 10		ΣS = 4.915	N = 12		ΣS = 29.390	
	Md_{x_t} = 30.2; Range X_t = 26.1-33.3			Md_{x_t} = 30.9; Range X_t = 26.3-38.4			Md_{x_t} = 30.3; Range X_t = 27.4-53.3			
	Md_S = 0.158; Range S = 0.070-0.260			Md_S = 0.493; Range S = 0.305-0.800			Md_S = 2.038; Range S = 1.085-5.875			

Total:			Total:			Total:			Total No. of countries = 83
N = 28		ΣS = 3.620	N = 27		ΣS = 12.775	N = 28		ΣS = 83.605	Median X_t = 20.4
Md_{x_t} = 21.8; Range X_t = 10.0-33.3			Md_{x_t} = 19.5; Range X_t = 10.1-38.4			Md_{x_t} = 20.6; Range X_t = 10.1-53.3			Range X_t = 10.0-53.3
Md_S = 0.095; Range S = 0.025-0.260			Md_S = 0.415; Range S = 0.290-0.800			Md_S = 2.0375; Range S = 0.955-12.200			Median S = 0.415
									Range S = 0.025-12.200
									ΣS = 100.0

medium, and high instability indexes of trade (down). Thus in the
upper left cell of the table are listed the 12 countries which contributed
as a group a mere 1.585 per cent of the international trade instability
and which had a median trade instability index of only 14.2 (with a
range of 10.0 to 16.7). At the opposite corner of the table, the cell at
the lower right, are the 12 countries which were in the highest third of
the contributors to world trade instability *and* in the highest third according
to their trade instability indexes. These countries were both unstable in
their trade relations and important in world trade instability. As a group,
they contributed 29.39 per cent of the international trade instability. They
had a median trade instability index of 30.3, with a range from 27.4

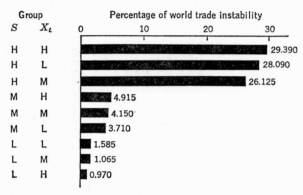

Figure 4-11. Percentage shares of world trade instability for groups of countries
classified according to percentage share of world trade instability (*S*) and trade
instability index (*X_t*). *Note:* H stands for highest third, M for middle third, and L
for lowest third. See Table 4-11 for further details.

to 53.3. Their median instability contribution was 2.038 per cent and
the range from 1.085 to 5.875 per cent. Not a single NATO country
and only one Western Hemisphere country is in this group. Four of
the twelve are Communist countries.

Figure 4-11 shows the percentages of world trade instability for all
nine groups of countries of Table 4-11. The extent to which instability
of world trade was concentrated is brought out very clearly in this chart.
The three groups (28 countries) in the highest third, by percentage of
world trade instability, accounted for five-sixths (83.6 per cent) of the
world trade instability. These countries had the same share of world
trade (83.6 per cent of exports and imports combined), but this close
relation is not a necessary one, since different instability indexes could
affect the results.

From the information available in Table 4-11 it is possible to rank
countries according to their percentage shares of world trade instability.

The 20 highest are singled out in Table 4-12 and Figure 4-12. Table 4-12 also shows the percentage of world trade conducted by each of these countries.

The United States is the largest single country factor in the instability of international trade, with about one-eighth of the world total (12.2

Table 4-12
Countries Accounting for Highest Percentages
of Instability of World International Trade

Country [Ranked by value in Col. (2)]	Percentage of world trade instability		Percentage of world trade (exports plus imports)		Rank by value in Col. (4)
	By country	Cumu-lative	By country	Cumu-lative	
(1)	(2)	(3)	(4)	(5)	(6)
1. United States (L)*.......	12.200	12.200	16.40	16.40	1
2. United Kingdom (M).....	8.270	20.470	9.75	26.15	2
3. Germany, West (L).......	6.200	26.670	7.40	33.55	3
4. U.S.S.R. (H)............	5.875	32.545	3.85	37.40	6
5. France (M)..............	5.260	37.805	5.15	42.55	5
6. Japan (H)..............	5.105	42.910	3.25	46.80	8
7. Netherlands (M).........	3.530	46.440	3.30	49.10	7
8. Canada (L)..............	2.850	49.290	5.45	54.55	4
9. Australia (H)............	2.845	52.135	1.90	56.45	14
10. China, mainland (H).....	2.815	54.950	2.05	58.50	12
11. Belgium-Luxembourg (L).	2.575	57.525	3.00	61.50	9
12. Italy (M)..............	2.510	60.035	2.85	64.35	10
13. Germany, East (H).......	2.210	62.245	1.55	65.90	15
14. Argentina (H)..........	2.055	64.300	1.05	66.95	17
15. Indonesia (H)..........	2.020	66.320	0.80	67.75	20
16. Venezuela (M)..........	2.010	68.330	1.95	69.70	13
17. Sweden (M).............	1.900	70.230	2.10	71.80	11
18. Brazil (M).............	1.690	71.920	1.30	73.10	16
19. Austria (H).............	1.515	73.435	0.95	74.05	19
20. Poland (H).............	1.445	74.880	1.00	75.05	18
20 countries..............	74.880	—	75.05	—	
63 other countries.........	25.120	—	24.95	—	
83 countries.............	100.000	100.000	100.00	100.00	

* Trade instability index in lowest third (*L*), middle third (*M*), or highest third (*H*) of the 83 countries. See Table 4-11 for details.
Sources: Tables 4-4, 4-5, and 4-11.

per cent). The United Kingdom is second (8.3 per cent), West Germany third (6.2 per cent), and the U.S.S.R. fourth (5.9 per cent). Canada is eighth in percentage of world instability but fourth in the percentage of world trade. The eight countries with the highest percentage contributions to instability accounted for almost half (49.3 per cent) of the world trade instability and conducted about 55 per cent of the world's trade. If the next eight countries are added—Australia through Venezuela in Table 4-12—just over two-thirds of the instability is accounted for and just under 70 per cent of the trade. The top 20 countries accounted for 75 per cent of the instability and 75 per cent of the trade.

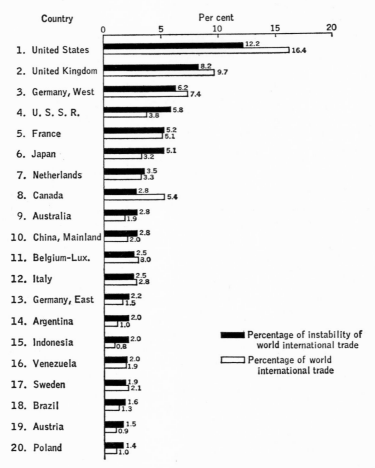

Figure 4-12. Countries accounting for highest percentages of instability of world international trade. Source: Table 4-12.

Only 4 of these 20 countries have "low" trade instability indexes— Canada (10.1), United States (14.4), West Germany (16.3), and Belgium (16.8). Seven of the countries had "medium" instability indexes and nine had "high." These 9 were all but 3 of the 12 countries in the highest third according to both classifications, trade instability index and percentage of world trade instability (lower right-hand cell in Table 4-11). Despite the weight of these 9 high-incidence countries, the 28 countries with the highest trade instability indexes, including the 9, accounted for only 35.3 per cent of the world trade instability. The presumption is, therefore, that *the reduction of instability for the countries with the highest instability indexes would not have a marked effect on the instability of international trade generally.*

Conclusions of Chapter

Certain important generalizations emerge from this chapter. Probably the most important is the distinction between (1) the incidence among countries of high instability of trade (exports, imports, or both) and (2) the incidence of a high percentage share of world instability of trade (exports, imports, or both). For example, Canada ranked very low (eighty-first) in instability of trade but very high (eighth) as a contributor to world trade instability. The policy implications of this distinction would seem to be that it is one thing to take measures designed to reduce the instability of exports or imports, or both, of countries with high instability indexes, but that it is something very different indeed to take measures to reduce the instability of world trade generally. It is conceivable that these two characteristics could show a high positive correlation among countries, but the fact is that they do not.

Perhaps the second most important point is that the United States is not as important a factor in international economic instability as has been widely assumed. The United States had a below-average export instability index (16.8) compared with the median of 19.4, the simple mean of 21.8, and the weighted mean of 20.0. Forty-eight countries had higher export instability indexes. Also, the United States had a below-average import instability index (11.9 compared with the median of 20.5, the simple mean of 22.8, and the weighted mean of 19.5). Seventy-nine of the eighty-three countries had higher import instability indexes. Moreover, the United States contributed only 16.6 per cent of world export instability, compared with its 20.0 per cent of world exports; 7.8 per cent of world import instability, compared with its 12.8 per cent of world imports; and 12.2 per cent of the world trade instability (exports plus imports), compared with its 16.4 per cent of world trade. Unless some special assumptions are introduced regarding trading relations, it seems incorrect to attribute much more than one-eighth of the world's international trade instability to the United States for this period.

Chapter 5

STATISTICAL ANALYSIS OF INSTABILITY OF EXPORT PROCEEDS

In the present chapter we start with the facts of export instability of various countries, as described in Chapter 4, and endeavor to explain these variations by methods which are in essence correlation or factor analysis. We try to discover what characteristics of countries are associated with high or low instability of export proceeds, and in what degree.

The results are influenced, of course, by the characteristics or variables selected. If one knew which variables to select, a large part of the problem would be solved, for it would remain only to measure their relative importance in determining export instability. Fundamentally, one selects the variables on the basis of his knowledge of the economic processes involved and on the basis of the explicit or implicit theories he holds regarding the processes. Some variables seem likely to turn out to be major determinants, a priori, while others hold dim prospects. There is obviously room for analytical experimentation.

After the investigator has enumerated the variables which seem likely to be relevant, he then has to pare down the list in the light of the available statistical materials, and possibly in the light of his own resources for investigation. In going through this process in the present study in the effort to obtain a list of plausible and usable variables for trying to explain the variability in export proceeds of the various countries, nearly 40 variables emerged. That data are available for such a large number reflects the great increase in statistical materials since the end of World War II. Many of these variables are only slightly or superficially different; they frequently relate to the same underlying forces. Even when they can be distinguished fairly clearly, they are often functionally interdependent.

Grouping of Variables

In order to provide some system in the discussion of these forces which determine instability of export proceeds, the variables are grouped under the following headings:

Size, growth, and importance of foreign trade

80

Direction of exports
Composition of exports
Size of national economy
Growth of national economy
Economic level of country
Prices, monetary factors

Method of Analysis

The first step in the analysis of the relation between the instability of export proceeds and these "determining" variables is to examine the relation between each of these variables and export instability. In several instances formal correlation analysis is used, but generally the countries are divided into two or more groups, with reference to the "independent" variable being considered, and then the differences, if any, in the typical export instability index values discovered. Enough detail is provided to show the variation around the measure of central tendency. The median is used most frequently in order to avoid the distorting influence of large numbers on means.

One does not have to know much about the phenomenon of international economic instability in order to realize that single-variable analysis is not likely to yield very high correlations, but persons who should know better sometimes seize on single-variable explanations, such as that linking variations in export proceeds with fluctuations in United States national income. It is highly desirable, therefore, to take two or more "determining" variables into account in measuring differences in instability of export proceeds. Sometimes two variables can be taken into account by using ratios, e.g., relating national income per capita to export proceeds rather than national income or population. Other times a two-way classification can be used. If each of the variables is a ratio, such as national income per capita, then a two-way classification really takes into account four variables. Three-way or higher classifications are generally not feasible in view of the fact that there are only 83 cases (countries), at a maximum, with which to work.

This chapter shows the relation between single variables and export proceeds. Chapter 6 takes up the multivariable analysis. The order in which the variables are considered has no particular significance.

SIZE, GROWTH, AND IMPORTANCE OF FOREIGN TRADE

Export Quantum Instability

Export proceeds of a country for a period of time are, by definition, $p_1 \cdot q_1 + p_2 \cdot q_2 + \cdots + p_n \cdot q_n$, when p stands for average price per unit of a particular exported good or service, q for the quantity of such good or service sold during the period, and the subscripts 1, 2, . . . , n the different goods and services. Hence, unless there are fully compensating changes in prices, changes in quantities will affect export receipts. If the country faces relatively elastic demands for its exports, which is the most probable situation, a reduction of quantity from one period to another will reduce total receipts, and an increase in quantity sold will increase receipts. If the country should be in the unusual monopolistic situation of facing demand curves with elasticities of less than unity in the relevant ranges, a reduction of quantity sold would increase receipts and an increase in quantity sold would decrease receipts. There is no a priori certainty as to which situation is in fact dominant, but there is a strong presumption in favor of a positive correlation between export proceeds and export volume, because of the fairly competitive character of most international markets.

Correlation analysis bears out this presumption. The coefficient of linear correlation between the instability index of export proceeds and the instability index of export volume is +.58. Seventy of the eighty-three countries were included in this calculation. Figure 5-1 shows the scatter diagram and the least-squares line of volume on export proceeds. The indexes of export volume are in Column X_8 of Appendix Table A-2.

When the countries were ranked with reference to instability of export quantum, the lowest third had a median index of instability of export proceeds (Y) of 15.1, the middle third a median Y of 16.6, and the highest third a median Y of 21.4. The 13 countries for which data on export volume were lacking had a median Y of 22.5. The dispersion around the median was quite large in each case, as shown under X_8 in Figure 5-11 and Table 5-4 in the summary section of this chapter.

The size of the correlation coefficient (.58) and the differences in the medians for the three thirds support the conclusion that there is a positive correlation between instability of export quantum and export proceeds. This correlation coefficient is higher than that between export proceeds and any other single variable. (Table 5-4, in the summary section of this chapter, shows the ranking.)

Import Instability

A common opinion is that a country's export proceeds vary quite closely with its expenditures on imports of goods and services, even for periods as short as a year. This has been expressed many times in connection with United States trade policy: "You cannot sell unless you buy," "Trade is a two-way street," etc.

Alternatively, if a country is short of international reserves, its imports might depend principally on its exports, on the assumption that exports vary and the country spends practically all of its current export proceeds on current imports, perhaps with a little lead or lag. Either of these lines of reasoning leads one to expect a close correlation between the indexes of import instability and of export instability.

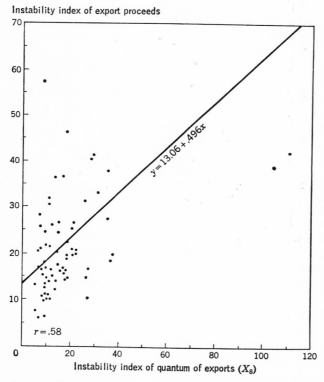

Figure 5-1. Scatter diagram: instability of quantum of exports and instability of export proceeds for 70 countries.

The correlation analysis reveals a correlation coefficient of $+.43$ between import instability and export instability (Y). Figure 5-2 shows the relation graphically. Column X_3 of Appendix Table A-2 contains the import instability index values. When the 83 countries were ranked with reference to the index of import instability, the lowest third had a median export instability index (Y) of 15.7, the middle third had a median Y of 22.1, and the highest third a median Y of 24.8. The positive relation

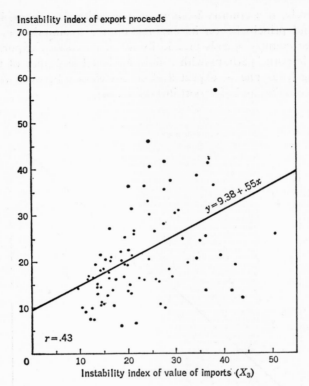

Figure 5-2. Scatter diagram: instability of value of imports and instability of export proceeds for 83 countries.

between these two variables is thus indicated. The correlation coefficient of +.43 and the dispersion around the median for each third (under X_3 in Figure 5-11 and Table 5-4 in summary section) reveal the influence of other factors than import instability as a determinant of export instability.

Foreign Trade as Per Cent of GNP

Exports plus imports (both goods and services) expressed as a percentage of gross national product or national income is a convenient measure of a country's involvement in international trade. The measure does not reveal, however, whether the foreign trade is concentrated in an enclave or whether it penetrates most segments of a national economy, nor does it indicate the degree of essentiality of imports to the country. Treated with caution, though, the "foreign trade percentage" is a useful measure, especially since statistical estimates of gross national product,

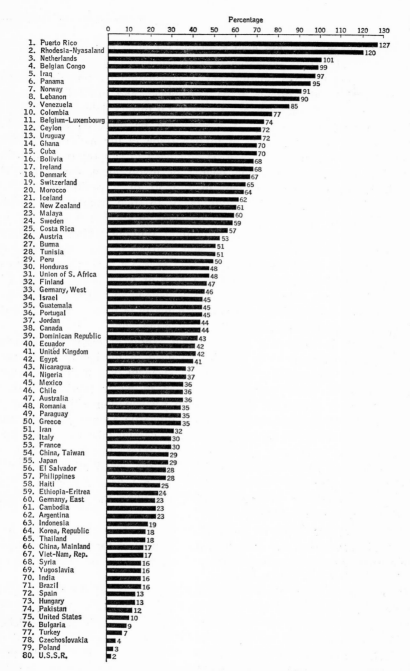

Figure 5-3. Foreign trade as a percentage of gross national product for 80 countries, 1957. Source: Column (X_4), Appendix Table A-2. See statistical note in Appendix for discussion of comparability of national product aggregates.

or related magnitudes, are now available for most countries. Figure 5-3 shows the foreign trade percentages for 80 countries in 1957.

The relation between involvement in international economic relations, as measured by the foreign trade percentage, and instability of export proceeds is one of much policy interest, for it throws light on the question of whether relative stability of exports can be obtained by increasing or decreasing the importance of foreign trade in the national economy. Plausible a priori arguments can be advanced in support of and against the view that the greater the degree of involvement the greater the export instability. The argument in support of a positive correlation between involvement and instability seems to stem from the undeniable proposition that if there is no involvement in foreign trade there will not be any export (or import) instability! Without taking this extreme position, proponents of this view would contend that a reduction in the relative importance of foreign trade would enable a government to pursue domestic stabilization policies without fear of their being disrupted by external influences. Advocates of centrally planned and managed economies would tend to support this position, particularly in view of the difficulties of planning international trade and executing the plans.

Arguments in support of the view that export proceeds will be more stable if a country is more heavily involved in foreign trade follow a different line. They assume that high involvement of a national economy in international trade means participation in wider markets, both as supplier and as demander, and that such participation will contribute to stability of export proceeds (and of the domestic economy) rather than lessen it. Advocates of laissez-faire, who generally take this view, stress the gains from geographic specialization and international trade, in terms of real incomes or satisfactions, rather than the contribution to stability. Unfortunately for this viewpoint, there are not firm conclusions, from economic analysis or empirical studies, regarding the relation between market structure and stability.

Spokesmen for countries with high foreign trade percentages have frequently contended that their high involvement in foreign trade subjects their economies to large instabilities of export proceeds, which generate undesirable internal repercussions.

What do the facts show? The coefficient of correlation between the foreign trade percentage and export instability (Y) is —.30. Figure 5-4 shows the relation. If one may place any confidence in this coefficient, it shows that the higher the foreign trade as a percentage of gross national product, the lower the export instability index. In other words, there is a tendency toward greater stability of export proceeds as involvement in foreign trade increases. In policy terms, a country is not likely to reduce the instability of its export proceeds by taking measures to cut down its involvement in international trade—unless it eliminates its foreign trade.

When the countries (80 of the 83) are ranked with reference to foreign trade as a percentage of gross national product, the median export instability index (Y) in 24.3 for the lowest third of the countries, 17.3 for the middle third, and 16.1 for the highest third. Thus the same negative correlation is revealed as in the formal correlation analysis. The dispersion

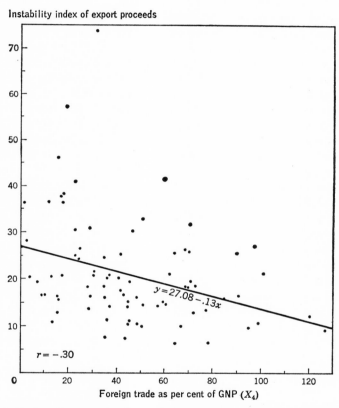

Figure 5-4. Scatter diagram: foreign trade as per cent of gross national product and instability of export proceeds for 80 countries.

around the medians is shown under X_4 in Figure 5-11 and Table 5-4 in the summary section of this chapter.

This variable—foreign trade as a percentage of GNP—has some additional significance in the context of this whole study. If a country had practically no economic relations with other countries, it would not be concerned with the problems of international economic instability. Changes in the economies of other countries would not affect it appreciably, and economic changes in it would not affect other countries. There would be only the possibility of psychological transmission of economic pulsations—a rather remote possibility in the absence of appreciable economic contacts. The country, in comparative isolation, might or might not have disturbingly large instabilities.

It seems plausible, at least at first blush, to suppose that countries with higher and higher foreign trade percentages would be more and more susceptible to instabilities from elsewhere. At one stage in the present study, an attempt was made, starting with the information provided in Figure 5-3 on foreign trade percentages for 80 countries, to eliminate countries from consideration on the basis of their low foreign trade percentages. This attempt was unsuccessful, for it was apparent, on the basis of other information, that even the countries with low foreign trade percentages were very much involved in foreign trade from other points of view. For example, the Soviet Union had a foreign trade percentage of only 2 per cent (or possibly 3, depending on the method of calculation) but it was the world's sixth largest exporter and eighth largest importer (1957). Also, its trade is extremely important to several countries, and it has a potential, in the form of its productive capacity, for greatly expanding its trade. It also has the political control and the self-sufficiency required to vary its trade rapidly and substantially for whatever reasons. Even the most casual knowledge of the economies of Turkey, the United States, Pakistan, and other countries with the lowest foreign trade percentages makes it apparent that it would be inappropriate to eliminate any of these countries from consideration in the present study on the basis of a low foreign trade percentage. Stated positively, this means that all countries covered by this study have a basis for concern with the problem of international economic instability. There is a presumption that the few remaining areas of the world have a similar basis for concern.

Foreign Economic Impact

The foreign trade percentage that we have been discussing in the preceding section is a measure of the impact of the foreign trade of a country upon its economy. It tells nothing of the impact of the foreign trade of one country upon the economies of other countries. We now turn to this other aspect of involvement.

A plausible single measure to show the impact of one country's foreign trade on other countries, as a group, is the sum of the country's exports and imports expressed as a percentage of the sum of the gross national products of all other countries. We shall call this measure the "global impact percentage." When the foreign trade of one country with a second country is expressed as a percentage of the gross national product of the second country, we have a "bilateral foreign impact percentage."[1]

If foreign trade were proportional to gross national product for each country, then the figures showing the percentage distribution of world international trade, or of world production, among countries would measure the *relative* impact of the trade of individual countries on other countries as a group. Figure 5-3 shows that there is so much variation in the ratio of trade to national production that this approach is not usable.

We are concerned in this section with the relation between the "global foreign impact percentage" and the export instability index. A country's foreign trade (exports and imports) in relation to the economic activity of the rest of the world is a rough measure of the "weight" a country "throws around" in the world economy. Column X_{11} of Table A-2 in the Appendix gives these percentages. What influence might this variable be expected to have on instability of export proceeds? The correlation analysis yielded a coefficient of —.09. When the countries were ranked from low to high with reference to the foreign impact percentage, the export instability index (Y) for the lowest third was 16.9, for the middle third 18.9, and for the highest third 19.4. There is thus some evidence of positive correlation between export instability and the foreign trade impact percentage, among the thirds, despite the nearly zero correlation coefficient. The correlation coefficient is much influenced by the weight of the United States, with its relatively high global impact percentage and its below-average export instability index. Figure 5-11 and Table 5-4 (part X_{11}) in the summary section of this chapter provide further details.

The conclusion seems to be that export instability tends to increase only slightly, if at all, with the relative impact of countries on the world economy. It should be observed, however, that a country with a high global foreign impact percentage, such as the United States, *can* spread much more instability than a country with a very small impact percentage; nevertheless, even the highest impact percentages were quite low: United States, 6.1; United Kingdom, 2.3; France, 1.3; West Germany, 1.2; and Canada, 1.2. (Appendix Table A-2, Column X_{11}, shows the values for all countries.) The small size of these figures makes it questionable to

---

[1] Conversion of gross national products or related magnitudes into a common currency in the manner required here is subject to well-known hazards. These are stated concisely in chap. 16 of P. Studenski, *The Income of Nations,* New York University Press, New York, 1958. His Statistical Appendix provided some of the data required for the calculations used here. More systematic discussion of the problems involved is contained in M. Gilbert and I. B. Kravis, *An International Comparison of National Products and the Purchasing Power of Currencies,* Organization for European Economic Cooperation, 1953.

impute to any one country, or even a few countries, the capability of spreading instability over the world.

Value of Foreign Trade

Another variable of plausible influence on the export instability index is the value of foreign trade for a country. In this case we use the 1957 figures, as converted into United States dollars by the International Monetary Fund. For purposes of correlation analysis, the percentage distribution of world international trade would serve equally well. Either exports alone, or imports alone, would give similar results, either on a monetary or a percentage basis. In fact, the "global foreign impact percentage" for each country provides a similar relative distribution of values, except for the differences caused by the few countries whose gross national products comprise a sizable fraction of world output. (The reason for this is that "gross world product," minus a country's own GNP, is the denominator of the fraction in calculating the "global foreign impact percentage.")

It is not surprising, therefore, that the correlation coefficient between the value of foreign trade and export instability is very close to that between the global foreign impact percentage and export instability. The coefficients are —.10 and —.09, respectively. The foreign trade figures are shown in Column X_{23} of Appendix Table A-2. When the 83 countries are ranked from low to high according to the value of their foreign trade in 1957, the median export instability index value (Y) is 20.9 for the lowest third, 19.4 for the middle third, and 19.0 for the highest third. Here is a slight negative trend in Y-values as foreign trade is larger, corresponding to the negative correlation coefficient. The correlation must be considered very weak, however. The dispersion is shown under X_{23} in Table 5-4 and Figure 5-11 in the final section of this chapter.

These statistical analyses thus yield little evidence of a significant relation between export instability and the value of a country's foreign trade. This is significant from a policy point of view in that it shows that there is no simple or clear correlation between instability of export proceeds and the value of trade. Countries with a small part of the world's international trade may have stable or unstable export receipts; countries with a relatively large fraction of the trade may have stable or unstable export proceeds. Size of trade, at least as a single variable, has nothing to do with export instability.

Foreign Trade Per Capita

Foreign trade per capita is a crude measure of the importance of foreign trade for a country. In 1957 the range was from $7 to $1,029 for the 83 countries. Column X_{31} of Appendix Table A-2 gives details.

There seems to be no plausible a priori connection between this measure and export instability, yet the statistical pattern is not a random one. When the 83 countries are ranked with reference to foreign trade per capita, in United States dollars, the lowest third has a median export instability index (Y) of 24.7, the middle third a Y of 18.2, and the highest third a median of 16.6. There is thus a trend: as foreign trade

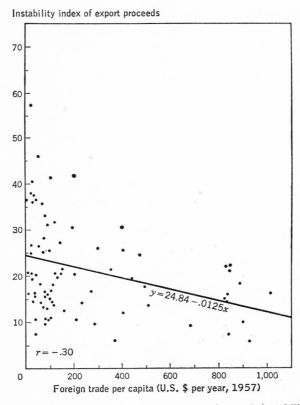

Figure 5-5. Scatter diagram: foreign trade per capita and instability of export proceeds for 83 countries.

per capita rises, the export instability index tends to fall. The correlation coefficient is —.30 and thus confirms this tendency. Figure 5-5 shows a scatter diagram. Figure 5-11 and Table 5-4 (part X_{31}) in the summary section show the dispersions for the trends.

The inference to be drawn is the same as in the case of the relation between export instability and foreign trade as a percentage of gross national product: a country is more likely to have fairly stable export receipts if foreign trade is relatively important to the country than if it is not. Stated negatively, the path to greater stability of export receipts is not through reduced trade, unless trade goes to zero.

Rate of Growth of Export Proceeds

It is interesting to try to discover whether instability of export proceeds is affected by the *trend* of export proceeds through time. During the post-

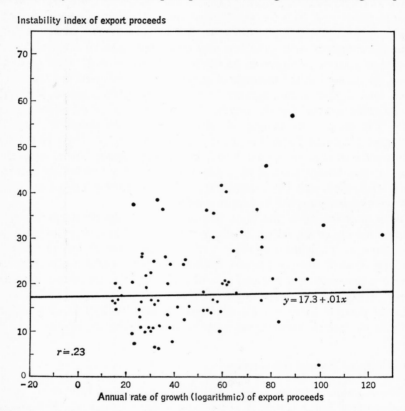

Figure 5-6. Scatter diagram: rate of growth of export proceeds and instability of export proceeds for 83 countries.

World War II period, 1946 to 1958, exports increased, on a trend basis, for all but 4 of the 83 countries—Iran, Argentina, Bolivia, and Uruguay.

We explore this question here with reference to a simple straight line and also with reference to a logarithmic straight line. The least-squares method was used in both instances. The correlation coefficient between the rate of growth on the simple basis and the export instability index (Y) is $+.07$, while between the rate of growth on a logarithmic basis and the export instability index, the correlation coefficient is $+.23$. Figure 5-6 provides a scatter diagram showing the relation between the logarithmic rate of growth of exports and export instability. The rates of growth for individual countries are given in Columns X_{21} and X_{25} of Appendix Table A-2. Comparison of the medians of the thirds of the distributions shows a roughly similar difference: When the countries are ranked from low to high with reference to the simple rate of growth, the median Y-value (export instability index) is 21.8 for the lowest third, 16.9 for the middle third, and 20.6 for the highest third. Evidently, countries with a moderate growth trend of exports tended to have greater export stability than the countries with quite low and quite high rates of growth exports. A similar pattern, not quite so pronounced, shows up when the logarithmic trend line is used as the measure of growth. When the countries are ranked from low to high with reference to this measure, the median Y for the lowest third is 16.9, for the middle third, 15.7, and for the highest third, 23.6. The dispersions around the medians are shown under X_{21} and X_{25} in Figure 5-11 and Table 5-4 at the end of this chapter. Three of the four countries with negative growth trends in export proceeds—Iran, Argentina, Bolivia, and Uruguay—had relatively high instability indexes for exports: 73.8, 41.3, 26.6, and 19.7, respectively; hence, declining foreign trade does not seem to be the route to export stability.

Both analyses show that there is a tendency for export instability to be greater for countries with a relatively high rate of growth of exports, but that those at the bottom of the growth scale are also subject to much instability. Except for this proviso, the findings here conform generally with the view that economic expansion tends to be uneven. Of course, countries experiencing a more rapid long-term rise in export proceeds should be in a better position to bear a greater degree of instability of exports. Apparently, a moderately rising trend is the most conducive to stability.

Instability of Capital Movements

The relation between export instability and the instability of capital movements is not a simple one, even on a theoretical basis. It is easy to think of a rise in net capital exports being associated with a rise in exports of goods and services, thus contributing to instability; but it is just as easy to imagine capital exports sustaining a level of exports and thus contributing to stability. These approaches are from the point of view of the capital-exporting country. If one thinks of net capital-importing countries—much more numerous in the contemporary world than net capital-exporting countries—capital imports would presumably vary inversely with exports. They would help fill the gaps in export earnings.

The correlation coefficient between the index of instability of net capital movements and export instability (Y) is $+.02$. The index values are in

Column X_{28} of Appendix Table A-2.[2] When the countries (67 in this instance) are ranked from low to high with reference to the measure of instability of capital movements, the median Y-value (export instability) for the lowest third is 16.0, for the middle third, 16.9, and for the highest third, 19.4. There is a tendency here for instability of exports to rise with instability of net capital movements, in line with a prior speculation. Figure 5-11 and Table 5-4 (part X_{28}) at the end of this chapter provide information in dispersion.

When the UN chain-relative method of measuring instability[3] is applied to capital movements, the correlation coefficient is $+.06$ (details in Column X_{30}, Appendix Table A-2). When the countries are ranked from low to high with reference to this measure, the countries in the lowest one-third of the distribution have a median export instability index (Y) of 17.3, those in the middle one-third a median Y-value of 16.1, and those in the highest one-third a median Y-value of 20.0.

There is thus only a modest tendency for export instability and instability of capital movements to be associated. Deficiencies in the data, which were assembled from the Balance of Payments Yearbooks of the International Monetary Fund, may account for part of the failure of this relation to live up to expectations. Another consideration is that net capital movements, which include donations here, are a small fraction of foreign trade for most countries for most years. Dispersion is shown under X_{30} in Table 5-4 and Figure 5-11 below.

Three other closely related variables were examined by means of scatter diagrams, but no discernible relation between them and export proceeds appeared, so they were not analyzed further. One was United States grants and credits to a country, July 1, 1945, through December 31, 1958. Another was United States grants and credits for this same period as a percentage of the foreign trade for the year 1957. The third was net capital movements, including donations, for the period 1947 to 1958, as a percentage of foreign trade for the year 1957.

DIRECTION OF EXPORTS

We now turn to another group of variables as a part of this single-determinant analysis of the variables associated with instability of export

[2] Measurement of instability presented some technical problems in this instance because of the presence of both negative and positive values in the time series for many individual countries. The logarithmic variance measure was not usable, so standard linear correlation analysis was used, with time on the x-axis and the net capital movements on the y-axis. A higher r-value indicates lower instability. Only five of the countries had r-values above .6. Thirty-one of the sixty-seven countries had negatively sloping regression lines for the period (1947 to 1958 in most cases).

[3] See p. 24.

proceeds. This group has to do with the direction of trade. Instability of a country's export proceeds could well be affected by the region or country of destination of its principal exports.

Percentage of Exports to One Region

The first measure we use is the percentage of a country's total exports which go to the region to which the country sells most of its exports. The regions and the percentages are those used by the International Monetary Fund:[4] United States and Canada, Latin America, Continental European Fund, Sterling Area, and Rest of World. The percentages range from 21 to 94. (See Appendix Table A-2, Column X_6, for figures for each country.)

There is no evident a priori indication as to the relation between regional concentration of exports and instability of export proceeds. High concentration might bring stability because of definite markets or it might bring instability because of changes in a country's bargaining position; low concentration might bring stability because of the presence of alternatives or it might bring instability because of the vicissitudes of the world market. These forces have different weights in different situations.

What do the postwar statistics show? The correlation coefficient between the regional concentration percentage and export instability (Y) is $-.18$. If any indication is provided by the minus sign, this value of r shows a mild tendency for export instability to be less for countries with high regional concentrations of exports than for those with low. Appendix Table A-2, Column X_6, shows country percentages.

When the countries are ranked from low to high by their highest regional concentration percentage, the lowest third has a median Y-value (export instability index) of 21.6, the middle third a median Y-value of 18.8, and the highest third a median Y-value of 16.1. This pattern supports the formal correlation analysis results, so it seems correct to state that there is, according to this measure, a weak inverse correlation between export instability and regional concentration of exports. Figure 5-11 and Table 5-4, part X_6, in the summary section, show the dispersion around the medians for the thirds.

Percentage of Exports to the United States

In view of the large place of the United States in the international economy, it is of interest to discover the relation between export instability and the percentage of a country's exports going to the United States. The popular supposition is that countries especially dependent on the United

[4] *International Financial Statistics*, e.g., March, 1960, pp. 28–32. The figures used are those for 1957. The United Nations *Yearbook of International Trade Statistics*, 1957, was the source in some cases.

States market for the sale of their exports are especially subject to fluctuations in their export proceeds.

The correlation coefficient between these two variables is —.27. Figure 5-7 shows the scatter diagram. With due allowance for the low *r* value, this indicates a tendency for export instability to be *less,* rather than more, when the percentage of a country's exports going to the United States is

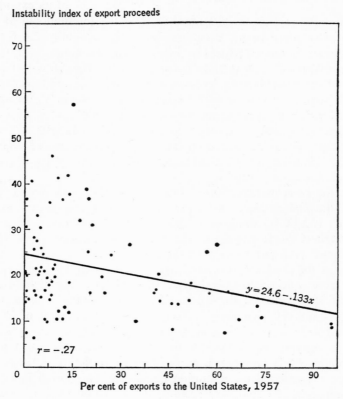

Instability index of export proceeds

$y = 24.6 - .133x$

$r = -.27$

Per cent of exports to the United States, 1957

Figure 5-7. Scatter diagram: per cent of exports to the United States and instability of export proceeds for 83 countries.

relatively high. Appendix Table A-2, Column X_7, shows the percentages of other countries' exports going to the United States in 1957.

The grouping of the countries by thirds shows the same tendency. The countries in the lowest third, by percentage of exports going to the United States, had a median *Y*-value (export instability index) of 20.9, those in the middle third a median *Y*-value of 19.0, and those in the highest third a median *Y*-value of 16.1. Dispersion around the medians is shown under X_7 in Table 5-4 and Figure 5-11 in the summary section of this chapter.

The statistical evidence provides no support for the view that countries selling heavily to the United States are especially subject to volatile earnings. This relative stability for such countries leaves out of account the financial aids available through close economic and political association with the United States.

Exports to United States as Per Cent of GNP

In this section we examine the hypothesis that a country's export receipts are especially unstable if a large fraction of its economic activity consists of exports to the United States. In order to give this notion more precision we have expressed each country's exports to the United States as a percentage of its gross national product (or similar magnitude). These percentages range from zero to 96.3 (Puerto Rico). Column X_{10} of Appendix Table A-2 gives the percentages for the various countries.

The statistical analysis shows that countries heavily involved with the United States tend to have *greater* stability of export receipts than do those only lightly involved in the United States market. The correlation coefficient is not high, however: —.20.

When the countries are ranked from low to high with reference to exports to the United States as a per cent of GNP, the export instability index (Y) is 20.6 for the lowest third, 19.4 for the middle third, and 16.1 for the highest third. The dispersion around the medians is shown under X_{10} in Figure 5-11 and Table 5-4 below.

Although the tendency described here is not strong by statistical standards, it serves effectively to invalidate the view that heavy trade involvement with the United States brings with it high instability of export proceeds. One rational economic explanation of the statistical result is that the United States constitutes a large and varied market, so that if another country is vigorous and adaptable in its export activities it can maintain fair stability of its earnings from the United States. Restrictive or discriminatory United States import policies can, of course, thwart these foreign initiatives.

Regional Export Concentration Index

In an attempt to obtain a more comprehensive measure of regional concentration, we employ a convenient concentration index that was developed some years ago.[5] The measure is the square root of the sum of the squares of the percentage shares provided by the regions (or other units that might be employed) and may conveniently be called the "Hirschman index."

[5] This measure is described in Albert O. Hirschman, *National Power and the Structure of Foreign Trade,* University of California Press, Berkeley, Calif., 1945, Appendix A.

This measure has the virtue of showing the influence of *both* the number of units and the percentage shares of the units. The maximum value is 100, since $\sqrt{100^2} = 100$; if 100 units have 1 per cent each, the value is $\sqrt{100}$ or 10.

The Monetary Fund regional classification was used in calculating a Hirschman index value for the exports of each of the 83 countries. The resulting values range from 45.5 to 94.1. (Appendix Table A-2, Column X_{27}, provides details.) This is a more refined and more comprehensive measure of the degree of directional concentration of exports than those provided in the preceding sections, so the correlation analysis should be a more reliable indication of the relation between export instability and regional concentration of exports. It is surprising, therefore, to discover that the correlation coefficient between the export instability index (Y) and the regional concentration index is only —.13.

When the countries are ranked from low to high with reference to the regional concentration index, the lowest third have a median Y-value (export instability index) of 20.0, the middle third a median Y-value of 18.3, and the highest third a median Y-value of 20.3. There is no directional tendency here and the differences between the medians are not large. (Dispersions are shown under X_{27} in Table 5-4 and Figure 5-11 below.) Hence, from both analyses it seems correct to conclude that a systematic relation between export instability and regional export concentration, as measured by the Hirschman index, does not exist. Stability of export proceeds is not likely to be affected one way or another by changing the regional destination "mix" of exports. This is an important variable, from the point of view of national policy, for it is within the power of governments to change the direction of trade, by a variety of devices; hence, it will be important to see whether the cross classifications, taken up in the next chapter, modify this first approximation.

COMPOSITION OF EXPORTS

We now move to commodity composition of exports in analyzing factors making for large or small export instability. Concentration of exports in one or a few commodities is another common "explanation" of instability of exports, so it is of particular interest to see what the statistical investigation yields.

Table 5-1 and Figure 5-8 show the three principal exports and their percentage of the value of all exports, for each of 62 of the 83 countries. Each of the 62 had over 30 per cent of its goods exports in as few as three commodities. Venezuela, with 98 per cent in three commodities and 92 per cent in petroleum alone, represents the peak.

Table 5-1
Countries Ranked According to Per Cent of Exports in Three
Commodities of Highest Value, 1957

| Country | Highest three | Percentage of total exports in: | | | Highest two; Col. (3) + Col. (4) |
| | | First | Second | Third | |
(1)	(2)	(3)	(4)	(5)	(6)
1. Venezuela.......	98	Petroleum 92	Iron ore 5	Coffee 1	97
2. Colombia........	95	Coffee 77	Petroleum 13	Bananas 5	90
3. El Salvador.....	94	Coffee 82	Cotton 11	Livestock 1	93
4. Costa Rica......	93	Coffee 49	Bananas 39	Cacao 5	88
5. Iraq............	93	Petroleum 88	Dates 3	Barley 2	91
6. Liberia..........	91	Rubber 68	Iron ore 18	Diamonds 5	86
7. Panama.........	91	Bananas 59	Fish 28	Cacao 4	87
8. Vietnam, Republic......	88	Rubber 60	Rice 25	Coal 3	85
9. Ecuador.........	88	Bananas 52	Coffee 22	Cacao 14	74
10. Ceylon..........	88	Tea 61	Rubber 18	Coconut products 9	79
11. Guatemala	88	Coffee 76	Bananas 9	Essential oils 3	85
12. Iceland.........	88	Fish 83	Meat 3	Hides 2	86
13. Haiti...........	88	Coffee 61	Sisal 18	Sugar 9	79
14. Chile...........	86	Copper 67	Nitrates 10	Iron ore 9	77
15. Ghana..........	85	Cacao 62	Wood 12	Diamonds 11	74
16. Dominican Rep..	83	Sugar 55	Coffee 16	Cacao 12	71
17. Egypt..........	83	Cotton 72	Textiles 7	Rice 4	79
18. Honduras.......	82	Bananas 52	Coffee 18	Wood 12	70
19. Ethiopia-Eritrea.	81	Coffee 64	Oil seeds 9	Hides 8	73
20. Nicaragua.......	81	Coffee 44	Cotton 34	Cottonseed 3	78
21. Burma..........	80	Rice 74	Rubber 4	Cotton 2	78
22. Uruguay........	79	Wool 50	Meat 21	Hides 8	71
23. China, Taiwan...	79	Sugar 63	Rice 12	Tea 4	75
24. Cambodia.......	79	Rice 37	Rubber 32	Maize 10	69
25. Finland.........	78	Wood, pulp 45	Paper 26	Boats 7	71
26. Rhodesia-Nyasaland....	78	Copper 54	Tobacco 18	Asbestos 6	72
27. Bolivia..........	76	Tin 60	Lead 9	Tungsten 7	69
28. Pakistan........	76	Jute 49	Cotton 21	Wool 6	70
29. Thailand........	74	Rice 48	Rubber 19	Tin 7	67
30. Iran............	72	Petroleum products 36	Petroleum, crude 29	Cotton 7	65
31. Indonesia.......	72	Rubber 36	Petroleum 30	Tin 6	66
32. Malaya.........	70	Rubber 49	Tin 11	Petroleum products 10	60
33. Cuba...........	69	Sugar 59	Tobacco 5	Molasses 5	64
34. Brazil..........	69	Coffee 61	Cacao 5	Cotton 3	66

Table 5-1 (*Continued*)

Country	Highest three	Percentage of total exports in:			Highest two; Col. (3) + Col. (4)
		First	Second	Third	
(1)	(2)	(3)	(4)	(5)	(6)
35. Philippines......	69	Coconut products 40	Sugar 19	Wood 10	59
36. Sudan..........	68	Cotton 47	Cottonseed 11	Gum 10	58
37. New Zealand....	68	Wool 38	Mutton 16	Butter 14	54
38. Greece..........	67	Tobacco 43	Raisins 17	Currants 7	60
39. Turkey.........	66	Tobacco 41	Hazelnuts 13	Cotton 12	54
40. Libya..........	65	Olive oil 25	Oil seeds 22	Peanuts 18	47
41. Israel..........	62	Citrus fruits 34	Diamonds, cut 24	Tires, tubes 4	58
42. Syria...........	62	Cotton 35	Wheat 17	Barley 10	52
43. Australia........	58	Wool 50	Wheat 6	Butter 2	56
44. Paraguay........	57	Timber 29	Cotton 14	Quebrecho 14	43
45. Argentina.......	55	Meat 26	Wheat 16	Wool 13	42
46. Nigeria.........	52	Cacao 21	Peanuts 16	Palm kernels 15	37
47. Ireland..........	52	Cattle 36	Meat 11	Alcoholic beverages 5	47
48. Belgian Congo...	52	Copper 32	Coffee 13	Diamonds 7	45
49. Poland..........	49	Coal, coke 39	Boats 5	Steel 5	44
50. Sweden........	47	Wood, pulp 27	Paper 10	Iron ore 10	37
51. Jordan..........	46	Fertilizer 21	Tomatoes 14	Olive oil 11	35
52. Peru............	46	Cotton 21	Sugar 16	Lead 9	37
53. India...........	45	Tea 25	Jute cloth 10	Cotton cloth 10	35
54. Mexico..........	45	Cotton 23	Coffee 15	Lead 7	38
55. Tunisia........	43	Olive oil 16	Alcoholic beverage 15	Fertilizer 12	31
56. Portugal........	38	Cork 17	Fish 12	Wine 9	29
57. Canada.........	38	Wood, pulp 15	Newsprint 14	Wheat 9	29
58. Union of South Africa	35	Wool 17	Fissionable material 12	Diamonds 6	29
59. Morocco........	34	Fertilizer 20	Barley 7	Fish 7	27
60. Norway.........	33	Fish 13	Wood, pulp 10	Paper 10	23
61. Switzerland.....	33	Watches 20	Drugs 8	Textile machines 5	28
62. Korea..........	32	Tungsten 14	Talc 12	Fish 6	26

14 other countries: More diversified
7 other countries: Inadequate information

Sources: UN, *Yearbook of International Trade Statistics 1957* and IMF, *International Financial Statistics*. Totals exclude exports of services.

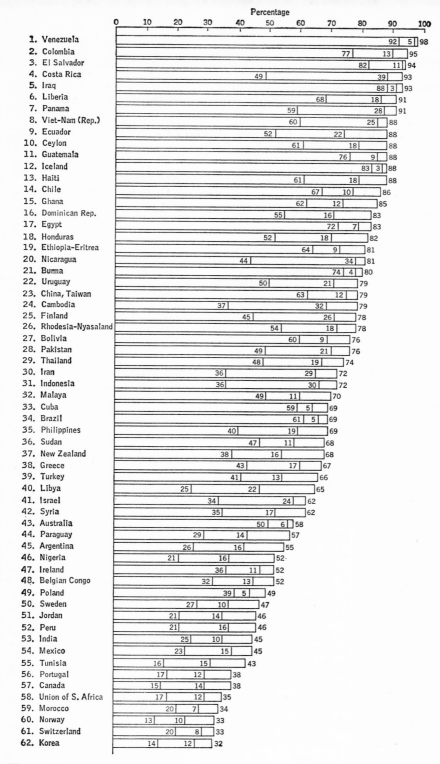

Figure 5-8. Percentage of export proceeds from three principal commodities for 62 countries, 1957. Fourteen other countries more diversified. Seven other countries, inadequate information. Totals exclude exports of services. Sources: UN, *Yearbook of International Trade Statistics 1957.* IMF, *International Financial Statistics.*

Table 5-2 provides a tabulation of the data of Table 5-1. Forty-eight of the eighty-three countries obtained 50 per cent or more of their (goods) export proceeds from three or less commodities. It is perhaps even more impressive that 26 countries should depend on only one commodity for 50 per cent or more of their export receipts, or that 21 countries should depend on only three commodities for 80 per cent or more of their receipts. Such concentrations reflect two things very clearly, first, the existence of many "economically small" countries and, second, the presence of large comparative differences in costs among countries which make extreme

Table 5-2
Number of Countries, by Percentage of Exports
in One, Two, and Three Commodities, 1957*

% of exports, 1957	One commodity		Two commodities		Three commodities	
	By class	Cumulative down	By class	Cumulative down	By class	Cumulative down
90–99	1	1	4	4	7	7
80–89	3	4	7	11	14	21
70–79	4	8	15	26	11	32
60–69	10	18	9	35	10	42
50–59	8	26	7	42	6	48
40–49	9	35	6	48	7	55
30–39	9	44	7	55	7	62

* This table differs somewhat from a similar table in *International Financial Statistics*, March, 1960, p. vi.

specialization advantageous. The method of classifying commodities affects the statistical results somewhat. For example, various grades and types of wheat are still classified as wheat, while various types of manufactured commodities, which might be produced by practically the same inputs, are classified as different products. But the general conclusion is clear enough.

In this discussion of the relation between export instability and export commodity concentration, we use three measures. One is in line with the compilation just presented; another uses the Standard International Trade Classification of commodities (SITC); the third uses the Hirschman concentration index with reference to the SITC categories.

Concentration of Exports in Few Individual Commodities

It is possible to calculate, for many of the 83 countries, the percentage of a country's total export proceeds provided by the single commodity which earns the most export proceeds. This was done. The results are shown in Column (3) of Table 5-1 and in Column X_{33} of Table A-2. This percentage was then correlated with the export instability index (Y). The correlation coefficient turned out to be $+.02$.

When the countries were ranked from low to high with respect to this percentage, the median Y-value for the lowest third of the countries was 19.4, for the middle third, 18.3, and for the highest third, 19.9. Quite evidently there is no direct connection between these two variables. Table 5-4 and Figure 5-11 (part X_{33}) in the concluding section of this chapter show the dispersions.

If the percentage of export proceeds provided by the *three* highest-yielding export commodities, for each country, is correlated with the index of export instability (76 countries in this case), the correlation coefficient turns out to be $+.11$. (See Appendix Table A-2, Column X_{32}, for details.) When the countries are ranked from low to high with respect to this variable, the lowest third have a median Y-value of 18.5, the middle third a median Y-value of 21.7, and the highest third a median Y-value of 19.7. Again, no relation is discernible. Dispersion figures are under X_{32} in Table 5-4 and Figure 5-11 below.

Types of Commodities in Exports

As discussed in Chapter 3, there is a common opinion that export receipts for primary goods—foods, raw materials, minerals—are more volatile than those for manufactured goods. In this section we test this proposition by comparing the export instability indexes of countries, when the countries are classified according to the principal type of commodities in their exports. Groups of the Standard International Trade Classification (SITC) were used for making the classification. The results are as follows:

Commodity group	*Median export instability index*
Minerals (including fuels)	26.6
Crude materials	20.8
Manufacturing (including machinery)	19.0
Food (including beverages, tobacco)	16.2

It is evident that minerals, but not crude materials and food, fit the stereotype. Indeed, countries with food as the principal export had the most stable export proceeds in the post-World War II period.

Commodity-group Export Concentration Index

Let us now refine the measurement of the degree of commodity concentration by employing the Hirschman concentration index—the square root of the sum of the squares of the percentage shares. The exports of each country, generally for 1957, were grouped according to the broad SITC classes and then the concentration index was calculated. The values ranged from 41.6 to 96.4 for the 78 countries for which data were available. See Appendix Table A-2, Column X_{26}, for details.

The correlation coefficient between the commodity concentration index and the export instability index (Y) is .04, a very low r-value. A pattern emerges, however, when the countries are ranked from low to high, by the commodity export concentration index, and the median Y-value (export instability index) determined. The lowest third have a median Y-value of 16.7, the middle third a median Y-value of 19.0, and the highest third a median Y-value of 20.6. Figure 5-11 and Table 5-4, part X_{26}, show the dispersions. This method of analysis gives some support for the view that the more highly concentrated the exports, by commodity groups, the greater the instability of export proceeds. This result is what one would expect, since diversification presumably reduces the chances of fluctuations, so it is surprising that the coefficient of correlation is so low.

SIZE OF NATIONAL ECONOMY

The group of variables we now consider with reference to instability of exports relates to the "size" of the national economy. Size, from an economic point of view, may be thought of in terms of inputs or of outputs. The obvious output measure is gross national product, or some related magnitude, expressed in some common measure for all countries. Inputs, according to the broadest classification, are human and material resources. Human resources are most readily measured by population figures, although these are obviously crude. Material resources might be measured by the capital value of all capital goods, including land, but this is not feasible. Area is an extremely crude but readily available measure which we shall use.

National Income

We are using national income rather than gross national product figures in this analysis because the figures were available for more countries.[6] They are shown in Column X_5 of Appendix Table A-2. It is interesting to speculate on the influence of size of a national economy on the stability of its export proceeds. There would seem to be no direct connection, but diversification is more likely in a larger economy, and presumably diversification makes for more stability, so a larger economy should, in general, have more stable export proceeds.

[6] See footnote [1] p. 89, for problems of using these measures.

The correlation analysis yields a coefficient extremely close to zero: $+.005$. When the countries (80 of the 83) are ranked from low to high with reference to national income, the lowest third has a median Y-value (export instability index) of 16.9, the middle third a median Y-value of 20.4, and the highest third a median Y-value of 18.5. There is no directional pattern to support the view that there is a systematic relation, though the smallest third of the economies have the lowest instability of exports. Hence the hypothesis is not supported. See Figure 5-11 and Table 5-4, part X_5, for dispersions around the medians.

Population

The relation between population and instability of exports is also weak, according to the correlation coefficient, which is $+.06$. Population figures are in Column X_{12} of Appendix Table A-2.

When the countries are ranked from low to high, by population, the lowest third of the countries has a median Y-value (export instability index) of 16.3, the middle third a median Y-value of 18.2, and the highest a median Y-value of 20.9. (Figure 5-11 and Table 5-4, part X_{12}, below, show dispersions.) Here is a distinct pattern, which indicates a tendency for instability to increase with increase in population. This result is also the opposite of plausible a priori analysis.

Area

Probably the crudest measure of size of a national economy is geographic size, so it is not surprising to find the correlation coefficient between area and export instability to be $+.07$ (area is shown in Column X_{13} of Appendix Table A-2); yet, when the countries are ranked and divided into thirds, the countries with the smallest areas have a typical export instability index lower than that for the larger areas. The lowest third of the countries has a median Y-value of 16.5, the middle third a median Y-value of 20.5, and the highest third a median Y-value of 20.5. See Figure 5-11 and Table 5-4, part X_{13}, below for dispersions.

It is apparent, therefore, from all three measures of size of an economy—national income, population, and area—that there is a tendency, though a weak one, for exports to be more unstable for larger economies than for smaller ones. A possible explanation is that small economies have to be more concerned about their export proceeds, so they may, through deliberate government policies or through built-in institutional arrangements, foster export stability.

It should be noted that "large," in this context, refers to the countries in the top one-third, according to each of these criteria of size, but that many countries are not very large by comparison with the United States, the U.S.S.R., China, or India. The top third begins with a 1957 national income of only $4.5 billion, a population of only 16.6 millions, and an area of only 514 million square kilometers.

GROWTH OF NATIONAL ECONOMY

We now examine the relation between the rate of growth of a national economy and the stability of its export proceeds. Analysis is limited by lack of data, but we have figures for 30 countries for the years 1951 to 1957. We used two measures: average percentage increase in gross national product, 1951 to 1957, and increase in per capita GNP per year, in United States dollars. Both series were adjusted for price changes.[7]

Rate of Growth of GNP

There is no well-established theoretical view regarding the rate of economic growth and the fluctuation in exports. Economic growth tends to be jerky rather than smooth, however, so there is a presumption that exports are likewise more unstable with high growth rates than with low growth rates.

The correlation coefficient again dashes this hypothesis: it is —.003 between rate of growth in the real GNP, 1951 to 1957, and instability index of export proceeds. Indeed, this is the lowest correlation coefficient obtained in the entire analysis! Arranging countries with reference to rate of growth in GNP also fails to show any pattern. The median Y-value (export instability index) for the bottom third is 16.2, for the middle third 15.0, and for the top third 18.2. There is only a slight tendency toward greater export instability among the highest growth countries. The rates of growth of the individual countries are shown in Column X_{18} of Appendix Table A-2; Figure 5-11 and Table 5-4, part X_{18}, at the end of this chapter, show the dispersions around the medians of the thirds.

Growth in Per Capita GNP

The correlation coefficient between export instability (Y) and growth in *per capita* real gross national product, 1951 to 1957, is —.15. (See Column X_{20} in Appendix Table A-2 for details.) This is higher than the growth figure, uncorrected for population, but it is very small. If the negative sign may be used as a directional indication, this means that

[7] The growth figures used in this section were supplied by Prof. H. D. Houthakker from his work in process on measurement of economic growth.

there is a slight tendency for export instability to be less than average in the countries with the higher per capita increases in gross national product.

When the countries are ranked from low to high with reference to per capita growth in gross national product, the opposite tendency appears! Countries in the lowest third have a median Y-value (export instability index) of 14.3, while those in the middle and highest thirds have median Y-values of 18.2 and 18.1, respectively. Figure 5-11 and Table 5-4, part X_{20}, show the dispersions.

The evidence does not indicate any relation between growth in per capita real income and export instability.

Instability of National Economy

Instability of a national economy, as measured by instability of its gross national product or national income, is often considered to be closely related to instability of export proceeds, according to theoretical analysis. The reasoning usually runs in terms of the Keynesian multiplier analysis, with the changes in the gross national product treated as dependent upon changes in exports. In more elaborate models, the export balance rather than gross exports is used, and consumption, domestic private investment, and government outlays are treated as other determining forces. In our analysis, we are seeking to discover what influence variations in national income have on gross exports, but the Keynesian framework makes this, for any one country, dependent upon the propensity of other countries to import. Exports are thus seen as dependent. A more elaborate general-equilibrium model is required in order to overcome these deficiencies, but statistical testing bcomes much more difficult.[8] If export proceeds are viewed as partially dependent upon national output, as they clearly are, it is then plausible, in a particular-equilibrium context, to inquire about the influence of fluctuations of national income on fluctuations of export proceeds.

When these two variables are correlated, one obtains, however, the shockingly low correlation coefficient of $+.07$. This is a surprise, whether one views the main causal forces as running from exports to national income or from national income to exports. (Column X_2 of Appendix Table A-2 gives the income instability indexes for individual countries.)

When the median export instability indexes (Y-values) are compared for the thirds of the countries, something of a pattern emerges. The median Y-value for the third of the countries with the lowest income

[8] Two attempts to deal with the problem in this framework are: Hans Neisser and Franco Modigliani, *National Incomes and International Trade,* The University of Illinois Press, Urbana, Ill., 1953, and Jacques J. Polak, *An International Economic System,* The University of Chicago Press, Chicago, 1953.

instability indexes is 16.5, for the third with moderate income instability, 16.3, and for the third with the highest income instability, 19.4. The value for the top third may be significantly different and thus indicate some tendency for high instability of national income to be associated with high instability of export proceeds, and vice versa. The dispersions around the medians are shown under X_2 in Table 5-4 and Figure 5-11 at the end of this chapter.

ECONOMIC LEVEL OF COUNTRY

In this section we relate several variables to export instability which reflect the level of economic well-being of a country. Some of them are output measures, others are input measures. A priori analysis seems to be inconclusive.

Per Capita GNP

The correlation coefficient relating per capita gross national product in 1957 and the export instability index is —.23. The better off a country is, the more stable are its exports. Figure 5-9 shows the scatter diagram and Column X_{22} of Appendix Table A-2 gives the country values.

When the countries (80) are ranked from low to high with reference to per capita GNP, the lowest third has a median export instability index (Y) of 20.8, the middle third a median of 17.6, and the highest third a median of 18.5. There is no clear pattern, but there is a negative drift, as indicated also by the correlation coefficient as well as the medians. See Table 5-4 and Figure 5-11, part X_{22}, for dispersions.

We also ran a correlation using the average per capita gross national product figures for the years 1951 to 1957, adjusted for price changes (Column X_{16} in Appendix Table A-2), against the export instability index. The r-value was —.04. When the countries (30) were ranked from low to high with reference to these average per capita GNP figures, the median Y-value (export instability index) for the lowest third of the countries was 15.4, for the middle third, 16.8, and for the highest third, 18.1. Here is a pattern, but it runs in the opposite direction from that obtained with only the 1957 figures! It seems, from these two sets of data and two types of measures, that there is probably a slight tendency toward negative correlation between export instability and per capita income. Details are available on dispersions around medians under X_{16} in Figure 5-11 and Table 5-4 below.

Capital Formation as Per Cent of GNP

Net fixed capital formation as a per cent of gross national product, averaged for the years 1951 to 1957, provides a fairly direct measure of the rate of saving and investment in a country and, indirectly, of changes in the level of well-being. Country figures are in Column X_{17} of Appendix Table A-2. The coefficient of correlation between this variable and the export instability index, for 30 countries, is $+.08$. When the countries are ranked from low to high with reference to this variable, the lowest third has a median Y-value (export instability index) of 17.0, the middle

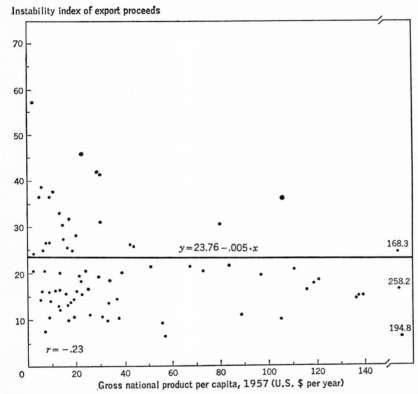

Figure 5-9. Scatter diagram: gross national product per capita and instability of export proceeds for 80 countries.

third a median Y-value of 15.0, and the highest third a median Y-value of 18.9. There is no directional pattern here. Dispersion figures around the medians are under X_{17} in Figure 5-11 and Table 5-4.

Energy Per Capita

Estimates of energy available in various countries have been made in a United Nations study.[9] Energy per capita is a rough measure of the

[9] *World Energy Supplies, 1954–57*, United Nations Statistical Papers, ser. J, no. 3, 1959.

productive capacity per person, and hence of the real income per person in a country. The correlation coefficient between energy per person in a country and export instability (Y) is $-.16$. Details are available in Appendix Table A-2, Column X_{19}.

When the 83 countries are ranked from low to high with reference to energy per capita, the median Y-value (export instability index) for the lowest third is 22.6, for the middle third, 19.4, and for the highest third, 18.1. The indication is that export instability declines with increases in energy per captia. See X_{19} in Table 5-4 and Figure 5-11 for dispersions.

Population Density

Population density, the man-land ratio, is a very crude measure of the relative scarcity of two means of production. If "land" stands for usable material resources including real capital, a low man-land ratio implies a high level of living. The correlation coefficient between the man-land ratio (persons per square kilometer) and the index of export instability, for the 83 countries, is $-.004$, one of the lowest values obtained. Country figures are in Column X_{14} in Appendix Table A-2.

When the countries are ranked from low to high with reference to population density, the median Y-value (export instability index) for the lowest third is 18.1, for the middle third, 19.4, and for the highest third, 19.8. There is a slight upward movement of the instability median value as the population density increases. This is equivalent to a slight downward movement as the land-man ratio increases and thus is consistent with the tendency for export instability to decrease as the energy per capita increases. Dispersions around medians are under X_{14} in Table 5-4 and Figure 5-11 at the end of this chapter.

The only safe generalization about the relation between the economic level of a country and instability of exports seems to be that there is a slight tendency for instability to decrease as the level of well-being increases. Most of the measures indicated this relationship.

PRICES, MONETARY FACTORS

Export Prices

As explained in an early section of this chapter, there is a logical basis for expecting the instability of prices of exports to show some connection with the instability of export receipts of a country. The correlation coefficient between these two variables is only $+.13$, however. Country values are in Column X_9 of Appendix Table A-2.

When the (67) countries are ranked from low to high with reference to the index of instability of export prices, the lowest third of the countries have a median Y-value (export instability index) of 16.1, the middle third a median Y-value of 19.0, and the highest third a median Y-value of 19.9. Dispersions around medians are in Figure 5-11 and Table 5-4, part X_9, below. Both measures give some indication of a positive correlation: export proceeds tend to become more unstable as export prices become more unstable.

This variable deserves a bit more comment, since so many schemes for stabilization of export proceeds generally or of trade in particular commodities consider stabilization of prices the principal method of achieving stabilization of export proceeds for countries or for particular producer-groups. *The evidence here falls far short of demonstrating a strong connection between instability of export prices and instability of export proceeds.* We consider this an important, though "negative," conclusion. The quantum of exports, with a correlation coefficient of $+.58$, is a much more influential factor. If the ratio of the correlation coefficients may be used as a rough indication of relative importance, export quantum instability is clearly much more important than export price instability in determining export proceeds instability. Of course, since both price and quantity are necessarily the two directly relevant variables in determining export proceeds (or outlays on imports), both would have to be regulated if there were a political determination really to stabilize export proceeds or import outlays with reference to some trend.

Terms of Trade

A country's terms of trade—the ratio of the index number of its export prices to the index number of its import prices—are frequently cited as a cause of fluctuations in its export proceeds. Changes in or chronically unfavorable terms of trade are also blamed for various other difficulties of countries. There is a certain plausibility in this point of view: if a country could command increasing quantities of foreign goods per unit of its own exports, more or less indefinitely, its economic troubles would just about be at an end. The fact is, of course, that the terms of trade are rarely a manipulable variable and are thus operationally almost irrelevant in an economic world in which prices move, and are generally expected to move, according to relative scarcities.

It is interesting, however, to see the connection between export proceeds instability and instability of the terms of trade. The coefficient of correlation between them is $+.38$. A scatter diagram is shown in Figure 5-10. Instability indexes of terms of trade of individual countries are in Column X_{36} of Appendix Table A-2.

When countries (41) are ranked from low to high with reference to instability of terms of trade, the median Y-value (export proceeds instability index) of the lowest third is 18.0, of the middle third, 14.9, and of the highest third, 18.3. Dispersions are under X_{36} in Figure 5-11 and Table 5-4 below.

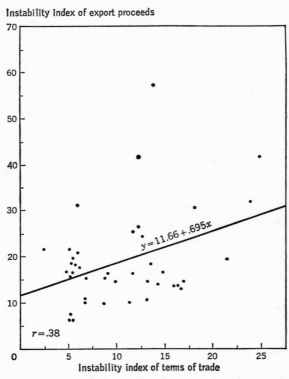

Figure 5-10. Scatter diagram: instability of terms of trade and instability of export proceeds for 41 countries.

Despite the uneven path of the medians the correlation coefficient is relatively high, so we may conclude that instability of export proceeds is positively correlated with instability of terms of trade.

Inflation, 1950 to 1958

It is plausible that relatively high levels of inflation should contribute to instability of export proceeds. The correlation of the increase in the level of domestic prices (usually cost of living indexes), 1950 to 1958, with the export instability index for 64 countries yields a coefficient of $+.14$. Column X_{24} in Appendix Table A-2 gives details.

The grouping of the countries into thirds provides more persuasive evidence. The third of the countries with the lowest rates of inflation had a median export instability value Y of 16.9, the middle third a median Y-value of 17.3, and the highest third a median Y-value of 19.7. Dispersion data are under X_{24} in Table 5-4 and Figure 5-11. If the inflation from 1946 to 1958 had been measured, it is probable that a higher positive correlation would have resulted.

Monetary Reserves as Per Cent of Imports

It seems plausible that there should be some relation between international monetary reserves and export instability. In order to make comparisons among countries, monetary reserves were expressed as a per cent of imports for each country for each of the postwar years for which the figures were available. Instability indexes were then calculated for this ratio and the resulting indexes correlated with the export instability index. The surprising result was a coefficient of correlation of $+.07$. Country figures are in Column X_{37} of Appendix Table A-2.

When the countries are ranked with respect to this percentage, from low to high, a stronger positive correlation emerges. The lowest third shows a median Y-value (export instability index) of 16.8, the middle third a median of 17.8, and the highest third a median of 18.3. Dispersion figures are under X_{37} in Table 5-4 and Figure 5-11 below.

SUMMARY AND CONCLUSION OF SINGLE-FACTOR ANALYSIS

We now bring to a close the analysis of the differences in export instability in terms of single independent variables. The empirical discussion has borne out the a priori expectation that export instability would not be highly correlated with any single factor. Yet the preceding discussion has indicated differences in the relative importance of the variables considered. For example, it has brought out the fact that instability of the physical volume of exports is a much more important factor than instability of export prices, or even terms of trade. It has also shown that regional concentration of exports, even concentration of exports to the United States, is not positively correlated with instability of export proceeds.

By way of summary of the single-factor analysis, a ranking of the factors with reference to the coefficients of correlation is provided in Table 5-3. The median export instability index value for each of the thirds of the countries is provided also. The table shows clearly that four

Table 5-3
Correlation Coefficients between (1) Export Instability Index (Y)
and (2) Other Variables, for Countries

Rank	Independent variable	r^*	Median Y-value†			Col. (6) as % of Col. (4)	No. of countries
			Lowest third	Middle third	Highest third		
(1)	(2)	(3)	(4)	(5)	(6)	(7)	(8)
1	Export quantum I-I (X_8)	+.58	15.1	16.6	21.4	142	70
2	Import value I-I (X_3)	+.43	15.7	22.1	24.8	158	83
3	Terms of trade I-I (X_{36})	+.38	18.0	14.9	18.3	102	41
4	Rate of growth (log.) of export proceeds (X_{25})	+.23	16.9	15.7	23.6	140	83
5	Change in domestic prices, 1950–1958 (X_{24})	+.14	16.9	17.3	19.7	117	64
6	Export prices I-I (X_9)	+.13	16.1	19.0	19.9	124	67
7	% exports in 3 commodities (X_{32})	+.11	18.5	21.7	19.7	106	66
8	Net fixed capital formation as % GNP (X_{17})	+.08	17.0	15.0	18.9	111	30
9	National income I-I (X_2)	+.07	16.5	16.3	19.4	118	60
10	I-I monetary reserves as % imports (X_{37})	+.07	16.8	17.8	18.3	101	62
11	Area of country (X_{13})	+.07	16.5	20.5	20.5	124	83
12	Rate of growth (linear) of export proceeds (X_{21})	+.07	21.8	16.9	20.6	94	83
13	Population (X_{12})	+.06	16.3	18.2	20.9	128	83
14	% exports in largest SITC group (X_{34})	+.04	16.6	19.6	20.6	124	79
15	Export commodity concentration index (X_{26})	+.03	17.3	19.0	20.2	117	78
16	I-I net capital movements (r) (X_{28})	+.02	16.0	16.9	19.4	121	67
17	Monetary reserves as per cent of imports (X_{35})	+.02	16.4	18.4	19.4	118	63
18	% exports in one commodity (X_{33})	+.02	19.4	18.3	19.9	103	66
19	National income (U.S.$) ($X_5$)	+.005	16.9	20.4	18.5	109	80
20	% increase per year in real GNP (X_{18})	−.003	16.2	15.0	18.2	113	30
21	Persons per sq km (X_{14})	−.004	18.1	19.4	19.8	109	83
22	Per capita GNP, 1951–1957 (X_{16})	−.04	15.4	16.8	18.1	118	30
23	Foreign impact % (X_{11})	−.09	16.9	18.9	19.4	115	80
24	Value of foreign trade (X_{23})	−.10	20.9	19.4	19.0	91	83
25	Regional export concentration index (X_{27})	−.13	20.0	18.3	20.3	102	83

Table 5-3 (*Continued*)

Rank	Independent variable	r^*	Median Y-value†			Col. (6) as % of Col. (4)	No. of coun-tries
			Lowest third	Middle third	Highest third		
(1)	(2)	(3)	(4)	(5)	(6)	(7)	(8)
26	Increase in per capita GNP, 1951–1957 (X_{20})	$-.15$	14.3	18.2	18.1	127	31
27	Energy per capita (X_{19})	$-.16$	22.6	19.4	18.1	80	83
28	% exports to region to which most exports go (X_6)	$-.18$	21.6	18.8	16.1	75	83
29	Trade with U.S. as % GNP (X_{10})	$-.20$	20.6	19.4	16.1	79	74
30	Country export concen-tration index (X_{38})	$-.20$	20.9	19.6	16.6	80	80
31	GNP per capita (X_{22})	$-.23$	20.8	17.6	18.5	89	80
32	% exports to U.S. (X_7)	$-.27$	20.9	19.0	16.1	77	81
33	Foreign trade as % GNP (X_4)	$-.30$	24.3	17.3	16.1	70	80
34	Foreign trade per capita (X_{31})	$-.30$	24.7	18.2	16.6	67	83

* Simple linear correlation coefficient between export instability index and other variable, for number of countries shown in Column (8).

† For countries ranked from low to high with reference to specified variable and divided into thirds. See Appendix Table A-4 and Table A-5 for details.

variables—instability of export quantum, the instability of value of imports, instability of terms of trade, and the logarithmic rate of growth of export proceeds—are relatively highly correlated positively with instability of export proceeds. This is indicated both by the correlation coefficients [Column (3)] and by the ratio of the median Y-values of the highest and lowest thirds of the countries [Column (7)].

The variables with relatively high negative correlations are three: foreign trade as a per cent of GNP, foreign trade per capita, and per cent of exports going to the United States. Higher values for these variables tend to be associated with lower export instability values. Per capita GNP, trade with the United States as a per cent of GNP, and per cent of exports to region to which most exports go show negative correlations nearly as high.

Included in this summary section are Table 5-4 and Figure 5-11, which show the medians for the "thirds" with respect to the several variables and the dispersions around these medians.

The fact that many variables show scarcely any relation at all with export stability is significant too. It must be mentioned once more that

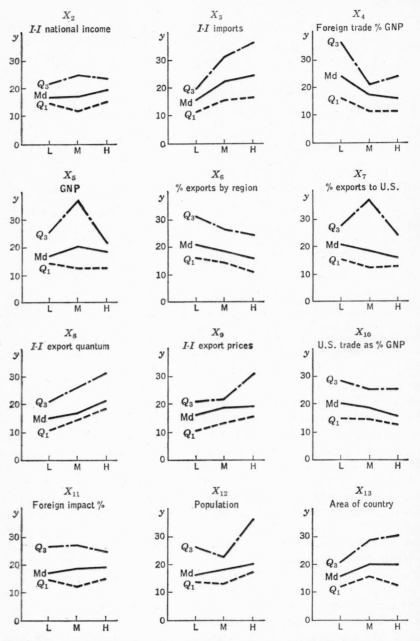

Figure 5-11. Median and quartile values of export instability index (Y) for coun-
values on y-axis. On x-axis, L stands for lowest third of countries ranked from low
third. Q_1 stands for first quartile y-value,

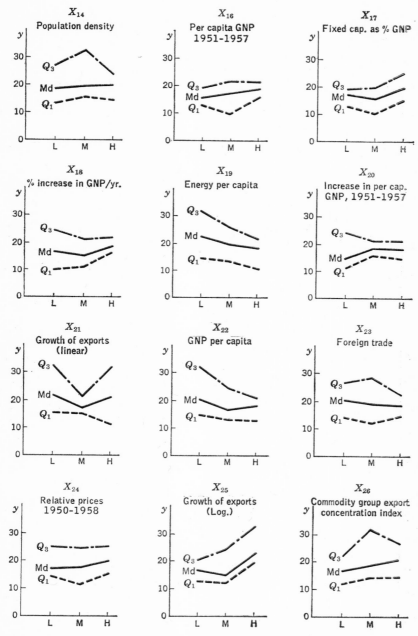

tries divided into thirds with respect to various variables. Export instability index
to high with respect to specified variable, *M* for middle third, and *H* for highest
Md the median, and Q_3 the third quartile.

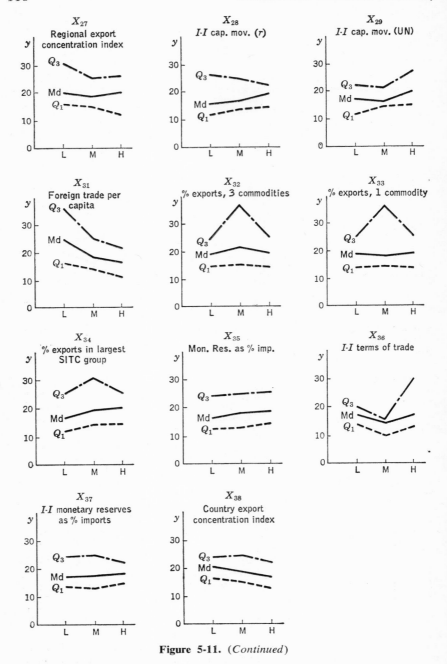

Figure 5-11. (*Continued*)

Table 5-4
Export Instability Index Values (Y) for Countries Divided into Thirds with Respect to Various Variables

Variable and r-value*	Third	Y-values				
		Lowest	Q_1	Median	Q_3	Highest
X_2 I-I, national income,	L	6.2	14.1	16.5	21.5	36.2
$r = +.07$	M	9.2	11.8	16.3	24.8	46.1
	H	10.0	14.7	19.4	23.7	36.6
X_3 I-I, imports (value),	L	7.5	11.0	15.7	19.0	27.2
$r = +.43$	M	6.2	15.4	22.1	31.1	46.1
	H	10.0	16.5	24.8	36.1	73.8
X_4 Foreign trade as % GNP,	L	10.9	16.5	24.3	36.6	57.2
$r = -.30$	M	7.5	11.6	17.3	20.9	73.8
	H	6.2	11.7	16.1	24.0	41.9
X_5 GNP, $r = +.005$	L	9.9	14.3	16.9	25.6	33.0
	M	6.3	12.6	20.4	37.2	73.8
	H	6.2	12.5	18.5	21.5	41.3
X_6 % exports to region to	L	7.5	16.5	21.6	31.5	57.2
which most exports go,	M	6.2	14.5	18.8	26.3	73.8
$r = -.18$	H	6.3	11.3	16.1	25.0	37.8
X_7 % exports to U.S.,	L	6.3	16.0	20.9	27.8	40.4
$r = -.27$	M	6.2	12.8	19.0	37.2	73.8
	H	7.5	13.4	16.1	25.1	36.6
X_8 I-I, export quantum,	L	6.2	10.7	15.1	20.7	57.2
$r = +.58$	M	10.0	14.5	16.6	26.3	41.9
	H	10.3	18.5	21.4	32.0	73.8
X_9 I-I, export prices,	L	6.2	10.9	16.1	21.5	73.8
$r = +.13$	M	10.3	13.7	19.0	22.1	46.1
	H	10.0	16.0	19.9	31.9	57.2
X_{10} Trade with U.S. as	L	6.3	15.8	20.6	29.2	46.1
% GNP, $r = -.20$	M	6.2	15.1	19.4	25.9	73.8
	H	7.5	13.4	16.1	26.0	57.2
X_{11} Foreign impact %,	L	9.9	14.3	16.9	26.6	38.4
$r = -.09$	M	6.3	12.0	18.9	27.2	73.8
	H	6.2	15.1	19.4	24.6	41.3
X_{12} Population, $r = +.06$	L	6.3	14.0	16.3	26.6	35.7
	M	6.2	13.6	18.2	23.0	41.9
	H	7.5	17.3	20.9	36.4	73.8

Table 5-4 (*Continued*)

Variable and *r*-value*	Third	Y-values				
		Lowest	Q_1	Median	Q_3	Highest
X_{13} Area of country,	L	6.2	12.5	16.5	21.8	38.4
$r = +.07$	M	7.7	16.2	20.5	29.3	46.1
	H	7.5	13.6	20.5	30.9	73.8
X_{14} Population density,	L	6.3	13.0	18.1	26.9	73.8
$r = -.004$	M	10.7	15.4	19.4	32.5	57.2
	H	6.2	14.6	19.8	23.7	38.4
X_{16} Per capita GNP,	L	10.0	13.0	15.4	18.3	25.7
1951–1957 average,	M	6.3	9.9	16.8	21.5	41.3
$r = -.04$	H	7.5	14.7	18.1	20.9	24.6
X_{17} Net fixed capital as %	L	9.9	13.0	17.0	18.5	25.2
GNP, 1951–1957 average,	M	6.3	10.0	15.0	19.4	41.3
$r = +.08$	H	7.5	14.3	18.9	24.6	31.0
X_{18} % increase in real GNP	L	6.3	10.0	16.2	24.6	41.3
per year, 1951–1957,	M	7.5	10.7	15.0	20.9	21.5
$r = -.003$	H	9.9	16.1	18.2	21.4	31.0
X_{19} Energy per capita,	L	10.7	14.5	22.6	32.5	40.4
$r = -.16$	M	9.9	13.9	19.4	25.9	73.8
	H	6.2	11.2	18.1	21.8	41.3
X_{20} Increase in per capita	L	6.3	10.7	14.3	24.6	28.1
real GNP per year,	M	9.2	16.0	18.2	21.5	41.3
1951–1957, $r = -.15$	H	7.5	14.7	18.1	20.9	21.4
X_{21} Rate of growth (linear)	L	10.7	15.4	21.8	33.8	73.8
of export proceeds,	M	6.3	14.9	16.9	20.9	27.2
$r = +.07$	H	6.2	11.6	20.6	30.7	57.2
X_{22} GNP per capita, 1957,	L	7.7	15.7	20.8	33.0	73.8
in U.S. \$, $r = -.23$	M	9.9	13.8	17.6	25.7	46.1
	H	6.2	13.4	18.5	21.5	36.2
X_{23} Foreign trade, 1957, in	L	9.9	15.9	22.1	26.7	40.4
U.S. \$, $r = -.10$	M	6.3	12.3	18.3	28.8	73.8
	H	6.2	14.9	18.0	23.1	41.3
X_{24} Relative prices (cost of	L	6.2	14.5	16.9	25.0	46.1
living), 1950–1958,	M	6.3	11.4	17.3	24.3	73.8
$r = +.14$	H	10.0	14.8	19.7	28.4	57.2

Table 5-4 (*Continued*)

Variable and *r*-value*	Third	Y-values				
		Lowest	Q_1	Median	Q_3	Highest
X_{25} Rate of growth (log) of export proceeds, $r = +.23$	L	7.5	13.4	16.9	21.4	73.8
	M	6.2	12.5	15.7	24.6	38.4
	H	10.0	20.0	23.6	32.5	57.2
X_{26} Commodity-group export concentration index, $r = +.03$	L	6.2	12.0	17.3	21.5	46.1
	M	6.3	14.2	19.0	31.9	73.8
	H	9.9	14.7	20.2	26.6	40.4
X_{27} Regional export concentration index, $r = -.13$	L	6.2	16.1	20.0	30.7	57.2
	M	7.5	15.1	18.3	25.9	73.8
	H	6.3	12.3	20.3	26.2	37.8
X_{28} I-I, capital movements (correlation method), $r = -.02$	L	10.0	12.0	16.0	26.6	73.8
	M	6.2	13.9	16.9	24.6	57.2
	H	9.9	14.7	19.4	22.5	43.1
X_{30} I-I, capital movements (UN method), $r = +.06$	L	6.3	12.0	17.3	22.5	73.8
	M	7.5	14.3	16.1	21.2	57.2
	H	6.2	14.7	20.0	27.2	41.3
X_{31} Foreign trade per capita, $r = -.30$	L	7.7	16.3	24.7	36.6	73.8
	M	10.0	14.0	18.2	25.7	41.3
	H	6.2	11.2	16.6	21.8	41.9
X_{32} % exports in 3 commodities, $r = +.11$	L	6.2	14.1	18.5	24.0	46.1
	M	6.3	15.1	21.7	36.5	73.8
	H	9.9	14.2	19.7	25.2	37.8
X_{33} % exports in one commodity, $r = +.02$	L	6.2	14.1	19.4	25.7	46.1
	M	6.3	14.7	18.3	36.5	73.8
	H	9.9	13.9	19.9	26.0	37.8
X_{34} % exports in largest SITC group, $r = +.04$	L	6.2	12.0	16.6	25.0	46.1
	M	6.3	14.3	19.6	31.5	73.8
	H	9.9	14.5	20.6	25.9	40.4
X_{35} Monetary reserves as % imports, 1956–57 average, $r = +.02$	L	10.0	13.1	16.4	24.4	46.1
	M	7.5	13.9	18.4	25.6	57.2
	H	6.2	15.0	19.4	26.6	73.8
X_{36} I-I, terms of trade, $r = +.38$	L	6.2	15.2	18.0	20.9	31.0
	M	9.9	10.7	14.9	16.2	41.3
	H	13.0	13.9	18.3	31.1	57.2

Table 5-4 (*Continued*)

Variable and r-value*	Third	Y-values				
		Lowest	Q_1	Median	Q_3	Highest
X_{37} I-I, monetary reserves as % imports, $r = +.07$	L	6.2	13.9	16.8	24.3	41.9
	M	9.9	13.2	17.8	24.4	73.8
	H	10.3	14.7	18.3	22.1	57.2
X_{38} Country export concentration index, $r = -.20$	L	6.2	16.6	20.9	30.7	33.8
	M	10.0	14.7	19.6	26.7	57.2
	H	6.3	13.4	16.6	26.0	38.4

* Correlation coefficient between export instability index (Y) and indicated variable.

all of these correlations are low, according to customary statistical tests, although confidence is increased when the path of the medians is clear and in the same direction as the coefficient of correlation. It should also be pointed out again that multifactor analysis might well reveal a relation between export instability and some of these variables which do not seem to be related according to the single-variable analysis. We now turn to the more complicated multifactor analysis.

Chapter 6

STATISTICAL ANALYSIS OF INSTABILITY OF EXPORT PROCEEDS (Continued)

The preceding chapter demonstrated the limitations of the attempt to explain the instability of export proceeds by means of single variables. We now turn to multivariable analysis in an effort to obtain a better explanation of the fluctuations in export proceeds. In theory, if the right variables could be selected and the necessary statistics assembled, the phenomenon could be largely explained. Or, in general equilibrium terms, if we had the right variables and the statistics for discovering the right relations among the variables, we could set up the equations for determining export instability as well as the values of other variables.

Obviously, lack of certainty regarding the correct variables and inadequacy of statistics make a much less ambitious approach necessary.

Two methods are used in the multivariable analysis. One is the standard multiple-correlation technique; the other is a cross-classification technique involving the grouping of the countries into thirds with respect to each of the several variables.

Selection of Variables

Twelve variables, in addition to instability of export proceeds (Y), were selected for analysis with the formal multiple-correlation technique. The following criteria were used in selecting them from the 34 variables used in the single-factor analysis (listed in Table 5-3): (1) relatively high correlation coefficient (r), either negative or positive, (2) analytical plausibility despite low r-values, and (3) availability of statistics for all of the selected variables for 60 or more of the 83 countries. These variables are:[1]

[1] National income instability index (X_2), which showed a relatively high r-value, is omitted from this list because by so doing the number of countries for which data were available could be increased from 50 to 63. Table 6-4 shows the intercorrelation r-values for this selected list of variables, with and without X_2.

X_3 Import value instability index
X_4 Foreign trade as per cent of GNP
X_5 National income
X_7 Per cent of exports to United States
X_8 Export quantum instability index
X_9 Export prices instability index
X_{22} GNP per capita
X_{23} Value of foreign trade
X_{25} Logarithmic rate of growth of export proceeds
X_{26} Commodity export concentration index
X_{27} Regional export concentration index
X_{31} Foreign trade per capita

All 34 variables were used in the cross-classification analysis—the second method.

Methods of Analysis

The formal multiple-correlation analysis was used first between the export instability index (Y) as the dependent variable, and all other combinations of pairs of the 12 selected independent variables. It was then used with all possible combinations of three independent variables and four independent variables.

The cross-classification method of analysis requires some explanation. Countries were first ranked, from low to high, with respect to each independent variable and divided into thirds, low (L), middle (M), and high (H).[2] For example, suppose the countries are so ranked with respect to variable X_2. Then the countries in each of the thirds are ranked from low to high with respect to another variable, say X_3, so that there are nine cells in all (aside from "not available" cells). Then the median Y-value (instability of export proceeds) is determined for the countries in each cell. The results are as follows for the cross classification of X_2 and X_3:

X_3 (I-I imports)	X_2 (I-I national income)		
	Median Y-values		
	Lowest third	Middle third	Highest third
Lowest third.........	16.4	13.0	18.8
Middle third.........	18.8	22.1	18.6
Highest third.......	16.5	19.6	20.4

[2] See Appendix Table A-4 for the ranges of values of the variables by thirds.

If this table is examined as a partial correlation table, it is apparent that there is no clear directional pattern across any row nor down any column. Neither is there a diagonal pattern. There is a substantial difference, however, between the lowest median of 13.0 and the highest median of 22.1.

Multiple-correlation Analysis, with Two Independent Variables

The coefficients of multiple correlation (R) between instability of export proceeds (Y), as the dependent variable, and all possible pairs of the 12 selected variables, as independent variables, are shown in Table 6-1. The most striking feature of this table is the failure of any R-values to be much high than .58, the simple correlation coefficient between the instability index of export proceeds (Y) and the instability index of export quantum (X_8). The highest R-value, .66, is that involving X_8 (export quantum) and X_{25} (logarithmic rate of growth of export proceeds). Indeed, the only R-values above .58 are for the 11 combinations having X_8 as one of the two independent variables as follows:

Variables	*R*
X_{25}–X_8	.662
X_3–X_8	.643
X_4–X_8	.614
X_{31}–X_8	.607
X_7–X_8	.606
X_{22}–X_8	.604
X_{27}–X_8	.603
X_9–X_8	.597
X_{26}–X_8	.587
X_{23}–X_8	.586
X_5–X_8	.584

The simple correlation coefficients between instability of export proceeds (Y) and the other variables are also shown in Column (3) of Table 6-2 in order to facilitate comparison of the simple and multiple correlation coefficients. See page 124 for the names of the variables.

It is worth noting that the variable with the second highest r-value, X_3 (import value instability index) with .42, did not yield much higher R-values when paired with the other variables (except for X_8, already discussed). The highest it reached was .48 [Column (1) of Table 6-1].

Multiple-correlation Analysis, with Three Independent Variables

It seems plausible that the correlation coefficient should be higher when three independent variables rather than two are used. Such is not the case,

Table 6-1
Coefficients of Multiple Correlation (R) between Instability Index of Exports (Y) and Various Pairs of Variables*

	R-values											
	X_3	X_4	X_5	X_7	X_8	X_9	X_{22}	X_{23}	X_{25}	X_{26}	X_{27}	X_{31}
X_3												
X_4	.452											
X_5	.420	.319										
X_7	.423	.388	.284									
X_8	.643	.614	.584	.606								
X_9	.423	.291	.119	.287	.597							
X_{22}	.480	.470	.287	.410	.604	.286						
X_{23}	.418	.301	.355	.265	.586	.137	.292					
X_{25}	.467	.391	.264	.424	.662	.274	.386	.277				
X_{26}	.416	.284	.106	.275	.587	.114	.298	.126	.248			
X_{27}	.425	.296	.200	.271	.603	.196	.351	.208	.300	.161		
X_{31}	.482	.341	.299	.421	.607	.299	.300	.300	.399	.309	.355	

* See p. 124 for names of variables.

Table 6-2
Multiple Correlation Coefficients between Instability Index of Exports (Y) and Various Sets of Three Independent Variables*

(1)	(2)	(3)
1. $R_{1.8,3,31} = .661$	$R_{1.8,3} = .64$	$r_{1.8} = +.585$
2. $R_{1.8,3,22} = .660$	$R_{1.8,3} = .64$	$r_{1.8} = +.585$
3. $R_{1.8,3,4} = .659$	$R_{1.8,3} = .64$	$r_{1.8} = +.585$
4. $R_{1.8,4,22} = .625$	$R_{1.8,4} = .61$	$r_{1.8} = +.585$
5. $R_{1.8,4,31} = .621$	$R_{1.8,4} = .61$	$r_{1.8} = +.585$
6. $R_{1.8,22,31} = .608$	$R_{1.8,22} = .60$	$r_{1.8} = +.585$
7. $R_{1.3,22,4} = .496$	$R_{1.3,22} = .48$	$r_{1.3} = +.417$
8. $R_{1.3,31,4} = .490$	$R_{1.3,31} = .48$	$r_{1.3} = +.417$
9. $R_{1.3,22,31} = .485$	$R_{1.3,22} = .48$	$r_{1.3} = +.417$
10. $R_{1.4,22,31} = .356$	$R_{1.4,22} = .47$	$r_{1.22} = -.285$

* See p. 124 for names of variables. See footnote to Table 6–4 on r-values.

however. The highest multiple correlation coefficients, with three independent variables, is .66, the same as the highest with two. See Table 6-2. Three combinations of variables approximated this value; all involved X_8, instability of export quantum, and X_3, instability index of import value. The highest involved these two and X_{31} (foreign trade per capita). The coefficient of correlation rose from .585 (simple) for X_8, to .64 for X_8 and

X_3, and then to .66 for X_8, X_3, and X_{31}. Table 6-2 shows at a glance, moving from Column (3) to Column (2) to Column (1), the improvement in the correlation coefficient as more variables are included.

Multiple-correlation Analysis, with Four Independent Variables

Despite the limited number of observations, multiple correlations were run with four independent variables. The results are shown in Table 6-3. For purposes of comparison, the next highest three-variable coefficient involving the same independent variables is shown in Column (2) and the difference in Column (3). The improvement in the coefficient of multiple correlation is nominal: from .6586 to .6677 in the case with the greatest difference. The variables involved for this highest R-value are instability index of import value (X_3), foreign trade as a percentage of GNP (X_4), export quantum instability index (X_8), and GNP per capita (X_{22}).

Table 6-3
Multiple Correlation Coefficients between Instability Index
of Exports (Y) and Various Sets of Four
Independent Variables*

	(1)		(2)	Col. (1) − Col. (2) (3)
1.	$R_{1.3,4,8,22}$ = .6677	$R_{1.3,4,8}$	= .6586	.0091
2.	$R_{1.3,4,8,31}$ = .6653	$R_{1.3,4,8}$	= .6586	.0067
3.	$R_{1.3,8,22,31}$ = .6614	$R_{1.3,8,22}$	= .6604	.0010
4.	$R_{1.4,8,22,31}$ = .6256	$R_{1.4,8,22}$	= .6248	.0008
5.	$R_{1.3,4,22,31}$ = .4964	$R_{1.3,4,22}$	= .4963	.0001

* See p. 124 for names of variables.

It is evident from Tables 6-1 to 6-3 that the multiple-correlation analysis adds little to our understanding of the factors determining the instability of export proceeds. The highest simple correlation coefficient ($r_{1.8}$) was .585 and the highest multiple correlation coefficient ($R_{1.3,4,8,22}$) was .6677. One possible explanation is that the proper variables were not used. Another is that the intercorrelations among the independent variables were so large that no net improvement could be expected from the multiple-correlation analysis. The next section explores this latter hypothesis.

Intercorrelations

The failure of the multiple-correlation analysis to yield higher R-values makes it interesting to inquire into the simple correlations between all the possible pairs of variables used in the multiple-correlation analysis. Table 6-4 shows these intercorrelations. They are of general interest, quite aside from the present attempt to explain variations in export proceeds.

Table 6-4 requires some explanation. There are two r-values for each cell. The r-values *not* in parentheses show the results of using the 63 countries for which data were available for the 13 variables (including Y) used in the multiple-correlation analysis. The r-values in parentheses show the results of including an additional variable, X_2 (national income instability index), for which data were available for only 50 countries. This reduction in the number of countries changed the r-values in varying degrees, although apparently not in any systematic way.

The highest intercorrelations in Table 6-4, excluding those involving instability of export proceeds (Y), are as follows:[3]

1. X_5 (national income) and X_{23} (foreign trade)............................ .927
2. X_{22} (GNP per capita) and X_{31} (foreign trade per capita)................. .914
3. X_{22} (GNP per capita) and X_{23} (foreign trade)........................... .571
4. X_4 (foreign trade as % GNP) and X_{31} (foreign trade per capita)........... .460
5. X_{23} (foreign trade) and X_{31} (foreign trade per capita).................... .453
6. X_7 (% exports to U.S.) and X_{26} (commodity export concentration index)... .429
7. X_5 (national income) and X_{22} (GNP per capita)........................... .425
8. X_{23} (foreign trade) and X_{26} (commodity export concentration index)....... .405
9. X_5 (national income) and X_{26} (commodity export concentration index)..... .377

The first two pairs are essentially the same, since X_{31} values are obtained by dividing GNP (roughly proportionate to national income) by population, and X_{31} values by dividing X_{23} values by population. The correlation coefficient between national income and foreign trade is surprisingly high. This high r-value is partly the result of the exclusion of the United States and the Soviet Union from these tabulations. The United States was excluded because it seemed desirable to include the variable X_7, per cent of exports to the United States, in the multiple-correlation analysis. The Soviet Union was excluded because of lack of figures for several variables.

On the question of whether high intercorrelations underlie the failure of the multiple correlations to raise the value of the correlation coefficient, Table 6-4 provides a fairly clear answer. Only with the pairs involving national income and foreign trade is the correlation coefficient high (.927 and .914); for the other independent variables which yielded relatively high multiple correlation coefficients, the intercorrelation r-values ranged between .115 and .275, except for X_4 (foreign trade as per cent of GNP) and X_{31} (foreign trade per capita), which was .460. But even the exclu-

---

[3] These are the r-values for 63 countries, *not* in parentheses in Table 6-4. The only cell in the table in which the r-value was higher for the 50 countries (shown in parentheses) was that relating to X_7 (per cent of exports to United States) and X_{27} (regional export concentration index): .427 as compared with .264.

Table 6-4
Intercorrelations of Pairs of 14 Variables*

r-values†

	Y	X_2	X_3	X_4	X_5	X_7	X_8	X_9	X_{22}	X_{23}	X_{25}	X_{26}	X_{27}	X_{31}
X_2	(.115) —													
X_3	(.315) .417	(.219) —												
X_4	(−.305) .282	(−.173) —	(−.329) .264											
X_5	(−.005) −.093	(−.113) —	(−.089) −.112	(−.261) −.197										
X_7	(−.242) −.253	(.255) —	(−.184) .226	(−.035) .050	(−.112) .088									
X_8	(.384) .585	(.310) —	(.300) .264	(−.208) −.165	(−.062) −.098	(−.161) .167								
X_9	(.059) .109	(.165) —	(.052) .093	(−.179) −.135	(−.222) −.229	(.117) .105	(−.020) −.027							
X_{22}	(−.212) .285	(−.286) —	(−.066) .115	(.245) .275	(.375) .425	(−.190) −.140	(−.283) .233	(−.307) .303						
X_{23}	(−.054) .110	(−.181) —	(−.168) .172	(−.013) .024	(.923) .927	(−.155) −.130	(−.103) −.117	(−.281) −.279	(.537) .571					
X_{25}	(.329) .244	(−.062) —	(.058) .080	(.159) .090	(.048) .032	(−.298) −.316	(−.024) −.109	(−.091) −.066	(.098) .056	(.107) .087				
X_{26}	(.061) −.012	(.067) —	(.055) −.112	(.136) .121	(−.400) −.377	(.387) .429	(.173) .053	(.221) .191	(−.276) .257	(−.426) −.405	(−.206) .225			
X_{27}	(−.346) −.160	(−.007) —	(−.288) −.184	(.369) .270	(−.142) −.161	(.427) .264	(−.105) −.021	(.097) .023	(−.099) −.151	(−.102) −.134	(−.112) .058	(.241) .200		
X_{31}	(−.259) .299	(−.336) —	(−.106) −.141	(.454) .460	(.198) .259	(−.180) −.135	(−.314) −.241	(−.311) −.303	(.904) .914	(.412) .453	(.107) .069	(−.231) −.220	(−.042) −.105	

* See p. 124 for names of variables.
† Figures in cells are simple correlation coefficients r. Those in parentheses are for 50 countries and include X_2 (national income instability index) as a variable; those not in parentheses are for 63 countries and exclude X_2. The r-values not in parentheses in Col. Y differ slightly from those shown earlier, e.g., in Table 5-4 because 63 rather than 83 countries were used.

129

sion of both X_{22} and X_{31}, as shown in Column (2), Rows 1 and 2 of Table 6-3, made very little difference in the R-value, so it seems correct to conclude that high intercorrelations were not the cause of the failure of the highest R-values to rise much above the best r-value. In short we have a large unexplained variance, which can be attributed in part to the variables used, in part to the statistics, and in part to the method of analysis.

Results of Cross-classification Tabulations

Because of the failure of the multiple-correlation analysis to throw much light on the factors influencing instability of export proceeds, it seemed desirable to subject the available data to the more detailed cross-classification analysis described earlier in this chapter. The essential data for this analysis are in the subtables of Appendix Table A-6. Each cell in each subtable shows the median export instability index (Y) for the countries falling in the designated thirds with respect to the two independent variables considered in each subtable. Highest and lowest median Y-values are underlined.

The method of discovering relations is to see whether the "paths of the medians" rise or fall with some regularity—first in each row, second in each column, and third for the two 3-point diagonals. The method may be illustrated with reference to subtable C-4-7 of Appendix Table A-6, reproduced here:

X_7 (% of exports to U.S.)	X_4 (foreign trade as % of GNP)		
	Median Y-values		
	Lowest third	Middle third	Highest third
Lowest third........	20.5	20.9	21.4
Middle third........	38.4	18.0	16.6
Highest third........	19.4	15.1	14.3

For the countries in the lowest third with respect to X_7, the median export instability index (Y) increases regularly, though slightly—from 20.5 to 20.9 to 21.4—as X_4 increases. For the middle and highest thirds, in contrast, the median Y-values decrease as X_4 increases. Looking at the columns, Column (1) shows no directional pattern, while Columns (2) and (3) both show that the median Y-value decreases as X_7 increases, with X_4 held constant. The diagonal from the northwest to the southeast

also shows decreasing median Y-values, which leads one toward the conclusion that export instability tends to decrease with increases in both
foreign trade as a per cent of GNP (X_4) and per cent of exports going to
the United States (X_7). The conclusion is qualified, however, by the fact
that the highest median, 38.4, is not in the upper left cell, though the
lowest, 14.3, is in the lower right, as the diagonal trend would indicate.

This method of analysis leaves a good bit to be desired in terms of precision, but it does permit the discovery of the interplay of the variables.
All of the subtables of Appendix Table A-6 were analyzed by this method.
There were not enough countries to warrant a three-way breakdown. Here
in the text we call attention first to those paths of medians which show a
consistent directional movement, up or down, with increases in *both* independent variables, and second to the cells with relatively high and relatively
low median I-I values: Table 6-5 presents the findings of the first. Tables
6-6 and 6-7 show the results for the second.

For convenience in identifying the variables indicated by X_2, etc., their
names and symbols are listed herewith:

X_2	I-I, national income	X_{22}	GNP per capita, 1957
X_3	I-I, value of imports	X_{23}	Foreign trade, 1957
X_4	Foreign trade as % GNP	X_{24}	Relative prices, 1950–1958
X_5	GNP	X_{25}	Rate of growth (logarithmic) of
X_6	% of exports to region to which		export proceeds
	most exports go	X_{26}	Commodity-group export concen-
X_7	% of exports to U.S.		tration index
X_8	I-I, export quantum	X_{27}	Regional export concentration
X_9	I-I, export prices		index
X_{10}	Trade with U.S. as % GNP	X_{28}	I-I, capital movements (correla-
X_{11}	Foreign impact %		tion method)
X_{12}	Population	X_{30}	I-I, capital movements
X_{13}	Area of country		(UN method)
X_{14}	Population density	X_{31}	Foreign trade per capita
X_{16}	Per capita GNP, 1951–1957	X_{32}	% exports in 3 commodities
X_{17}	Net fixed capital as % of GNP,	X_{33}	% exports in 1 commodity
	1951–1957 average	X_{34}	% exports in largest SITC group
X_{18}	% increase in real GNP per year,	X_{35}	Monetary reserves as % imports,
	1951–1957		1956–1957
X_{19}	Energy per capita	X_{36}	I-I, terms of trade
X_{20}	Increase in per capita real GNP per	X_{37}	I-I, monetary reserves as % imports
	year, 1951–1957	X_{38}	Country export concentration
X_{21}	Rate of growth (linear) of export		index
	proceeds		

The two variables which have the greatest influence on export instability
(Y), according to this analysis, are percentage growth in GNP per year
(X_{18}) and instability index of capital movements (X_{30}): the median Y-
values increased from 7.8 to 14.7 to 31.0 as X_{18} and X_{30} increased (Table

Table 6-5
Pairs of Variables Which Affect the Export Instability Index (Y), According to Cross-classification Analysis*

Pairs of variables	Median Y-values			Percentage change, low to high
	Low	Middle	High	
(a) With Increases in Median Y-values as Two Variables Increase				
18, 30	7.8	14.7	31.0	299
8, 9	9.9	16.4	19.7	199
8, 25	10.7	16.0	29.1	172
8, 36	7.5	14.7	19.0	153
13, 30	15.2	16.9	36.6	141
3, 25	13.0	15.7	29.2	125
8, 30	12.5	16.1	27.2	118
6, 24	16.8	18.2	34.4	105
25, 32	16.2	19.1	29.6	83
3, 30	15.2	18.1	25.7	69
38, 8	15.1	24.3	25.2	67
3, 19	14.2	20.1	23.0	62
7, 27	30.4	18.2	12.2	60
4, 9	16.8	19.2	26.6	58
38, 25	17.7	24.3	28.0	58
20, 25	13.0	16.3	20.2	55
8, 20	13.0	16.0	20.2	55
3, 27	16.6	21.4	25.7	55
3, 31	14.1	18.2	21.4	52
20, 27	13.8	18.2	20.9	51
3, 23	14.2	20.1	21.4	51
8, 26	15.1	15.7	22.1	46
3, 22	15.2	20.6	21.4	41
8, 22	14.6	14.7	20.2	38
7, 30	16.3	19.4	22.3	37
9, 27	16.1	16.7	20.1	31
2, 25	16.1	16.4	20.9	30
12, 32	16.4	18.2	20.1	29
2, 8	15.6	16.8	19.8	27
8, 19	16.6	17.9	20.9	26
3, 36	17.7	20.7	22.2	25
2, 19	16.5	16.8	20.7	25
22, 26	16.6	19.6	20.2	22
27, 30	16.4	17.6	18.2	11
18, 19	17.2	18.2	18.8	9

* The median Y-values are from the subtables of Appendix Table A-6. They are the diagonal paths of medians which increase or decrease from the lower left cell to the upper right or from the upper left to the lower right. The pairs of variables are ranked according to the percentage change from high to low or low to high. Part (a) of the table contains the results when the median Y-values increase, part (b) when the median Y-values decrease. Names of variables are given on p. 131.

Table 6-5 (*Continued*)

Pairs of variables	Median Y-values			Percentage change, high to low
	Low	Middle	High	
(b) With Decreases in Median Y-values as Two Variables Increase				
38, 31	36.5	20.2	14.1	61
38, 22	28.3	19.7	11.1	61
4, 14	36.2	16.5	15.3	58
4, 21	27.6	19.9	12.1	56
4, 32	31.0	19.6	14.7	53
6, 7	28.1	17.3	13.4	52
7, 20	24.6	21.5	11.8	52
27, 31	24.3	15.2	12.1	50
5, 32	29.5	23.5	16.1	45
23, 32	29.5	20.2	16.1	45
4, 18	27.6	15.7	15.2	45
38, 4	25.8	16.0	14.3	45
38, 5	22.1	17.2	12.5	43
31, 32	26.2	17.0	15.2	42
38, 23	24.0	19.4	14.3	40
19, 31	26.6	17.4	16.4	38
4, 19	25.0	19.2	15.6	38
23, 31	25.2	16.7	16.6	34
4, 10	24.7	19.2	16.4	34
38, 7	21.4	18.2	14.2	34
4, 23	24.3	19.2	16.3	33
5, 31	25.0	20.2	16.8	33
4, 13	20.5	18.8	14.0	32
18, 27	17.7	14.1	12.1	32
7, 31	20.1	18.2	13.8	31
7, 10	20.8	17.3	14.3	31
4, 7	20.5	18.0	14.3	30
23, 26	21.3	18.2	15.0	30
4, 12	20.4	16.8	14.7	28
22, 31	23.0	17.6	16.8	27
26, 31	20.7	18.2	15.2	27
7, 9	21.2	17.3	16.1	24
38, 36	18.5	16.1	14.1	24
38, 26	20.9	18.8	16.1	23
7, 26	21.4	19.4	16.5	23
4, 10	20.6	18.2	16.1	22
32, 36	18.1	15.1	14.2	22
6, 13	18.5	18.3	14.7	21
4, 28	20.2	17.3	16.4	19
23, 30	22.5	20.1	18.5	18
4, 20	21.0	18.2	17.3	18
26, 36	16.8	14.7	13.9	17
13, 32	18.5	18.2	15.4	17
19, 26	21.0	19.7	18.1	14
4, 5	18.6	17.7	16.1	13
22, 23	20.8	18.3	18.1	13
4, 30	18.8	18.6	18.5	2

6-5a). Other pairs which yield large percentage increases in Y as the independent variables increase, as shown in Table 6-5a, are: instability index of export quantum (X_8) and logarithmic growth of exports (X_{25}); instability index of export quantum (X_8) and instability index of terms of trade (X_{36}); area of country (X_{13}) and instability index of capital movements (X_{30}); instability index of imports (X_3) and logarithmic growth of exports (X_{25}); instability index of export quantum (X_8) and instability index of capital movements (X_{30}); and percentage concentration of exports by region (X_6) and relative price-level changes, 1950–1958 (X_{24}). Manifestly, sizable changes in the instability index of exports are associated with several pairs of variables.

Pairs of independent variables which yield relatively large *decreases* in the median instability index of export proceeds (Y) as the independent variables increase are shown in Table 6-5b. The pair of variables yielding the largest percentage decrease in the median instability index of export proceeds (Y) is the concentration index of exports by country of destination (X_{38}) and foreign trade per capita (X_{31}). The median Y-values fall from 36.5 to 20.2 to 14.1 as the independent variables increase. Other pairs which yield relatively large percentage *decreases* in Y as the independent variables increase, as shown in Table 6-5b, are: concentration index of exports by country of destination (X_{38}) and GNP per capita (X_{22}); foreign trade as a per cent of GNP (X_4) and population density (X_{14}); foreign trade as a per cent of GNP (X_4) and growth of exports (X_{21}); foreign trade as a per cent of GNP (X_4) and per cent of exports in three commodities (X_{32}); per cent of exports to any one region (X_6) and per cent of exports to the United States (X_7); per cent of exports to the United States (X_7) and increase in per capita GNP (X_{20}); and regional export concentration index (X_{27}) and foreign trade per capita (X_{31}). Again, the variety of variables associated with changes in export instability may be noted.

In comparing the variables which were associated fairly closely with export instability under the multiple-correlation technique and under the cross-classification technique, it appears that several more variables revealed themselves as influential forces under the cross-classification technique.[4]

Table 6-6 and Table 6-7 employ the cross-classification analysis in another way, namely, to determine what two-way combinations of high,

---

[4] Specifically, the seven highest percentage changes in Table 6-5a and the eight highest percentage changes in Table 6-5b included 11 variables not included in the multiple-correlation analysis: X_6, X_{13}, X_{14}, X_{18}, X_{20}, X_{21}, X_{24}, X_{30}, X_{32}, X_{36}, and X_{38}. It should be noted, however, that some variables were eliminated from the multiple correlation exercise because of low simple correlation coefficients. See the preceding list, p. 131, for names of variables.

Table 6-6
Highest Median *Y*-values in Two-way
Cross Classification

Rank	Variables and thirds*	Median *Y*-value	No. of countries in cell
1	$X_{5,M}-X_{8,H}$	42.2	4
2	$X_{10,H}-X_{25,H}$	41.9	3
3	$X_{8,H}-X_{32,M}$	40.4	5
4	$X_{4,L}-X_{7,M}$	38.4	7
5	$X_{4,L}-X_{5,M}$	37.8	7
6	$X_{5,M}-X_{7,M}$	37.8	11
7	$X_{3,H}-X_{7,M}$	37.2	12
8	$X_{4,L}-X_{24,H}$	37.2	8
9	$X_{7,M}-X_{22,L}$	37.2	8
10	$X_{25,H}-X_{36,H}$	36.9	4

* $X_{5,M}$ denotes variable X_5 (GNP) and the middle third (M) of countries ranked from low to high with respect to X_5-values; likewise for others. L and H stand for lowest and highest thirds.

Source: Appendix Table A-6. See p. 131 for names of variables.

Table 6-7
Lowest Median *Y*-values in Two-way
Cross Classification

Rank	Variables and thirds*	Median *Y*-value	No. of countries in cell
1	$X_{8,L}-X_{36,L}$	7.5	5
2	$X_{18,L}-X_{23,M}$	9.2	3
3	$X_{18,L}-X_{27,H}$	9.2	3
4	$X_{4,H}-X_{17,M}$	9.6	4
5	$X_{3,M}-X_{8,L}$	9.8	4
6	$X_{4,H}-X_{16,M}$	9.9	5
7	$X_{8,L}-X_{9,L}$	9.9	7
8	$X_{8,L}-X_{31,H}$	9.9	7
9	$X_{2,L}-X_{26,M}$	10.0	3
10	$X_{7,H}-X_{18,M}$	10.0	3

* $X_{8,L}$ denotes variable X_8 (instability index of export quantum) and the lowest third (L) of countries ranked from low to high with respect to X_8-values; likewise for others. M and H stand for middle and highest thirds.

Source: Appendix Table A-6. See p. 131 for names of variables.

middle, and low values of the independent variables are associated with very high and very low median export instability indexes (Y). Thus, the highest median instability index value is associated with the middle third of the countries ranked with reference to gross national product (X_5) and with the highest third of the countries ranked with reference to instability of export quantum (X_8). Table 6-6 shows the other high median instability indexes according to this method of analysis. Table 6-7 shows the lowest median instability index values found in any of the cells of Appendix Table A-6. The lowest median Y-value involves, interestingly, the two variables, and the values of those variables, which might be expected, a priori, to yield a low Y-value, namely, the lowest third for the instability index of export quantum (X_8) and the lowest third for the instability index of terms of trade (X_{36}). Only two other cells among the lowest ten involved X_8, and none X_{36}.

Again it is necessary to note the variety of variables—and variety of values of these variables—associated with very high or very low export instability index values. Part of this variety results from the large number of variables, many of which reflect the same or similar basic forces at work.

Characteristics of Countries with High and Low Export Instability Indexes

Another way to try to determine which characteristics are associated with high and low instability of export proceeds is to compare, with reference to various characteristics, the countries which have very low and very high export instability indexes. Table 6-8 shows, for the six countries with the highest export instability indexes and for the six with the lowest export instability indexes, the "third" (first, second, or third) within which each of these countries falls when all countries (as available) are ranked from low to high with respect to each of the indicated variables.

The "average ranking" (explained in the footnote to Table 6-8) is used for comparing the two groups of countries.

The countries with high export instability are *higher* than the countries with low export instability with respect to the following characteristics, ranked according to ratios of their average rankings:

Instability of export quantum (X_8)............ 2.5
Instability of imports (X_3).................. 2.3
Instability of export prices (X_9).............. 2.2
Instability of terms of trade (X_{36})............ 2.0
Area of country (X_{13})....................... 1.8
Population (X_{12})............................ 1.5
Logarithmic growth of exports (X_{25})........... 1.5
Instability of national income (X_2)............ 1.4

Table 6-8

Characteristics of Countries with Highest and Lowest Instability of Exports*

Third in which country falls

Countries with highest instability (ranked by Y)	Y (I-I)	X_2	X_3	X_4	X_5	X_6	X_7	X_8	X_9	X_{12}	X_{13}	X_{14}	X_{19}	X_{22}	X_{23}	X_{25}	X_{26}	X_{27}	X_{30}	X_{31}	X_{32}	X_{36}	X_{38}
1. Iran	73.8	—	3	2	2	2	2	3	1	3	3	1	2	1	2	1	2	2	1	1	2	—	1
2. Indonesia	57.2	—	3	1	2	1	2	1	3	3	3	2	1	1	2	3	2	1	2	1	2	3	2
3. Yugoslavia	46.1	2	2	1	2	1	2	3	2	3	2	2	2	2	2	3	1	2	1	1	1	—	1
4. Malaya	41.9	3	3	1	2	1	2	2	3	2	2	2	2	2	2	3	1	1	—	3	2	3	1
5. Argentina	41.3	2	3	1	3	1	2	3	1	3	3	1	3	2	3	1	2	1	3	2	2	2	2
6. Sudan	40.4	—	2	—	—	1	1	3	3	2	3	1	1	—	1	3	3	1	3	1	2	—	1
A. Average ranking‡		2.0	2.7	1.6	2.2	1.2	1.8	2.5	2.2	2.7	2.7	1.5	1.8	1.6	2.0	2.3	1.8	1.3	2.0	1.5	1.8	2.7	1.3
Countries with lowest instability																							
7. Panama	9.9	2	1	3	1	3	3	1	1	1	1	1	2	2	1	1	3	3	2	3	3	2	3
8. Puerto Rico	9.2	2	1	3	2	3	3	—	—	1	1	3	3	3	2	1	—	3	1	3	—	—	—
9. Romania	7.7	—	1	2	2	3	1	—	—	3	2	3	3	1	2	2	—	3	—	1	—	—	—
10. Canada	7.5	1	1	2	3	1	3	1	1	3	3	1	3	3	3	1	1	2	2	3	1	1	3
11. Ireland	6.3	1	2	3	2	3	2	1	1	1	1	3	3	3	2	2	2	3	1	3	2	1	3
12. Switzerland	6.2	1	2	3	3	2	2	1	1	2	1	3	3	3	3	2	1	1	3	3	1	1	1
B. Average ranking‡		1.4	1.2	2.7	2.2	2.5	2.2	1.0	1.0	1.8	1.5	2.0	2.8	2.5	2.2	1.5	1.8	2.5	1.8	2.7	1.8	1.3	2.5
C. A divided by B		1.4	2.3	0.6	1.0	0.5	0.8	2.5	2.2	1.5	1.8	0.7	0.6	0.6	0.9	1.5	1.0	0.5	1.1	0.6	1.0	2.0	0.5
D. G, if A greater than B; S, if A smaller than B		G	G	S	Equal	S	S	G	G	G	G	S	S	S	Equal	G	Equal	S	Equal	S	Equal	G	S

* From Appendix Table A-5. Dash (—) for not available.

† Names of variables are given on p. 131.

‡ Obtained by averaging the "third" in which countries fall.

137

The countries with high export instability are *lower* than those with low export instability with respect to the following characteristics, ranked according to ratios of their average rankings:

Per cent of exports to the United States (X_7)....... 0.8
Population density (X_{14})......................... 0.7
Foreign trade as per cent of GNP (X_4)............. 0.6
Energy per capita (X_{19}).......................... 0.6
GNP per capita (X_{22})............................ 0.6
Foreign trade per capita (X_{31}).................... 0.6
Per cent of exports to single region (X_6)............ 0.5
Regional export concentration index (X_{27}).......... 0.5
Country export concentration index (X_{38}).......... 0.5

The average ranking is approximately the *same* for GNP (X_5), value of foreign trade (X_{23}), commodity-group export concentration index (X_{26}), instability of capital movements (X_{30}), and per cent of exports in three commodities (X_{32}).

The characteristics linking high export instability with high ratios of average rankings—instability of export quantum, instability of imports, instability of export prices, instability of terms of trade, etc.—are also characteristics which are relatively highly correlated with export instability according to the standard correlation techniques. The results of the present scheme of analysis therefore largely corroborate the earlier analysis.

Conclusion of Chapter

The purpose of this chapter has been to improve upon the single-variable analysis for explaining instability of export proceeds by bringing more variables into the analysis.

Multiple-factor analysis was able to achieve a coefficient of multiple correlation R of only .67, as compared with the highest simple correlation coefficient r of $+.58$. All combinations of variables that yielded R-values above .50 included instability of export volume, which was the variable which yielded the highest r-value. The additional variables which raised the R-value the most (to .66) when two independent variables were used, were the logarithmic rate of growth of export proceeds and the terms of trade instability index. With three independent variables, the highest R-value also (.66) was obtained with three combinations, all of which included instability of export volume, and instability of import outlays, but also, respectively, foreign trade as a per cent of GNP, GNP per capita, and foreign trade per capita. The multiple correlation coefficient was edged up less than one percentage point (to .67) by using combinations of four of these factors as independent variables.

The cross-classification analysis, which involved only two independent variables, turned up other variables as most influential on instability of export proceeds than those revealed in the multiple-correlation analysis. Percentage increase in GNP per year and instability of capital movements were the most powerful, according to the cross-classification technique, whereas instability of export quantum and instability of terms of trade (as well as instability of export quantum and logarithmic growth of export proceeds) brought the highest multiple correlation coefficients with two independent variables. Instability of export quantum and logarithmic growth of exports were second highest by the cross-classification technique. Several other variables were obviously important, as shown in Table 6-5.

The analysis comparing the characteristics of countries with high instability of exports with those of countries with low instability of exports showed that four variables—instability of export quantum, instability of imports, instability of export prices, and instability of terms of trade—were most closely associated with high export instability, and that regional concentration of export destination, measured in three different ways, was the characteristic most closely connected with stability of exports. It seems worth mentioning again that it is not tautologous to have instability of export quantum and instability of export prices as determining variables of instability of export proceeds, since quantum and price *could be* perfectly compensating variables, leaving proceeds perfectly stable. They are not, however.

The statistical analysis of this chapter, though far from satisfying, brings out some significant points. The two variables which by their nature directly determine variations in export proceeds, namely, variations in export quantum and variations in export prices, yielded a multiple correlation coefficient of only .60 (as compared with values up to .66 for seven other pairs all involving instability of export quantum) and were only the second highest pair of variables under the cross-classification technique. These less than perfect results arise from the deficiencies in the data and in the methods of analysis. Beyond these formal determinants of instability of export proceeds, however, the analysis shows that high instability is associated with various combinations of characteristics. We should not be too surprised at this result. A phenomenon can be the resultant of various combinations of variable forces.

Chapter 7

SUMMARY AND CONCLUSIONS

In this final chapter the principal findings are summarized and some concluding observations are made regarding policies for reducing international economic instability.

SUMMARY

Purpose

The purpose of this study has been to discover and measure the different degrees of instability in international economic relations after World War II (usually 1946 to 1958) and to explain them by relating them to some other measurable variables. It was expected that the detailed factual inquiry would throw light on policy measures for mitigating international economic instability. An underlying purpose was also to carry the understanding of this subject beyond the formal mechanics of the foreign trade multiplier and related national income analysis (Chapter 1).

Method

Export proceeds—the money value of exports of goods (and services)— were used as the principal variable indicative of international economic instability. The measurement of the fluctuations in export proceeds (and other variables) was done principally by means of a logarithmic variance index. The instability index shows the typical year-to-year relative changes corrected for trend influences. Relatively high index numbers show relatively high degrees of instability (Chapter 2).

Instability in Selected World Aggregates

The instability index (I-I) had a value of 9.1 for world exports of all goods, 1947 to 1958. The corresponding I-I for quantum of world exports was 4.2 and for price (unit value) was 7.6. Hence, the instabilities of quantum and price reinforced each other. The instability indexes for the value and volume of world production (non-Communist countries) were both 4.7 in the postwar period. For the years 1925 to 1938, the I-I for quantum of world production was 5.8 and for quantum of exports was 7.8.

The comparisons of instabilities of primary goods and manufactured goods are particularly interesting. World exports of primary goods, by value, 1948 to 1958, had an I-I of 3.8, while the corresponding I-I for manufactured goods was 6.8. Since world trade was about evenly divided between primary and manufactured goods, manufactured goods thus contributed about two-thirds of the world export instability. The instability indexes for quantum of exports differed almost as much, but in reverse order: 4.7 for primary goods and 7.1 for manufactured goods. World production of primary goods, by volume, 1948 to 1958, had an I-I of only 1.9, while the corresponding I-I for manufactured goods was 4.8. The terms of trade between primary and manufactured goods—showing changes in relative prices—had an I-I for the same period of 7.4.

Statistics were available to make possible the comparison of instability indexes for eight broad groups of exports, by value, for the years 1952 to 1957, for the non-Communist countries. The most unstable were base metals, with an I-I of 10.5, and the most stable were agricultural raw materials, with an I-I of 4.1. Other indexes were: minerals, 9.9; "other" manufactures, 6.6; capital goods, 6.1; fuels, 5.9; food, 5.1; and consumer goods, 4.6. When world exports in these groups were weighted by these indexes, capital goods, food, and base materials turned out to be the greatest contributors to world export instability (Chapter 3).

Individual Primary Commodities

Instability indexes of export proceeds could be calculated for the non-Communist countries for 29 primary commodities, 1950 to 1958 (Table 3-7). Pulp and paper (I-I of 41.4) and rubber (I-I of 40.3) stood at the top, while fish (I-I of 6.5) and butter (I-I of 8.2) were at the bottom. Seven of the 29 commodities—pulp and paper, rubber, wool, wheat, cotton, coffee, and petroleum—accounted for five-eighths of the instability contributed by these 29 commodities. Price instability was fairly closely associated with export-value instability (correlation coefficient of $+.72$). Cocoa (I-I of 49.4), rubber (I-I of 46.2), and pulp and paper (I-I of 36.3) had the highest price instabilities; bananas (I-I of 2.3) and tobacco (I-I of 3.5) had the lowest (Chapter 3).

Instability of Exports of Individual Countries

Individual countries had export instability indexes ranging from 73.8 (Iran) and 57.2 (Indonesia) to 6.2 (Switzerland) and 6.3 (Ireland).

The median for the 83 countries was 19.4, the simple mean 21.8, and the weighted mean (weighted by value of exports) 20.0. Figure 4-1 provides the details. The six countries supplying just over half of the world's exports had export instability indexes as follows: United States, 16.8; United Kingdom, 17.7; West Germany, 19.4; Canada, 7.5; France, 20.9; U.S.S.R., 36.2. When exports are weighted by the instability indexes, the largest percentage contributors to world export instability are, in percentages: United States, 16.6; United Kingdom, 8.1; West Germany, 7.9; U.S.S.R., 7.5; France, 5.1; Japan, 4.2. These six countries accounted for 49 per cent of world exports and 49 per cent of world export instability (Chapter 4).

Instability of Imports of Individual Countries

Instability of exports was not highly correlated with instability of imports for the 83 countries ($r = +.43$), so it is informative to note the instability indexes for imports. The import instability index numbers ranged from 50.7 (Lebanon) and 44.2 (Israel) to 9.6 (Jordan) and 10.7 (Denmark). The median was 20.5, the simple mean 22.8, and the weighted mean (weighted by value of imports in 1957) 19.5. Figure 4-7 provides the details. The eight countries taking just over half of the world's imports had import instability indexes as follows: United States, 11.9; United Kingdom, 16.1; West Germany, 13.2; Canada, 12.9; France, 19.3; Japan, 30.5; Netherlands, 20.8; U.S.S.R., 23.5. When imports (1957) are weighted by the import instability indexes, the largest percentage contributors to world import instability are: United Kingdom, 8.0; United States, 7.8; Japan, 6.0; France, 5.5; West Germany, 4.5; U.S.S.R., 4.3; Netherlands, 3.9; and Canada, 3.8. These countries accounted for 43.8 per cent of the world import instability. World import instability was not as concentrated among countries as was world export instability (Chapter 4).

Contribution of Individual Countries to World Trade Instability

When the percentage shares of individual countries in world export instability and world import instability are averaged, we obtain a measure of the percentage contribution of individual countries to world trade as a whole (Table 4-12). Eight countries supplied half of the instability: United States, 12.2; United Kingdom, 8.3; West Germany, 6.2; U.S.S.R., 5.9; France, 5.3; Japan, 5.1; Netherlands, 3.5; and Canada, 2.8. The highest 20 countries accounted for 75 per cent of the instability and 75 per cent of world trade. Looked at from the other end, 63 of the 83 countries furnished only 25 per cent of the trade instability and of the trade, but many of these had very high export instability indexes (Chapter 4).

Factors Correlated with Instability of Exports

The single factor most closely associated with instability of export proceeds is physical volume of exports. The coefficient of correlation between instability of export proceeds and instability of quantum of exports, by countries, is $+.58$. Three other variables—instability of value of imports, instability of terms of trade, and the logarithmic rate of growth of export proceeds—have lower but relatively high *positive* correlations with export proceeds. The variables with relatively high *negative* correlations are foreign trade as a per cent of GNP, foreign trade per capita, and per cent of exports going to the United States. These three negative correlations are particularly interesting in view of the common view that high involvement in foreign trade, particularly with the United States, makes for instability of exports. The opposite is the case. The correlation coefficients for 30 other single variables were quite low (Chapter 5).

Multifactor analysis—standard multiple-correlation technique and a rather special cross-classification technique—does not throw much additional light on the determinants of export instability. The highest coefficient of multiple correlation is .67, as compared with the highest simple correlation coefficient of .58. Five different variables, in addition to instability of export quantum, contributed to these higher coefficient values: instability of import outlays, foreign trade as a per cent of GNP, GNP per capita, logarithmic growth of exports, and foreign trade per capita. The cross-classification analysis turned up several other variables of significance. The pair which gave rise to the greatest change in instability of exports consisted of percentage growth in GNP per year and the instability index of capital movements.

Comparison of the six countries with the highest export instability indexes and the six countries with the lowest export instability indexes, with respect to the other variables for which we had data, gave the following results. High export instability is positively correlated with instability of export quantum, instability of import outlays, instability of export prices, and instability of terms of trade; it is negatively correlated with geographic concentration of exports, foreign trade per capita, GNP per capita, foreign trade as a per cent of GNP, and energy per capita (Chapter 6).

Relevance of Findings for Policy

This empirical study of international economic instability provides few positive prescriptions for governmental or intergovernmental policy for reducing international economic instability. Statistical analysis is not needed in order to know that the stabilization of prices *and* quantities will stabilize proceeds. This study does provide some important negative points with respect to policy, however. One is that manipulation of some single, indirectly connected variable, that is, other than price and quantity, is very unlikely to have much influence on export instability. For example, stabilization of imports by a country would not have much effect on its export instability.

Another conclusion relevant for government policy is that stabilization efforts concentrated on a few countries or a few commodities are very unlikely to make much difference in international trade instability generally. For example, the United States accounted for only one-twelfth of the world trade instability in the postwar period. All primary commodities accounted for only about one-third of world trade instability.

Manifestly, measures for reducing international economic instability do not flow directly from this study, though the facts and relations brought together here can serve as checks or tests for proposals for reducing instability. We now turn to a brief discussion of the types of measures which might be effective in reducing international economic instability or in mitigating its effects.

POLICIES FOR DEALING WITH INTERNATIONAL ECONOMIC INSTABILITY

In this final section we shall consider briefly the principal types of governmental or intergovernmental measures for reducing or adjusting to international economic instability. We assume that such measures are not to be directed toward changing basic trends in international trade. In fact, the measures should facilitate adjustment to trends. Neither are the measures considered here directed toward removal of seasonal variations, although reduction of some seasonal variations would be desirable.

Measures for dealing with international economic instability may be classified in various ways. The most useful classification for policy purposes seems to be the one that distinguishes between *trade-control* measures and *financial* measures. The distinction can be maintained fairly consistently. The trade-control measures emphasize direct and indirect actions to affect demand, supply, or price so as to reduce fluctuations around the trend. The financial measures are essentially devices for easing the impact of instability or facilitating adaptation to instability, though they do have some stabilizing influence.

Trade-control Measures

Trade-control measures fall into two broad subgroups. The first subgroup consists of measures designed to improve the market mechanism.

The second subgroup involves controls or actions that affect demand, supply, or price.

Improving the Market Mechanism. These measures would improve international monetary arrangements, broaden international capital markets, lower international trade barriers, broaden the opportunities for international movements of technology and enterprise, and facilitate the internal adjustment of industries to changing world-market conditions. They also include measures for promoting stable economic growth within countries. Progress in these ways is slow and it is frequently resisted. Also, some improvements in world markets might bring new instabilities, particularly if they were not accompanied by increased domestic adaptability to change. In any case, the governments and the economic groups that seek reduction of international economic instability are unlikely to be satisfied with the rate of progress that can be achieved by efforts to improve the market mechanism and to promote steady economic growth.

Government Intervention in Markets. The second subgroup involves government intervention in markets. The intervention can take the form of direct or indirect controls. Direct controls are government regulation of prices, production, storage, or marketing; indirect controls are taxes, subsidies, or governmental production or marketing activities. Many combinations are possible. Administrative feasibility, the costs, and the effectiveness of the various possibilities can be evaluated only with reference to specific proposals. A high degree of intergovernmental cooperation is necessary to make an intervention system even moderately successful. Hence, single-commodity rather than multicommodity arrangements are more promising.

The problems of direct control are well known. Effective control over production is extremely difficult to achieve; price control, in the form of either ceilings or floors, is almost impossible in the absence of standard grades and a police force, although if governments themselves monopolize the marketing arrangements they can maintain the negotiated prices internationally for short periods; effective marketing controls generally require definite international commitments to buy and sell, although export quotas may work in some situations. Control arrangements are practically impossible if the commodities are not storable for a considerable period of time; storage makes it possible for commitments to be met by both consumer and producer, buyer and seller. Control arrangements tend to be predominantly influenced by producer-countries, with the result that the objective of reduction of instability tends to be supplanted by that of obtaining maximum profits. A strong combination of buyers could of course exert monopsonistic pressure on suppliers, but it is more difficult to organize buyers than sellers because buyers are usually more numerous and less dependent on a particular commodity. Although a few private international cartels might be considered reasonably successful in controlling trade, no intergovernmental commodity control arrangements have been successful for very long.

Direct control arrangements involving firm commitments with respect to quantity and price can, if proper agreements are negotiated and if members live up to them, assure absolute stability of export proceeds around some trend. These are very demanding international requirements. If the control arrangements relate to only price *or* quantity, the effects on proceeds are much less certain because of the difficulty of estimating the elasticity and stability of the demand and supply functions involved. Control arrangements which concentrate mainly on price—as most tend to do—imply high flexibility of supply to counter shifting demand, and thus, under most plausible demand-supply conditions, increase rather than decrease the instability of export proceeds.

Indirect governmental controls—taxes, subsidies, governmental market operations—have not been used much for international stabilization purposes. The big exception to this generalization is the case of gold, which has been subjected to price control by means of buying and selling operations by governments in connection with the management of money. Suggestions for the use of buffer stocks—that is, adding to and subtracting from stockpiles—to reduce instability are essentially variations on the technique of maintaining the international gold standard. To support a price at a specified level requires "sufficient"—usually very large—financial resources; to keep a price from rising above a specified level requires sufficient stocks of the commodity in question. There is a strong tendency for the specified level or range of prices to be set above the normal market prices because of the pressure of the producer-seller interests, who are the principal supporters of the price stabilization arrangements. When this pressure is expressed through governments, the prestige of national states becomes involved. This pressure for above-normal prices is the greatest weakness of the buffer-stock system. The buffer-stock system does have the virtue, however, of operating without production or marketing controls, a matter of great administrative importance. Criticisms of the United States and other agricultural aid programs are not all directly applicable to buffer-stock schemes because the agricultural programs have been aimed primarily at achieving a target price or income relation with other commodities or nonagricultural groups. Reduction of instability of the gross proceeds of agriculture has been a subsidiary objective.

It is conceivable that a coordinated system of taxes and subsidies, operated by the governments of the principal exporting and importing countries of a particular commodity, could reduce instability of export proceeds (and payments for imports), but such schemes seem difficult to devise and more difficult to administer. Unilateral arrangements involving taxes and subsidies usually include international price discrimination as an incident to domestic stabilization or price-raising efforts and tend to be destabilizing beyond very short periods because of the reactions they elicit.

Financial Measures

The second broad type of measure for dealing with international economic instability does not involve efforts to perfect international markets or control them: it simply tries to cushion the impact of instability on the victims of it. It is not inconsistent with the measures of the trade-control type, but it is much more feasible on an international basis. In essence, financial measures reduce fluctuations in foreign exchange *availabilities,* whereas trade-control measures, if successful, reduce fluctuations in export *earnings.*

Foreign exchange availabilities can be made more stable by a government on its own by building up its foreign exchange reserves during good times and by drawing on them as needed during lean times; or they can be made more stable by means of cooperative international financial arrangements which make it relatively easy for a country to acquire foreign exchange when its export earnings fall off and to repay the funds at a later time, if repayment is required. Countries likely to want financial assistance to counteract a decline in export earnings are likely to be countries generally short of international monetary reserves and credit sources and are likely to find domestic compensatory measures difficult to establish. Hence, if much is to be accomplished in this field it will probably have to be done by means of international arrangements.

Foreign exchange availabilities would be maintained or supported, then, by providing international credits or grants to countries suffering a substantial decline in their exports. If the advances are credits, it is desirable to distinguish between "short-term" and "long-term" credits. Short-term credits would be repaid during the next upswing in exports or within a few years. Grants to offset instability of export earnings would be unacceptable because they would put a premium on instability! Long-term credits or grants would usually be the foreign exchange requirements of productive investments which would yield their fruits over several years.

Long-term Credits

Such countercyclical long-term investments would be designed to counteract declines in private foreign investment which tend to be associated with declining foreign exchange earnings of capital-importing and international-debtor countries. Countercyclical international grants for development purposes could serve as the balance-wheel just as well as long-term loans.

There are several international lending organizations, most prominently the International Bank for Reconstruction and Development, and aid arrangements, most prominently the aid programs of the United States, geared to making loans or grants to less developed countries as supplements to private long-term investment. They are technically able to step up their advances to countries suffering export declines; the question is whether they will have the funds to make the advances in such circumstances and whether they will be willing to do so, even if they have the funds. The decline of exports generally takes place in the recession or depression phase of the business cycle, so pessimism tends to prevail when the funds are needed. It seems impractical to try to devise a formula to bring about the maintenance or increase of such long-term investments. The most important steps have already been taken, namely, the creation of international and national agencies to promote foreign investment. The next most important thing is for the boards and managements of these agencies to recognize as one of their guiding principles the avoidance of sharp downturns in foreign investment in particular countries. This is a matter of policy and a matter of sufficiency of financial resources, not a matter of organization. Financial resources are more likely to be sufficient in a depression period if they have been acquired or authorized in advance.

Short-term Credits

Short-term credits would enable a country to maintain its imports—other than those financed by long-term credits—despite a reduction in its export earnings. Such credits could be provided by private sources, national agencies such as the Export-Import Bank, or intergovernmental sources such as the International Monetary Fund. The assumption we are making is that private sources of credit are insufficient. The Export-Import Bank is able to make such loans, as are agencies of governments of some other industrial countries, but it seems equitable to expect the burden of financing the dips for poorer countries to be shared by various countries. Multicountry arrangements could be formal or informal, but convenience, equity, and economy point to formal arrangements.

The International Monetary Fund could meet the needs for these instability short-term credits to some degree. Its methods of operation rather than the size of its resources or the restrictions imposed by its Articles of Agreement tend to disqualify it from serving this purpose, however. Rather than set up a separate institution to provide international short-term credits, it would seem desirable, if the Fund cannot adapt itself to this need of many of its members, to establish a subsidiary or affiliate of the Fund which would be explicitly authorized to make short-term loans in case of a sizable reduction in export earnings. Such a subsidiary would have the advantage of providing a means of adding to total international credit resources.

A Proposal for an International Short-term Credit Corporation

On the assumption that the International Monetary Fund will not adapt its lending policies sufficiently to meet the problem of instability of export proceeds within the next few years, it seems desirable to outline in some detail the nature and functions of a possible "International Short-term Credit Corporation" (ISTCC) that would be an affiliate of the International Monetary Fund. This discussion draws from various proposals that have been made for providing such credits.[1]

The reason for making the ISTCC an affiliate of the International Monetary Fund is that it would avoid duplication of the Fund organization. The Fund already collects the information that would be needed by the ISTCC and it has officers who are experienced in this kind of work. The officers would simply apply different lending standards when functioning under the ISTCC.

Membership. Members of the ISTCC would be members of the International Monetary Fund who subscribed capital to the Corporation and agreed to abide by the articles of incorporation. Other countries not members of the Fund could become members of the ISTCC with the understanding that they would become members of the Fund within perhaps three years.

Sources of Funds. Funds for making advances would come from paid-in capital, borrowings, and earnings. Principal reliance would be on paid-in capital. Borrowings would be obtained by selling short-term notes, pending receipt of previously pledged or new capital. Earnings would of course be from interest on loans made to members. Only convertible currencies would be accepted or used in any of the transactions.

Eligibility for Loans. Member countries eligible for loans would be those with actual export earnings in a given year a certain percentage below a statistically determined normal level of export earnings. For example, if export earnings of a country in a given year were more than 10 per cent below the calculated normal value, the country would be eligible for a loan. It might seem plausible to consider eligible only those countries with an historical record of high export instability, as indicated

[1] "International Compensation for Fluctuations in Commodity Trade," United Nations, New York, 1961; "Latin American Export Commodities: Market Problems. Report of the Group of Experts," Pan American Union, Washington, 1961; Joseph D. Coppock, "Cushioning the International Impact of U.S. Depressions," *Journal of Finance*, May, 1959.

by such measures of instability as those described in Chapter 2, but politically it would seem preferable not to disqualify any member country because of a good historical record of stability. Presumably, the generally stable countries would not often have occasion to borrow from the Corporation. The financial resources needed would be much smaller if the six or eight countries with the largest exports were not ordinarily eligible for loans.

The determination of the normal value of exports for any particular year could be done by any of various methods of trend fitting. The linear logarithmic trend line used for measuring instability in this study would be feasible, but it might be too insensitive to changes in the trend of exports. Five-year or three-year moving averages would be more sensitive and more easily understood. One empirical investigation indicated that for the 1950s the five-year and three-year moving averages of exports yielded very similar results.

Amounts and Terms of Loans. The expectation would be that loans would be made almost automatically after the eligible countries applied for them. Countries otherwise eligible should not be denied loans because they had built up their monetary reserves. The amount of the credit to which a country would be entitled would be some fraction, say one-half, of the amount by which actual export proceeds in any one year fell short of, say, 90 per cent of the normal export figure, however determined. For illustrative purposes the three-year moving average of exports is used here. For example, if "Primarania" had exports in Years 1, 2, and 3 averaging $100 million and in Year 4 $84 million, it would be eligible for a loan of as much as $3 million, that is, 0.5 (0.90 × $100 million — $84 million). It would not be able to get the loan until the statistics were available for Year 4.

The loan would be due in equal installments, say in the middle of the third, fourth, and fifth years after the date of the loan at the latest, but repayments would be required earlier to the extent of 50 per cent of the amount by which export earnings ran more than 10 per cent above the moving average. For example, if in Year 5 Primarania's export earnings amounted to $108 million, as compared with the average for Years 2, 3, and 4 of $95 million, it would be required to pay back, if the loan were that large, 50 per cent of the excess of $108 million over 110 per cent of the $95 million. This would be one-half of the difference between $108,000,000 and $104,500,000, or $1,750,000, and would be due in the middle of Year 6, after the statistics for Year 5 became available. This automatic repayment arrangement would be the counterpart of the automatic lending arrangement and would help maintain the revolving character of the fund. The board should probably have the power to alter the 50 per cent provision, say between 50 and 100 per cent according to the availability of funds, but the effective percentage would apply to all borrowers and on their repayments as well as their borrowings. It should also have the power to suspend the automatic repayment provisions in unusual circumstances. In case a country failed to meet the regular schedule of repayments, it would lose its right to further loans until repayments were back on schedule.

No collateral security would be required. If a country had good financial collateral available, it would not have to turn to the ISTCC for credit; if it had to pledge commodities of some sort, the ISTCC would find itself with heavy administrative burdens connected with the collateral and might even find itself in the business of buying and selling commodities. Hence, the good faith of the member governments rather than collateral security seems the proper reliance.

Interest Charges. Interest would be on the actual amount of a loan outstanding and should be, say, 25 per cent higher than going rates of interest for similar kinds of credit. A special fee or surcharge would serve the same purpose. The reason for the higher rate would be to discourage resort to the ISTCC for credit before other sources had been tried. This higher rate is an important feature of the plan. Conceivably, the rate could be altered annually on loans outstanding in the light of going rates. If after some years the interest charges should result in profits for the ISTCC well in excess of administrative and similar expenses, rebates could be made to members on the basis of their capital contributions.

Total Funds Required. The total funds required would depend on (1) the countries eligible for loans, (2) the fluctuations around the moving averages, and (3) the extent to which countries eligible for loans would actually request them. A statistical study based on the experience of the non-Communist countries which would have been eligible to request such loans during the 1950s showed that the credits outstanding would not have exceeded $1 billion at any time. This calculation was based on loans of 50 per cent of the shortfall below 90 per cent of the three-year moving average. If the loans had been based on 75 per cent of the shortfall below 95 per cent of the three-year moving average, the maximum credits outstanding would have amounted to $1.7 billion. If credits amounting to a full 100 per cent of the shortfall below 90 per cent of the three-year moving average had been used, nearly $2.5 billion would have been required.

International trade is likely to expand, in both volume and money terms, in the several years ahead more or less as it has in the past, and there is little reason to believe that the degree of instability around the expansion trend will decrease much, if any. The multiplication of national states is almost certain to increase the instability for individual countries. Also, international trade was more stable—around the trend—

in the 1950s than it had been in the preceding four decades, so the figures cited almost certainly understate the needs for the 1960s and the 1970s. Hence, a total capital subscription amounting to 3 per cent of a moving average of members' commodity exports, about $3 billion, for the three years 1958 to 1960, would seem to be an appropriate fund for most of the 1960s. Capital subscriptions would be called as needed. Emergency needs could be met by borrowings by the ISTCC. The fund would be a revolving one, and the capital subscription would be automatically expanded. The moving-average base for determining the size of loans would provide protection against very large increases in requirements for funds.

Country Shares of Total Capital. On the assumption that practically all non-Communist countries joined the Corporation, the percentage shares of the total capital subscription (corresponding to export shares in 1960) would be 18 for the United States, 10 for the United Kingdom, 10 for West Germany, 6 for Canada, 4 for Japan, 25 for Western Europe (excluding the United Kingdom and West Germany), and 27 for the remaining countries. Hence, the countries which would not ordinarily be borrowers would furnish about three-fourths of the funds. With the capital subscriptions amounting to 3 per cent of total exports of $100 billion, or $3 billion, the United States share (18 per cent) would be $540 million, that of the United Kingdom $100 million, etc.

It seems desirable to keep the basis for assessment on a single standard, namely, an equal percentage of average exports in a recent period. A system of assessment that allowed for differences in income, national or per capita, would put even more of the control in the hands of the relatively prosperous countries and would be more difficult to determine.

Provisions for Changed Needs. It is quite possible that after some years the International Monetary Fund would follow lending policies which would be flexible enough to make unnecessary the maintenance of a separate affiliate, in which case the ISTCC resources could be merged into those of the Fund proper. If not, the ISTCC could be revised.

Probable Effects of ISTCC Operations

The credit arrangements described in the preceding section would enable the less developed countries outside the Communist bloc to maintain their imports quite well in the face of declining exports. Imports of say $25 billion in one year would fall to $21 billion in the following year in the absence of these special credits but could be sustained at about $23 billion if the credits were fully used. Since the imports of the borrowing countries are largely from the industrial countries, it would be the exports of the industrial countries which would be sustained, *not* those of the less developed countries, with minor exceptions. Barring unlikely repercussion effects, export instability of the less developed countries would not be affected. During the repayment phase, exports of goods from industrial to less developed countries would be lower than they otherwise would be. The reduction in aggregate international trade instability would evidently approximate that represented by the ratio of credit advances in a period to the total international trade of the period. With total world exports of $100 billion and credits of $2 billion, the improvement would be around 2 per cent. The assurance of available credits would be important for many countries, however.

Stronger Measures for Reducing International Economic Instability

If the nearly automatic scheme for providing short-term credits and the hoped-for countercyclical loan and aid policies of the principal institutions failed to provide an acceptable international contribution toward trade stability, other measures could be employed.

More Credits. For one thing the long-term and short-term credit measures could be strengthened. These could be available to all member countries and the amounts available could be increased. Such credits could enable all countries to maintain imports (and thus the exports of other countries) if countries were disposed to borrow.

Maintenance of Demand by Buffer Stocks. Demand may be lacking, however, regardless of the availability of credit. Hence, the only sure way to maintain exports is for other countries, individually or in groups, to buy them. Maintenance of demand for exports provides the exporting country with two things: (1) the foreign exchange and (2) the continued utilization of the resources employed in producing the exports. The ramifications for the domestic economy of the exporting country are important too, and the tendency would be for its import demand to be supported also as a result of the support of its export demand. The difficulty with maintaining demand, aside from financing, is that the goods purchased would have to be stored, destroyed, left to deteriorate, or disposed of in noncommercial channels. If they were disposed of in commercial channels, the special sales would simply substitute largely for commercial sales. It is difficult to establish noncommercial channels for disposal; destruction and deterioration through neglect seem distressingly wasteful; and storage is feasible only for durable, staple products. Hence, proposals for the maintenance of demand for exports tend to simmer down to proposals for establishing buffer stocks of storable, primary commodities.

The most important objection to buffer stocks is the one cited earlier, namely, that the price range tends to be set too high and that supplying countries bitterly resent sales by the stockpiling authorities. With large enough financial resources and a directive to do only two things—reduce fluctuations in prices *and* maintain the purchasing power value of its capital—a buffer-stock agency might succeed in reducing the instability of export earnings of the suppliers of the commodities involved. Unneedy as well as needy countries (and producers) benefit, however. What is needed for policy guidance is some actual experience with a well-conceived, adequately financed operation involving a major primary commodity. It would be preferable to experiment first with a primary commodity which is very durable and unlikely to become technologically obsolete. Hence, a mineral rather than an agricultural product would seem to be the best candidate. The brief buffer-stock experience with tin should not disqualify it.

Direct Controls. If buffer stocks should be unsatisfactory for one reason or another, the next recourse is to direct control measures of the general form represented by international commodity agreements or international cartels. Intergovernmental long-term contracts are in this same category. There has been enough experience with these arrangements to reveal the principal problems involved. Participation by nearly all actually or potentially important supplying countries is required—a difficult matter. Importing countries just about have to be included in order to keep the stronger of them from driving separate bargains with particular suppliers. Prices, even though negotiated at the start of the agreement, are almost certain to cease to be acceptable to buyers or sellers before much time has elapsed. The generally stronger bargaining power of sellers tends to put prices above "equilibrium" levels, so new production is encouraged. Also, it is difficult to confine the negotiation to reduction of instability. Guaranteed import and export quotas impose rigid conditions on both buyers and sellers which they may not be able or anxious to fulfill for very long. Export quotas, if they are to be met, tend to require domestic production control arrangements, either to assure the supply or to limit it. Maintenance of stocks at satisfactory levels is difficult. Effective agreements tend to increase government controls within countries. It is very difficult to allocate production according to lowest costs. There is no way to enforce compliance with an agreement, since a country can always drop out. Collapse of an agreement tends to bring new instability. Renegotiation is difficult. National prestige is involved in the arrangements, and considerations extraneous to the problems of the particular commodity may easily be determining factors.

These difficulties may be surmountable, but they are real. It seems very unlikely that commodity control arrangements could be negotiated for more than a few commodities. Hence, only a small fraction of international trade would be affected.

Conclusion on Policies

This discussion of policies should make it clear that measures to cushion countries against the shock of changes in their export earnings are much more feasible than measures to maintain export earnings. Institutional arrangements already exist for providing countercyclical long-term loans or grants to countries likely to need foreign exchange in periods of export decline. Institutional arrangements for providing almost automatic short-term credits can be provided as an adjunct to the International Monetary Fund, pending the time when the Fund is in a position to provide these short-term resources itself.

If maintenance of demand seems desirable, in addition to the cushioning measures, the buffer stock is the most promising vehicle, but it has limited applicability and benefits the unneedy as well as the needy. Intergovernmental control or cartel arrangements hold little promise for reducing international economic instability. They might be temporarily useful for other purposes.

Beyond any of these measures are those fundamental changes in national economies which increase their adaptability to changing demand conditions, increase the level of production so that temporary adversity can be borne, and provide internal arrangements which cushion the inevitable shocks of economic life. Such changes would almost certainly broaden the range of products in the various countries. Funds and energies would be better used, by and large, in bringing about these fundamental changes than in trying to stabilize or otherwise control world markets.

APPENDIX

Note on Statistical Sources

Sources of information are shown here rather than at every point in the text. The principal sources were: *International Financial Statistics,* the monthly publication of the International Monetary Fund; *Balance of Payments Yearbook,* annual publication of the International Monetary Fund; *Monthly Bulletin of Statistics,* United Nations; *Statistical Yearbook,* United Nations; *International Trade,* annual publication of Contracting Parties to the General Agreement on Tariffs and Trade; *World Economic Survey,* annual publication of the United Nations; *Direction of International Trade,* December issues, United Nations; *Commodity Trade Statistics,* annual publication of the United Nations; *Trade Yearbook,* Food and Agriculture Organization of the United Nations; *Yearbook of International Trade Statistics,* United Nations; publications of the regional economic commissions of the United Nations; *Yearbook of National Accounts Statistics,* United Nations; *World Energy Supplies, 1954–57,* United Nations.

Despite the great improvement in international statistics since 1945, there are many gaps, particularly in commodity and commodity-group

(*Text continues on page* 167)

Table A-1
Export Proceeds of 83 Countries, by Years, 1946–1958*
(In millions of currency units specified, except as noted)

Country	1946	1947	1948	1949	1950	1951	1952	1953	1954	1955	1956	1957	1958
1. Argentina (U.S. $)	1,256	1,689	1,698	730	1,190	1,399	866	1,240	1,161	1,071	1,169	1,148	1,106
2. Australia (Australian £)	279	326	466	581	647	1,038	755	946	918	879	897	1,125	889
3. Austria (U.S. $)	n.a.	111	229	329	385	532	606	676	794	878	1,166	1,275	1,252
4. Belgian Congo (franc), billions	n.a.	n.a.	14.5	14.7	17.6	22.8	25.3	25.0	27.1	30.2	33.6	30.9	28.9
5. Belgium-Luxembourg (franc), billions	48	77	89	95	102	159	149	139	146	175	204	211	204
6. Bolivia (U.S. $)	78	77	104	93	81	126	98	67	75	87	86	79	57
7. Brazil (U.S. $)	n.a.	1,226	1,250	1,165	1,403	1,833	1,485	1,654	1,662	1,542	1,635	1,591	1,410
8. Bulgaria (U.S. $)	n.a.	n.a.	n.a.	n.a.	124	128	171	206	233	230	339	500	506
9. Burma (kyat)	n.a.	n.a.	n.a.	n.a.	765	1,001	1,261	1,265	1,184	1,179	1,165	1,238	1,036
10. Cambodia (riel), thousands	n.a.	n.a.	n.a.	968	1,316	1,602	1,778	1,937	2,188	1,402	1,282	1,811	1,852
11. Canada (dollar)	3,268	3,678	4,067	4,005	4,183	5,089	5,571	5,397	5,145	5,764	6,365	6,394	6,332
12. Ceylon (rupee)	958	967	1,167	1,217	1,584	1,934	1,584	1,726	1,940	2,125	2,007	1,916	1,946
13. Chile (U.S. $)	266	329	384	300	331	419	512	382	446	537	535	457	401
14. China, mainland (U.S. $)	n.a.	418	488	426	535	525	368	433	380	487	641	652	751
15. China, Taiwan (U.S. $)	n.a.	n.a.	n.a.	n.a.	100	101	125	134	105	137	141	174	185
16. Colombia (U.S. $)	216	286	323	359	432	506	523	666	716	634	727	678	609
17. Costa Rica (U.S. $)	26	37	49	52	67	72	83	92	98	95	81	99	110
18. Cuba (U.S. $)	411	820	785	644	714	852	730	715	614	674	780	947	860
19. Czechoslovakia (U.S. $)	287	573	753	806	779	845	874	994	1,005	1,176	1,387	1,358	1,513
20. Denmark (krone)	2,300	3,133	3,594	4,536	5,875	7,634	7,807	8,072	8,633	9,535	10,315	11,207	11,675
21. Dominican Republic (U.S. $)	71	89	87	78	90	131	128	119	132	130	140	182	155
22. Ecuador (U.S. $)	45	49	56	46	86	77	115	107	140	127	130	148	154
23. Egypt (£)	90	109	184	211	269	291	219	215	222	227	219	237	250
24. El Salvador (colon)	70	111	123	154	186	225	235	252	281	288	332	349	320
25. Ethiopia-Eritrea (dollar)	63	94	89	83	83	129	120	188	184	193	177	220	182

158

26. Finland (markka), billions	35	64	79	93	107	226	195	157	184	197	197	271	290
27. France (U.S. $)	789	1,484	1,522	2,109	2,461	3,157	2,872	3,196	3,827	4,646	4,701	4,594	4,460
28. Germany, East (rouble), billions	n.a.	n.a.	n.a.	n.a.	1.6	2.9	3.0	3.9	2.8	2.8	3.1	4.5	4.7
29. Germany, West (U.S. $)	n.a.	n.a.	796	1,424	2,153	3,875	4,691	5,323	6,471	7,676	9,272	11,118	11,658
30. Ghana (£)	15	23	50	43	68	83	77	80	105	91	78	84	97
31. Greece (U.S. $)	64	116	134	119	129	154	180	201	241	322	345	402	392
32. Guatemala (U.S. $)	53	69	72	67	84	88	94	98	105	110	133	128	123
33. Haiti (gourde)	126	175	169	171	211	270	287	220	313	228	300	220	261
34. Honduras (U.S. $)	37	49	55	62	64	72	70	75	60	58	81	71	77
35. Hungary (U.S. $)	n.a.	n.a.	165	280	329	396	443	503	525	609	493	488	680
36. Iceland (U.S. $)	45	58	79	58	42	52	55	72	80	83	92	85	98
37. India (rupee)	4,654	5,371	5,101	4,982	6,586	8,783	7,895	6,702	6,835	7,796	7,621	8,334	6,904
38. Indonesia (U.S. $)	58	129	372	353	831	1,326	956	712	813	923	896	899	695
39. Iran (U.S. $)	333	371	592	519	757	761	309	91	111	217	351	504	764
40. Iraq (dinar)	38	40	30	36	64	83	115	159	192	209	195	157	227
41. Ireland (£)	82	95	109	115	126	140	168	181	184	183	180	201	204
42. Israel (U.S. $)	n.a.	n.a.	n.a.	43	46	55	86	102	133	144	178	223	239
43. Italy (U.S. $)	432	773	1,357	1,411	1,602	2,121	1,958	2,289	2,439	2,776	3,208	3,910	3,998
44. Japan (U.S. $)	105	184	287	601	1,054	2,139	2,192	2,192	2,372	2,720	3,304	3,719	3,662
45. Jordan (dinar)	n.a.	n.a.	n.a.	n.a.	4	4	5	6	8	10	10	13	12
46. Korea, Republic (U.S. $)	n.a.	n.a.	n.a.	n.a.	47	81	124	72	65	71	60	76	86
47. Lebanon (£)	n.a.	n.a.	n.a.	n.a.	52	90	77	88	93	108	130	133	101
48. Liberia (U.S. $)	12	13	16	16	28	52	37	31	26	43	45	40	57
49. Libya (£)	2.2	1.9	2.9	2.7	3.6	4.7	4.6	3.5	3.8	4.6	4.2	5.4	5.1
50. Malaya (dollar)	720	1,323	1,764	1,721	4,014	6,074	3,917	3,020	3,105	4,156	4,166	4,171	3,726
51. Mexico (U.S. $)	531	672	699	647	803	981	974	938	1,055	1,304	1,388	1,386	1,374
52. Morocco (French franc), billions	10	18	38	54	66	88	96	94	100	115	119	118	147
53. Netherlands (guilder), billions	1.4	3	4	5	7	9	10	11	12	13	13	14	16
54. New Zealand (£)	148	164	136	151	206	270	266	257	234	266	296	301	293
55. Nicaragua (U.S. $)	20	25	31	28	38	50	55	59	67	87	81	89	86

159

* Export proceeds from both goods and services.

Table A-1 (*Continued*)

Country	1946	1947	1948	1949	1950	1951	1952	1953	1954	1955	1956	1957	1958
56. Nigeria (£)	25	44	62	81	90	120	130	124	150	132	135	128	136
57. Norway (krone), billions	2.5	3.5	4.4	4.6	5.8	8.7	8.7	7.9	8.6	9.8	12.0	13.0	11.8
58. Pakistan (rupee), billions	n.a.	n.a.	0.8	1.0	1.3	2.8	1.9	1.5	1.3	1.7	1.9	2.0	1.8
59. Panama (U.S. $)	71	67	85	90	82	84	96	103	124	139	141	145	158
60. Paraguay (U.S. $)	28	23	31	30	35	44	37	34	40	40	38	41	43
61. Peru (U.S. $)	153	178	185	187	210	274	282	268	287	317	359	374	332
62. Philippines (U.S. $)	390	568	630	444	477	581	523	594	562	568	619	611	629
63. Poland (U.S. $)	127	248	533	619	630	762	776	831	869	913	975	975	1,060
64. Portugal (escudo)	n.a.	n.a.	5.7	5.7	8.0	11.1	10.0	10.9	11.7	12.0	14.8	15.2	14.8
65. Puerto Rico (U.S. $)	373	352	357	372	330	387	434	537	552	559	618	687	696
66. Rhodesia-Nyasaland (£)	n.a.	55	70	84	103	129	146	156	177	203	211	189	168
67. Romania (U.S. $)	n.a.	n.a.	n.a.	n.a.	207	259	298	341	350	391	395	390	430
68. Spain (peseta)	734	886	1,141	1,234	1,192	1,476	1,402	1,476	1,422	1,366	1,353	1,457	1,487
69. Sudan (£)	10	17	29	33	38	83	51	48	44	54	71	61	54
70. Sweden (krona), billions	4.0	4.7	5.5	5.8	7.4	11.8	10.9	10.4	11.2	12.2	13.9	15.7	15.2
71. Switzerland (franc)	2,676	3,268	3,435	3,457	3,911	4,690	4,748	5,163	5,264	5,616	6,195	6,702	6,615
72. Syria (U.S. $)	45	n.a.		n.a.	93	109	120	142	192	201	221	206	167
73. Thailand (U.S. $)		87	218	274	308	376	345	336	291	359	388	430	349
74. Tunisia (franc), billions	3.9	6.5	12.7	27.2	40.0	37.5	40.1	38.8	44.2	37.2	39.1	54.0	64.4
75. Turkey (U.S. $)	159	240	215	267	282	350	405	431	365	396	456	455	349
76. Union of South Africa (£)	227	226	265	290	393	478	478	492	537	603	678	734	671
77. United Kingdom (U.S. $), billions	5.8	6.8	9.2	10.4	9.0	10.7	10.8	10.5	11.2	12.0	13.4	13.8	9.6
78. United States (dollar), billions	14.7	19.7	16.8	15.9	13.9	18.9	18.1	17.1	17.9	20.0	23.5	26.5	23.1
79. Uruguay (U.S. $)	192	210	226	229	296	276	239	297	279	210	228	157	170
80. U.S.S.R. (U.S. $)	n.a.	274	494	281	252	391	468	382	501	633	812	1,043	1,036
81. Venezuela (U.S. $)	530	715	1,126	997	1,198	1,386	1,501	1,570	1,728	1,970	2,308	2,857	2,610
82. Vietnam, Republic (piastre), billions	n.a.	n.a.	1.1	1.1	1.6	2.5	2.0	1.9	2.0	2.4	2.8	2.8	1.9
83. Yugoslavia (U.S. $)	62	179	348	226	191	230	296	231	296	336	423	514	532

Explanatory Note to Table A-2

The variables shown in Table A-2 are defined in Chapter 5, except as noted below.

Y Instability index (I-I) of export proceeds: logarithmic variance measure described in Chap. 2

X_2 I-I of national income: same

X_3 I-I of imports: same

X_4 Foreign trade as % of GNP: calculated in national currencies

X_5 GNP: in U.S. dollars

X_6 % of exports to region receiving most of country's exports

X_7 % of exports to the United States

X_8 I-I of export quantum: logarithmic variance measure applied to export value, deflated by export price index

X_9 I-I of export prices: logarithmic variance measure applied to indexes of export prices

X_{10} Exports to the United States as % of GNP

X_{11} Foreign impact %: exports plus imports of a country expressed as % of sum of gross national products of all other countries

X_{12} Population: millions of persons

X_{13} Area of country: in units of 10,000 kilometers

X_{14} Population density: persons per square kilometer

X_{15} I-I of average deviation from trend of export proceeds: described in Chap. 2

X_{16} Per capita GNP, 1951–1957: in U.S. dollars, adjusted for price changes in each country

X_{17} Fixed capital investment as % of GNP, averaged for the years 1951–1957

X_{18} % increase in GNP per year, 1951–1957, adjusted for price changes

X_{19} Energy per capita: kilograms per year (1957), divided by 10

X_{20} Increase in per capita GNP, 1951–1957, adjusted for price changes

X_{21} Growth of exports: slope of least-squares line through annual export proceeds

X_{22} GNP per capita, 1957: in U.S. dollars

X_{23} Foreign trade: exports and imports of goods and services, 1957, in U.S. dollars

X_{24} Relative prices, 1950–1958: 1958 cost-of-living index as percentage of 1950 cost-of-living index

X_{25} Growth of exports: slope of least-squares line through logarithms of annual export proceeds

X_{26} Commodity-group export concentration index: Hirschman index (Chap. 5) applied to exports by broad SITC classes

X_{27} Regional export concentration index: Hirschman index (Chap. 5) applied to exports by principal regional destinations

X_{28} I-I of capital movements: correlation coefficient (r), with a low value representing high instability

X_{29} I-I of export proceeds, measured by UN Secretariat method (Chap. 2)

X_{30} I-I of capital movements, measured by UN Secretariat method (Chap. 2)

X_{31} Foreign trade per capita: in 1957, in U.S. dollars

X_{32} % of exports in 3 commodities of highest total money value, 1957

X_{33} % of exports in 1 commodity, of highest total money value, 1957

X_{34} % of exports in SITC group having highest export proceeds, 1957

X_{35} Monetary reserves as % of imports: average of 1956 and 1957 figures

X_{36} I-I of terms of trade: logarithmic variance method, annual figures

X_{37} I-I of monetary reserves as % of imports: logarithmic variance method, annual figures

X_{38} Country export concentration index: Hirschman index (Chap. 5) applied to exports of each country to all other countries

Table A-3
Percentages of World International Trade Instability and Related Variables for 83 Countries

| Country | Per cent of total instability | | | | Instability index of trade (X_t) | | Per cent of total trade | | | Rank by Col. (9) |
| | Exports | Imports | Exports plus imports (S) | Rank (S) (low to high) | Index | Rank | Exports | Imports | Exports plus imports | |
	(1)	(2)	(3)	(4)	(5)	(6)	(7)	(8)	(9)	(10)
1. Argentina	1.90	2.21	2.055	71	39.1	81	0.9	1.17	1.035	62
2. Australia	2.56	3.13	2.845	76	29.8	66	2.1	1.74	1.92	70
3. Austria	0.99	2.04	1.515	66	30.4	69	0.9	1.01	.955	59
4. Belgian Congo	0.24	0.53	.385	42	18.6	35	0.4	0.39	.395	42
5. Belgium-Luxembourg	2.79	2.36	2.575	74	16.8	28	3.0	3.07	3.035	75
6. Bolivia	0.09	0.11	.100	15	26.1	56	0.1	0.08	.09	11
7. Brazil	0.91	2.47	1.690	67	24.9	54	1.3	1.33	1.33	65
8. Bulgaria	0.29	0.20	.245	24	15.8	21	0.4	0.30	.35	38
9. Burma	0.16	0.56	.360	38	28.1	62	0.2	0.27	.235	27
10. Cambodia	0.06	0.08	.070	10	28.2	63	0.05	0.05	.05	6
11. Canada	1.94	3.76	2.850	77	10.1	2	5.2	5.67	5.435	80
12. Ceylon	0.22	0.24	.230	23	13.4	11	0.3	0.34	.32	30
13. Chile	0.43	0.33	.380	40	18.3	34	0.4	0.39	.395	43
14. China, mainland	2.29	3.34	2.815	75	27.4	58	2.2	1.91	2.055	72
15. China, Taiwan	0.11	0.22	.165	19	19.4	37	0.1	0.19	.145	20
16. Colombia	0.32	0.44	.380	41	16.7	25	0.5	0.43	.47	46
17. Costa Rica	0.06	0.06	.060	8	14.0	13	0.1	0.09	.095	13
18. Cuba	1.04	0.87	.955	57	23.6	51	0.8	0.80	.80	56
19. Czechoslovakia	1.32	0.83	1.075	60	16.7	27	1.3	1.24	1.27	64
20. Denmark	0.56	0.67	.615	51	10.4	4	1.1	1.21	1.155	63

21. Dominican Republic	0.13	0.18	.155	18	23.0	50	0.2	0.12	.16	22
22. Ecuador	0.16	0.10	.130	16	22.3	48	0.1	0.10	.10	15
23. Egypt	0.47	0.48	.475	44	19.5	38	0.5	0.49	.495	48
24. El Salvador	0.09	0.09	.090	14	15.4	20	0.1	0.10	.10	14
25. Ethiopia-Eritrea	0.09	0.07	.080	12	22.4	49	0.1	0.06	.08	8
26. Finland	1.21	1.24	1.225	64	30.2	68	0.8	0.80	.80	55
27. France	5.05	5.47	5.260	27	20.1	41	4.8	5.52	5.16	79
28. Germany, East	2.59	1.83	2.210	72	27.5	59	1.7	1.44	1.57	67
29. Germany, West	7.87	4.54	6.200	81	16.3	23	8.1	6.70	7.40	81
30. Ghana	0.35	0.26	.305	31	26.3	57	0.2	0.24	.22	26
31. Greece	0.19	0.34	.265	29	16.3	22	0.2	0.47	.335	34
32. Guatemala	0.06	0.10	.080	13	12.6	8	0.1	0.13	.115	16
33. Haiti	0.04	0.04	.040	3	24.0	53	0.03	0.04	.035	3
34. Honduras	0.05	0.06	.055	7	16.7	26	0.1	0.07	.085	9
35. Hungary	0.48	0.47	.475	45	18.0	33	0.5	0.59	.545	51
36. Iceland	0.06	0.07	.065	9	20.4	42	0.1	0.08	.09	12
37. India	1.06	1.22	1.140	62	14.1	15	1.3	2.00	1.65	69
38. Indonesia	2.62	1.42	2.020	70	47.8	82	0.9	0.72	.81	57
39. Iran	1.76	0.63	1.195	63	53.3	83	0.5	0.37	.435	44
40. Iraq	0.46	0.25	.355	37	21.7	47	0.3	0.30	.30	29
41. Ireland	0.11	0.51	.310	32	14.0	14	0.3	0.46	.38	40
42. Israel	0.08	0.88	.480	46	28.1	61	0.1	0.39	.245	28
43. Italy	2.59	2.43	2.510	73	18.0	32	2.4	3.28	2.84	74
44. Japan	4.19	6.02	5.105	79	30.8	70	2.7	3.83	3.265	76
45. Jordan	0.01	0.04	.025	2	11.9	6	0.02	0.08	.05	5
46. Korea, Republic	0.04	0.70	.370	39	36.4	78	0.02	0.40	.21	25
47. Lebanon	0.05	0.58	.315	33	38.4	80	0.04	0.22	.13	17
48. Liberia	0.07	0.05	.075	11	31.7	73	0.04	0.03	.035	2
49. Libya	0.02	0.07	.045	4	21.3	46	0.01	0.07	.04	4
50. Malaya	1.41	0.76	1.085	61	34.9	76	0.7	0.53	.615	53

Table A-3 (*Continued*)

Country	Per cent of total instability				Instability index of trade (X_t)		Per cent of total trade			Rank by Col. (9)
	Exports	Imports	Exports plus imports (S)	Rank (S) (low to high)	Index	Rank	Exports	Imports	Exports plus imports	
	(1)	(2)	(3)	(4)	(5)	(6)	(7)	(8)	(9)	(10)
51. Mexico	0.38	0.78	.580	50	12.9	10	0.7	1.03	.865	58
52. Morocco	0.40	0.68	.540	48	30.9	72	0.3	0.37	.335	35
53. Netherlands	3.14	3.92	3.530	78	21.1	45	2.9	3.67	3.285	77
54. New Zealand	0.54	1.00	.770	54	20.5	43	0.7	0.74	.72	54
55. Nicaragua	0.04	0.05	.045	5	14.3	17	0.1	0.07	.085	10
56. Nigeria	0.35	0.32	.335	36	18.8	36	0.3	0.38	.34	36
57. Norway	0.64	0.94	.790	55	16.3	24	0.8	1.14	.97	60
58. Pakistan	0.62	0.77	.695	53	37.2	79	0.3	0.39	.345	37
59. Panama	0.02	0.07	.045	6	11.3	5	0.03	0.10	.065	7
60. Paraguay	0.02	0.03	.025	1	19.7	39	0.03	0.03	.03	1
61. Peru	0.15	0.51	.330	34	19.9	40	0.3	0.36	.33	33
62. Philippines	0.37	0.92	.645	52	23.9	52	0.4	0.65	.525	50
63. Poland	1.31	1.58	1.445	65	27.8	60	0.9	1.12	1.01	61
64. Portugal	0.217	0.31	.260	28	14.4	19	0.3	0.45	.375	39
65. Puerto Rico	0.215	0.37	.290	30	10.1	3	0.4	0.65	.525	49
66. Rhodesia-Nyasaland	0.26	0.40	.330	35	14.1	16	0.4	0.50	.45	45
67. Romania	0.14	0.23	.185	20	10.0	1	0.4	0.37	.385	41
68. Spain	0.25	0.58	.415	43	12.8	9	0.4	0.77	.585	52
69. Sudan	0.28	0.22	.250	25	32.5	74	0.1	0.17	.135	19
70. Sweden	1.53	2.27	1.900	68	17.8	31	2.0	2.17	2.085	73

164

	(1)	(2)	(3)	(4)	(5)	(6)	(7)	(8)	(9)	(10)
71. Switzerland	0.46	1.69	1.075	59	12.5	7	1.5	1.76	1.63	68
72. Syria	0.12	0.15	.135	17	17.4	30	0.2	0.15	.175	23
73. Thailand	0.63	0.38	.505	47	28.5	64	0.3	0.36	.33	32
74. Tunisia	0.23	0.20	.215	21	28.6	65	0.1	0.16	.13	18
75. Turkey	0.32	0.77	.545	49	30.9	71	0.3	0.35	.325	31
76. Union of South Africa	0.63	1.32	.975	58	13.7	12	1.2	1.51	1.355	66
77. United Kingdom	8.11	8.44	8.270	82	16.9	29	9.3	10.22	9.76	82
78. United States	16.58	7.83	12.200	83	14.4	18	20.0	12.81	16.405	83
79. Uruguay	0.12	0.33	.225	22	25.9	55	0.1	0.20	.15	21
80. U.S.S.R.	7.50	4.25	5.875	80	29.8	67	4.2	3.52	3.86	78
81. Venezuela	1.80	2.22	2.010	69	21.0	44	2.2	1.67	1.935	71
82. Vietnam	0.14	0.38	.260	26	33.3	75	0.1	0.26	.18	24
83. Yugoslavia	0.86	0.74	.800	56	35.2	77	0.4	0.59	.495	47
Total	100.00	100.00	100.000				100.00	100.00	100.000	

165

Column (1): Instability index of export proceeds times the percentage of world exports (1957), for each country; this product expressed as a per cent of the sum of the products for all countries.

Column (2): Instability index of import value times the percentage of world imports (1957), for each country; this product expressed as a per cent of the sum of the products for all countries.

Column (3): Average of percentages in Columns (1) and (2); referred to as S in text.

Column (4): S-values of Column (3), ranked from low to high.

Column (5): Instability index of export proceeds plus instability index of value of imports (X_t).

Column (6): Ranking of countries according to X_t.

Column (7): Percentage of world exports (goods only) supplied by each country, 1957.

Column (8): Percentage of world imports (goods only) taken by each country, 1957.

Column (9): Average of Column (7) and Column (8).

Column (10): Ranking of countries according to values in Column (9).

Table A-4
Range Table of Values of Variables X_2 to X_{38} for Countries Ranked by Thirds

Variable		Range			Total number available	Number not available
		Lowest third	Middle third	Highest third		
X_2	I-I—national income	1.6–4.7	4.8–9.6	10.3–66.8		
		$n = 20$	$n = 20$	$n = 20$	60	23
X_3	I-I—imports	9.6–16.5	16.9–25.5	25.9–50.7		
		$n = 28$	$n = 27$	$n = 28$	83	0
X_4	Foreign trade as % GNP	2.0–29.0	30.1–50.5	51.0–127.4		
		$n = 26$	$n = 26$	$n = 27$	80	3
X_5	National income in	150–1181	1204–4251	4531–441,659		
	millions of U.S. $	$n = 26$	$n = 26$	$n = 27$	79	4
X_6	% exports to region	21–45	46–57	58–94		
	receiving most exports*	$n = 26$	$n = 28$	$n = 29$	83	0
X_7	% of exports to U.S.	0.0–5.9	6.0–19.0	19.7–95.8		
		$n = 27$	$n = 28$	$n = 27$	82	1
X_8	I-I—export quantum	5.3–10.1	10.3–18.1	18.4–110.2		
		$n = 23$	$n = 24$	$n = 23$	70	13
X_9	I-I—export prices	3.0–11.6	11.8–16.5	16.7–74.2		
		$n = 22$	$n = 22$	$n = 22$	66	17
X_{10}	Trade with U.S. as %	0.0–3.8	3.9–8.0	8.5–96.3		
	GNP*	$n = 28$	$n = 25$	$n = 26$	79	4
X_{11}	Foreign impact %	.005–.059	.062–.153	.162–6.063		
		$n = 27$	$n = 26$	$n = 27$	80	3
X_{12}	Population (millions)	0.2–4.8	5.1–14.2	16.6–640.0		
		$n = 28$	$n = 27$	$n = 28$	83	0
X_{13}	Area, sq km (millions)	8–114	125–503	514–22,403		
		$n = 28$	$n = 27$	$n = 28$	83	0
X_{14}	Population density,	1–15	16–70	75–690		
	persons/sq km	$n = 28$	$n = 27$	$n = 28$	83	0
X_{15}	I-I—exports (av. dev.	3.2–8.8	9.0–14.3	14.3–45.2		
	from trend)*	$n = 27$	$n = 29$	$n = 27$	83	0
X_{16}	Per capita GNP adjusted	47–194	203–552	668–1713		
	for prices (U.S. $)	$n = 10$	$n = 10$	$n = 10$	30	53
X_{17}	Net fixed capital as	2.4–9.1	9.5–11.8	12.4–20.8		
	% GNP	$n = 10$	$n = 10$	$n = 10$	30	53
X_{18}	% Δ GNP per year	(−)0.5–3.1	3.3–5.8	6.3–11.4		
	adjusted for prices	$n = 10$	$n = 10$	$n = 9$	29	54
X_{19}	Energy per capita	6–163	173–931	939–7787		
		$n = 28$	$n = 27$	$n = 28$	83	0
X_{20}	Δ per capita GNP	(−)2.0–7.4	9.9–23.2	24.0–99.1		
	(U.S. $)	$n = 10$	$n = 11$	$n = 10$	31	52
X_{21}	Rate of growth of export	(−)73–75	76–181	183–3304		
	proceeds (linear)	$n = 28$	$n = 27$	$n = 28$	83	0
X_{22}	GNP per capita 1957	25–159.0	167–377	382–2582		
	(U.S. $)	$n = 26$	$n = 26$	$n = 27$	79	4
X_{23}	Foreign trade (in millions	65–702	742–1773	1842–45,976		
	of U.S. $)	$n = 28$	$n = 27$	$n = 28$	83	0
X_{24}	Relative prices	100–118	120–162	164–8333		
	(index 1950–1958)	$n = 21$	$n = 22$	$n = 21$	64	19
X_{25}	Rate of growth of export	(−)4.4–30.2	30.4–56.2	56.4–126.8		
	proceeds (log)	$n = 28$	$n = 27$	$n = 28$	83	0
X_{26}	Commodity export con-	41.6–62.4	62.5–75.8	76.1–96.4		
	centration index	$n = 26$	$n = 26$	$n = 26$	78	5

Table A-4 (*Continued*)

Variable	Range			Total number available	Number not available
	Lowest third	Middle third	Highest third		
X_{27} Regional export concentration index	45.5–57.1 $n = 28$	57.5–68.7 $n = 27$	69.0–94.1 $n = 28$	83	0
X_{28} I-I—capital movements (r)†	.003–.166 $n = 22$	.192–.340 $n = 23$	.341–.879 $n = 22$	67	16
X_{29} I-I—exports (UN method)	6.82–12.46 $n = 28$	12.53–16.46 $n = 27$	16.65–32.60 $n = 28$	83	0
X_{30} I-I—capital movements (UN method)	14.8–81.5 $n = 22$	82.2–155.4 $n = 23$	161.4–463.0 $n = 22$	67	16
X_{31} Foreign trade per capita 1957 (U.S. \$)	7.0–75.9 $n = 28$	78.9–206.4 $n = 27$	206.8–1029.1 $n = 28$	83	0
X_{32} % exports in 3 commodities	–45 $n = 25$	46–76 $n = 26$	77–98 $n = 25$	76	7
X_{33} % exports in one commodity	–21 $n = 25$	23–49 $n = 25$	50–93 $n = 26$	76	7
X_{34} % exports in largest SITC group	22–51 $n = 27$	52–71 $n = 26$	72–98 $n = 26$	79	4
X_{35} Monetary reserves as % imports*	3–24 $n = 21$	25–44 $n = 20$	46–161 $n = 22$	63	20
X_{36} I-I—terms of trade	2.4–6.2 $n = 14$	6.6–13.1 $n = 14$	13.3–24.9 $n = 13$	41	42
X_{37} I-I—monetary reserves as % imports	7.1–28.0 $n = 21$	29.1–47.5 $n = 20$	48.0–143.1 $n = 21$	62	21
X_{38} Country export concentration index	19.9–33.6 $n = 27$	34.2–49.1 $n = 26$	50.1–96.6 $n = 27$	80	3

* Thirds not even to avoid overlapping classes.
† High $\pm r$ means low instability.

statistics, largely because the Standard International Trade Classification has not been widely enough adopted. Exchange-rate changes cause difficulties in compiling statistics. Methods of classifying items change over time, for example, in balance-of-payments records.

The appendix to GATT's *International Trade 1957–58* is informative on sources. P. Lamartine Yates, in *Forty Years of Foreign Trade,* The Macmillian Company, New York, 1959, has a useful critical appendix. The research work of individuals and institutions would be greatly facilitated by further standardizing of categories, reconciliation of various series, and carrying the changes backward as well as forward in time in order to lengthen the usable time series. The user of the statistics can rarely make these changes; the task must be that of the original compilers.

Future investigators will be able to benefit from the commodity time series being set up by the United Nations Secretariat.

Table A-5
The Third in Which a Country Falls, for Selected Variables for 83 Countries
(Ranked from low to high; "0" means "not available.")

Country	Y export proceeds I-I	X_2 I-I national income	X_3 I-I imports	X_4 Foreign trade % GNP	X_5 GNP	X_6 % exports by region	X_7 % exports to U.S.	X_8 I-I export quantum	X_9 I-I export prices	X_{12} Population	X_{13} Area of country	X_{14} Population density	X_{18} % increase in GNP per year	X_{19} Energy per capita	X_{22} GNP per capita	X_{23} Foreign trade	X_{25} Growth of exports (Log)	X_{26} Commodity-group export concen-tration index	X_{27} Regional export concentration index	X_{29} I-I UN method	X_{30} I-I capital move-ments (UN)	X_{31} Foreign trade per capita	X_{32} % exports, 3 commodities	X_{36} I-I terms of trade	X_{38} Country export concentration index
1. Argentina	41.3	2	3	1	3	1	2	3	1	3	3	1	1	3	2	3	1	2	1	3	3	2	2	2	2
2. Australia	24.6	2	3	2	3	2	1	1	3	3	3	1	1	3	3	3	2	2	1	3	2	3	2	3	2
3. Austria	21.4	3	3	3	3	3	1	3	2	2	1	3	3	3	3	3	3	1	2	3	2	3	1	0	1
4. Belgian Congo	10.7	2	3	3	2	3	2	3	1	0	2	3	1	2	1	1	2	1	2	3	1	2	2	0	2
5. Belgium-Luxembourg	18.5	1	1	3	3	3	2	3	3	2	2	1	3	1	3	3	3	2	2	2	1	2	3	1	1
6. Bolivia	26.6	0	2	3	1	2	3	3	2	3	1	3	1	0	1	1	1	1	3	2	3	1	1	2	3
7. Brazil	13.8	1	3	1	3	2	3	3	2	3	2	3	1	1	1	2	3	1	3	1	3	1	3	2	3
8. Bulgaria	16.6	0	1	1	1	3	1	1	0	0	2	1	2	0	2	1	1	3	1	2	2	0	2	0	3
9. Burma	14.7	2	3	3	1	3	1	1	3	3	3	2	2	2	1	1	1	1	3	1	3	0	1	3	0	2
10. Cambodia	25.0	2	3	3	3	1	1	3	0	0	1	1	2	0	1	1	1	2	3	1	3	0	1	3	0	2
11. Canada	7.5	1	1	3	2	3	1	3	1	1	2	3	1	2	3	3	3	1	1	2	1	2	3	1	1	3
12. Ceylon	13.0	2	1	3	3	1	2	2	3	2	1	1	3	3	1	1	2	1	2	2	1	3	2	3	3	2
13. Chile	20.2	3	1	2	2	1	1	1	2	2	2	3	1	0	2	3	2	1	3	1	2	3	2	2	0	2
14. China, mainland	20.7	0	3	1	3	3	3	1	0	0	3	3	2	0	3	3	3	1	1	3	1	0	1	0	3	0
15. China, Taiwan	16.3	3	2	1	1	1	2	2	3	1	2	1	3	1	3	3	3	2	2	1	1	1	3	1	2	2
16. Colombia	13.4	3	2	3	3	2	3	3	1	3	2	3	1	0	1	2	2	1	3	2	2	2	2	3	3	3
17. Costa Rica	14.3	1	1	3	3	1	3	3	3	2	1	1	2	3	1	2	1	1	3	2	2	2	1	3	2	3
18. Cuba	26.0	3	2	3	3	3	3	1	2	3	2	1	3	0	2	3	3	1	1	3	2	3	1	2	0	3
19. Czechoslovakia	20.5	1	1	1	1	1	2	1	1	1	2	2	2	0	3	3	3	3	2	2	2	0	2	0	3	1
20. Denmark	10.0	3	1	3	3	1	2	2	2	1	1	1	3	1	3	3	3	3	2	1	1	3	1	2	0	2
21. Dominican Republic	16.9	1	3	2	2	1	1	3	1	3	1	1	2	0	1	2	1	1	3	2	1	2	2	3	3	3
22. Ecuador	25.2	1	3	2	2	1	3	3	3	2	1	2	1	3	1	2	1	2	3	2	2	2	1	3	2	3
23. Egypt	20.1	2	2	2	2	1	1	1	2	3	3	1	3	0	2	1	2	2	3	3	1	3	1	3	0	1
24. El Salvador	13.9	0	2	2	1	2	2	3	2	2	1	1	3	0	1	2	1	2	3	2	2	3	2	3	3	3
25. Ethiopia-Eritrea	24.3	0	2	2	1	0	1	3	2	2	3	3	2	0	1	0	1	2	3	1	2	3	1	3	0	2

168

#	Country																									Value
26	Finland	1	3	2	3	3	3	1	1	3	2	3	3	0	1	2	1	3	2	1	1	2	2	3	3	30.4
27	France	1	1	1	3	2	2	3	1	3	3	3	3	2	3	3	3	1	3	1	1	3	2	2	3	20.9
28	Germany, East	3	0	0	2	0	3	3	0	3	3	1	3	0	3	1	3	0	0	1	2	2	1	2	1	30.2
29	Germany, West	1	1	1	3	2	3	2	2	3	3	3	3	0	3	2	3	0	3	2	1	3	2	1	3	19.4
30	Ghana	2	3	3	2	0	3	1	2	3	1	2	1	0	2	2	1	3	2	2	1	1	3	2	2	31.9
31	Greece	2	1	2	2	1	2	2	2	3	2	2	2	3	2	2	2	2	1	2	2	1	2	1	3	18.2
32	Guatemala	3	2	3	2	3	1	3	3	2	1	2	1	0	2	1	1	3	1	3	3	1	2	1	3	10.7
33	Haiti	2	0	3	1	2	3	3	3	1	1	1	1	0	3	1	1	3	3	3	2	1	1	2	0	26.7
34	Honduras	3	2	3	2	2	1	3	3	1	1	2	1	2	2	1	1	1	2	3	3	1	2	2	1	16.1
35	Hungary	1	0	0	2	0	2	3	0	3	2	2	3	0	3	1	2	0	0	1	3	2	1	1	3	20.5
36	Iceland	1	0	3	3	1	2	1	3	1	1	3	3	0	1	1	1	2	3	2	1	1	3	2	2	22.1
37	India	2	2	1	1	1	1	1	1	1	3	1	1	0	3	3	3	3	1	3	2	3	1	1	2	16.2
38	Indonesia	2	3	2	1	2	3	1	2	3	2	1	1	0	2	3	3	3	1	2	1	2	1	3	0	57.2
39	Iran	1	0	2	1	1	3	2	3	1	2	1	2	0	1	3	3	1	3	2	2	2	2	3	0	73.8
40	Iraq	2	0	3	2	3	3	2	3	3	2	1	2	0	1	2	2	1	3	1	2	1	3	1	2	27.2
41	Ireland	3	1	2	3	1	1	3	2	2	2	3	3	1	1	1	1	1	1	1	3	2	3	2	1	6.3
42	Israel	1	0	2	3	1	3	1	1	3	2	3	3	0	3	1	1	1	2	2	1	2	2	3	3	12.0
43	Italy	1	1	1	2	1	3	1	1	3	3	3	2	2	3	2	3	1	1	2	2	3	2	1	1	21.5
44	Japan	1	1	1	2	3	3	1	2	3	3	2	2	3	3	1	1	2	3	3	1	3	1	3	3	31.0
45	Jordan	2	0	1	1	1	2	3	2	3	1	1	1	0	2	1	1	0	0	1	3	2	2	1	0	14.1
46	Korea, Republic	3	0	1	1	1	3	2	2	2	1	1	2	0	3	1	3	0	0	2	2	2	1	3	0	38.4
47	Lebanon	1	0	1	3	1	2	2	1	2	1	3	1	0	3	1	1	0	0	1	2	1	3	3	1	25.9
48	Liberia	3	0	3	1	0	3	3	3	3	1	0	2	0	1	1	1	0	0	2	3	0	0	3	0	35.7
49	Libya	3	0	2	3	1	2	3	3	2	1	0	1	0	1	3	1	0	0	1	3	0	0	2	0	22.5
50	Malaya	1	3	2	3	0	1	1	1	3	2	2	2	0	2	2	2	3	2	2	1	2	3	3	0	41.9
51	Mexico	3	0	1	2	1	1	3	1	2	3	2	2	0	2	3	3	2	1	3	3	3	2	1	2	11.1
52	Morocco	3	0	1	2	3	3	3	1	3	2	2	1	1	2	2	2	1	1	1	3	2	3	3	0	25.7
53	Netherlands	1	1	1	3	3	3	2	1	3	3	3	3	2	3	1	2	1	2	1	2	3	3	2	1	21.4
54	New Zealand	3	2	2	3	3	1	2	2	1	3	3	3	1	1	2	1	2	2	2	3	3	3	3	2	14.7
55	Nicaragua	3	3	2	2	2	2	2	2	2	1	2	1	0	1	2	1	3	2	3	1	1	2	1	0	14.2
56	Nigeria	3	0	2	1	0	2	3	3	3	2	1	1	0	2	3	3	2	1	1	3	2	2	1	0	20.9
57	Norway	1	1	1	3	1	2	1	1	2	3	3	3	0	1	2	1	2	2	2	2	2	3	1	2	16.4
58	Pakistan	1	0	2	1	2	3	1	3	2	2	1	1	0	3	3	3	3	2	2	1	3	1	3	3	36.5
59	Panama	3	2	2	3	2	1	3	3	1	1	2	2	3	1	1	1	1	1	3	3	1	3	1	2	9.9
60	Paraguay	2	0	2	1	2	1	1	2	1	1	1	1	0	1	2	1	3	2	3	1	1	2	2	3	16.0

Table A-5 *(Continued)*

Country	Y I-I export proceeds	X_2 I-I national income	X_3 I-I imports	X_4 Foreign trade % GNP	X_5 GNP	X_6 % exports by region	X_7 % exports to U.S.	X_8 I-I export quantum	X_9 I-I export prices	X_{12} Population	X_{13} Area of country	X_{14} Population density	X_{18} % increase in GNP per year	X_{19} Energy per capita	X_{22} GNP per capita	X_{23} Foreign trade	X_{25} Growth of exports (Log)	X_{26} Commodity-group export concentration index	X_{27} Regional export concentration index	X_{29} I-I UN method	X_{30} I-I capital movements (UN)	X_{31} Foreign trade per capita	X_{32} % exports, 3 commodities	X_{36} I-I terms of trade	X_{38} Country export concentration index
61. Peru	10.0	3	3	2	2	1	3	1	3	2	3	1	2	2	2	2	1	1	1	1	1	2	2	2	2
62. Philippines	18.3	3	3	1	3	2	3	3	3	3	2	3	3	1	2	2	1	2	2	1	1	1	2	3	3
63. Poland	28.1	0	3	1	3	1	1	1	0	3	1	3	0	3	2	3	3	0	3	2	0	2	2	0	2
64. Portugal	15.2	1	1	2	2	3	2	2	1	2	1	3	2	2	2	2	2	1	2	1	3	2	1	1	1
65. Puerto Rico	9.2	2	1	3	2	3	3	0	0	1	1	3	1	3	3	2	1	0	3	1	1	3	0	0	0
66. Rhodesia-Nyasaland	12.5	2	1	3	1	3	2	1	2	2	3	1	0	2	1	2	2	2	2	2	1	2	3	0	3
67. Romania	7.7	0	1	2	2	3	1	0	0	2	2	3	0	3	1	2	2	0	3	1	0	1	0	0	0
68. Spain	10.9	3	1	1	3	2	2	2	1	3	2	2	0	2	3	1	1	1	1	1	0	1	1	2	1
69. Sudan	40.4	0	2	0	0	1	1	3	3	2	3	1	0	1	0	1	3	3	1	3	3	1	2	0	1
70. Sweden	15.1	1	2	3	3	2	1	1	2	2	2	2	0	3	3	3	2	1	2	1	3	3	2	2	1
71. Switzerland	6.2	1	2	3	3	2	2	1	1	2	1	3	0	3	3	3	2	1	1	1	3	3	1	1	1
72. Syria	15.7	0	2	1	1	2	1	2	1	1	2	2	0	2	1	1	2	2	2	2	2	2	2	0	1
73. Thailand	36.6	3	2	1	2	2	3	2	1	3	3	2	0	1	1	2	3	3	3	3	3	1	1	0	2
74. Tunisia	33.0	0	2	2	1	3	1	3	3	1	2	2	0	1	1	1	3	2	3	3	0	2	1	0	3
75. Turkey	19.4	3	3	1	3	1	3	3	2	2	3	2	0	2	2	2	1	2	1	2	1	1	2	0	2
76. Union of South Africa	10.3	2	2	2	3	2	2	3	2	2	3	1	0	3	3	3	2	1	2	1	1	3	1	0	2
77. United Kingdom	17.7	1	1	2	3	1	2	2	1	3	2	3	1	3	3	3	1	1	1	1	2	3	1	1	1
78. United States	16.8	2	1	1	3	1	0	2	1	3	3	2	0	3	3	3	1	1	1	1	3	3	1	1	1
79. Uruguay	19.7	0	3	3	1	2	2	3	3	1	2	1	0	2	2	1	1	2	1	2	0	2	3	3	2
80. U.S.S.R.	36.2	1	2	1	3	3	1	0	0	2	3	1	0	3	3	3	2	1	3	3	0	1	1	0	1
81. Venezuela	16.1	1	3	3	3	1	3	3	1	1	3	1	3	3	3	3	3	3	1	1	2	3	3	2	2
82. Vietnam, Republic	37.8	0	3	1	2	3	2	2	3	2	2	2	0	1	1	1	1	2	3	3	0	1	3	0	3
83. Yugoslavia	46.1	2	2	1	2	1	2	3	2	3	2	2	0	2	2	2	3	1	2	3	1	1	1	0	1

170

Table A-6
Median Export Instability Index Values (*Y*) for Two-way Classifications of Countries Ranked by Thirds with Respect to Selected Variables*

	L	*M*	*H*	*L*	*M*	*H*	*L*	*M*	*H*
		C-2-3			C-2-9			C-2-20	
L	16.4	13.0	18.8	15.2	22.0	19.4	13.8	13.8	10.1
M	18.8	22.1	18.6	18.5	13.8	20.2	18.8	25.2	18.2
H	16.5	19.6	20.4	15.4	20.1	16.3	16.9	14.7	20.9
		C-2-4			C-2-12			C-2-22	
L	25.6	16.9	15.1	16.1	16.4	14.0	30.2	15.4	26.4
M	25.0	14.0	14.7	15.6	12.8	19.2	15.6	31.9	18.2
H	20.0	18.2	21.4	21.5	16.8	20.2	17.7	16.4	20.9
		C-2-5			C-2-14			C-2-23	
L	18.7	18.4	16.2	15.0	15.6	16.0	16.9	22.1	16.0
M	15.2	15.6	20.4	15.6	20.9	18.8	10.8	13.0	18.8
H	16.1	16.5	20.2	19.5	14.6	20.5	17.7	16.6	21.4
		C-2-7			C-2-18			C-2-25	
L	21.4	22.4	20.9	13.8	19.7	0	16.1	14.7	18.3
M	16.4	15.6	18.2	16.1	13.0	15.5	15.2	16.4	15.4
H	16.1	11.1	18.8	16.1	9.9	18.3	21.0	31.9	20.9
		C-2-8			C-2-19			C-2-26	
L	15.6	12.5	12.0	16.5	15.5	18.3	19.1	16.3	16.4
M	15.6	16.8	26.0	18.4	16.8	18.2	10.0	14.7	19.4
H	18.5	24.6	19.8	16.9	16.2	20.7	16.1	21.1	18.2
		C-2-27			C-3-4			C-3-10	
L	15.4	23.8	19.4	16.7	15.2	13.0	16.6	31.6	24.6
M	17.7	13.8	19.4	26.7	20.1	21.4	17.3	20.9	28.4
H	18.3	10.9	17.0	29.6	20.8	19.7	10.9	20.6	17.6

* *L* for lowest third of countries when they are ranked from low to high with respect to specified variable; *M* for middle third; *H* for highest third. Subtable C-2-3 indicates variable X_2 in caption and variable X_3 in stub; similarly for other subtables. Names of variables are in Appendix Table A-2. Numbers in body of each subtable are median export instability index values for countries in each cell. Underlining shows highest and lowest cell values. The number of countries in each cell (not shown here) was rarely under 3 and rarely over 15.

Table A-6 (*Continued*)

	L	M	H	L	M	H	L	M	H
	C-2-30			C-3-5			C-3-12		
L	21.5	14.4	17.3	14.2	23.2	19.7	16.5	16.6	20.2
M	16.1	15.8	20.2	15.8	26.0	30.4	15.6	15.5	10.7
H	15.2	21.0	28.2	16.5	18.0	21.4	15.4	24.6	18.3
	C-2-31			C-3-7			C-3-18		
L	30.7	20.1	17.3	20.5	21.2	25.2	13.9	6.3	24.6
M	18.7	13.0	19.2	16.4	22.1	37.2	14.1	20.9	10.7
H	14.8	15.6	21.2	11.1	24.8	17.6	14.3	20.8	19.9
	C-2-32			C-3-8			C-3-19		
L	18.6	16.3	20.9	13.0	9.8	20.8	14.2	26.6	25.7
M	13.8	19.7	18.9	15.2	21.4	22.6	15.2	20.1	25.9
H	16.1	20.1	14.9	19.4	25.2	21.4	16.8	20.9	23.0
	C-2-36			C-3-9			C-3-20		
L	16.5	16.6	20.2	14.8	16.1	25.7	14.1	6.3	14.7
M	15.6	15.5	10.7	17.3	22.1	21.4	16.2	16.2	31.0
H	15.4	24.6	18.3	14.2	26.7	19.7	17.7	21.2	16.1
	C-3-22			C-3-30			C-4-6		
L	15.2	25.4	36.5	15.2	22.1	19.4	29.6	16.9	27.0
M	14.2	20.6	19.7	14.3	18.1	18.8	17.3	20.5	18.1
H	17.7	20.9	21.4	15.2	22.9	25.7	20.7	15.2	14.3
	C-3-23			C-3-31			C-4-7		
L	14.2	23.4	25.5	14.1	25.9	35.7	20.5	20.9	21.4
M	15.2	20.1	25.7	16.6	18.2	22.7	38.4	18.0	16.6
H	16.8	21.2	21.4	15.4	20.9	21.4	19.4	15.1	14.3
	C-3-25			C-3-32			C-4-8		
L	13.0	24.0	18.3	16.2	21.4	25.9	24.3	16.9	12.8
M	14.2	15.7	25.9	19.6	22.5	24.6	16.3	16.5	23.7
H	20.0	32.4	29.2	13.6	21.1	19.7	28.9	20.9	19.7

Table A-6 (*Continued*)

	L	M	H	L	M	H	L	M	H
		C-3-26			C-3-36			C-4-9	
L	16.4	20.9	23.6	17.7	13.6	<u>31.0</u>	16.8	17.7	<u>14.3</u>
M	<u>14.2</u>	21.0	<u>27.3</u>	<u>10.8</u>	20.7	15.4	<u>27.7</u>	19.2	15.8
H	17.2	22.5	16.9	13.6	13.9	22.2	18.3	16.9	26.6
		C-3-27			C-4-5			C-4-10	
L	16.6	23.2	24.8	18.6	16.5	19.7	20.6	20.5	14.7
M	15.2	21.4	21.4	<u>37.8</u>	17.7	<u>14.7</u>	<u>28.0</u>	18.2	17.5
H	<u>14.1</u>	21.7	<u>25.7</u>	20.1	18.6	16.1	22.5	<u>14.2</u>	16.1
		C-4-11			C-4-17			C-4-22	
L	<u>24.7</u>	16.1	19.7	17.3	17.7	13.0	<u>25.9</u>	20.1	<u>13.9</u>
M	20.5	19.2	<u>13.0</u>	27.6	18.8	<u>9.6</u>	20.0	15.2	19.7
H	24.4	18.6	16.4	<u>31.0</u>	15.1	16.1	20.5	19.8	16.3
		C-4-12			C-4-18			C-4-23	
L	20.4	16.1	15.5	<u>27.6</u>	21.2	<u>12.4</u>	24.3	16.1	20.9
M	18.6	16.8	17.3	0	15.7	13.8	<u>28.5</u>	19.2	<u>13.0</u>
H	<u>30.2</u>	19.8	<u>14.7</u>	18.3	19.4	15.2	24.4	18.6	16.3
		C-4-13			C-4-19			C-4-24	
L	20.5	15.2	<u>14.3</u>	25.0	16.1	20.2	18.3	16.9	16.1
M	<u>25.0</u>	18.8	22.7	19.4	19.2	19.7	20.6	17.7	<u>15.1</u>
H	24.3	20.2	14.0	<u>28.1</u>	17.7	<u>15.6</u>	<u>37.2</u>	17.1	19.7
		C-4-14			C-4-20			C-4-25	
L	<u>36.2</u>	18.1	15.4	21.0	15.2	13.0	18.8	16.5	14.7
M	22.5	16.5	25.7	<u>24.7</u>	18.2	<u>11.8</u>	24.6	<u>14.2</u>	14.3
H	23.6	18.6	<u>15.3</u>	0	18.6	17.3	<u>30.2</u>	20.9	23.6
		C-4-16			C-4-21			C-4-26	
L	16.3	16.1	13.9	27.6	16.0	21.8	18.6	<u>13.6</u>	21.4
M	<u>36.2</u>	18.2	<u>9.9</u>	19.4	19.8	15.1	<u>34.4</u>	18.8	13.9
H	0	19.4	16.1	<u>28.1</u>	18.2	<u>12.1</u>	24.7	20.1	15.4

Table A-6 (*Continued*)

	L	M	H	L	M	H	L	M	H
		C-4-27			C-4-36			C-5-19	
L	13.8	<u>11.0</u>	<u>36.9</u>	13.9	18.2	16.4	<u>14.7</u>	<u>25.7</u>	16.1
M	18.3	16.9	21.4	16.2	<u>13.4</u>	14.7	16.5	23.1	20.1
H	26.7	16.1	12.1	16.1	20.9	<u>19.7</u>	20.8	<u>14.7</u>	18.5
		C-4-28			C-5-7			C-5-20	
L	20.2	15.2	15.4	18.6	20.5	21.4	13.8	10.7	24.6
M	<u>26.7</u>	17.3	<u>11.5</u>	19.0	<u>37.8</u>	18.1	16.2	<u>9.2</u>	<u>26.2</u>
H	24.7	14.8	16.4	<u>16.1</u>	16.8	16.2	0	14.7	18.5
		C-4-30			C-5-8			C-5-22	
L	18.8	<u>13.0</u>	16.4	<u>13.0</u>	13.4	16.1	16.6	<u>30.2</u>	20.7
M	21.8	18.6	14.3	16.0	20.1	16.8	16.1	20.5	18.8
H	<u>31.0</u>	16.9	18.5	22.1	<u>42.2</u>	19.4	22.1	<u>15.6</u>	18.1
		C-4-31			C-5-9			C-5-23	
L	<u>25.8</u>	20.1	<u>14.7</u>	<u>15.7</u>	20.5	16.8	16.6	<u>37.8</u>	0
M	20.5	16.1	19.7	16.1	20.6	18.5	<u>15.6</u>	20.2	18.9
H	15.3	18.6	16.1	16.9	<u>30.4</u>	18.3	20.5	21.2	18.5
		C-4-32			C-5-18			C-5-25	
L	<u>31.0</u>	16.5	20.0	0	12.0	18.1	16.5	17.4	17.2
M	28.1	19.6	15.1	14.7	<u>10.7</u>	<u>21.2</u>	15.7	<u>15.2</u>	16.8
H	24.7	16.9	<u>14.7</u>	16.3	0	19.9	23.8	<u>30.2</u>	21.4
		C-5-26			C-5-36			C-6-23	
L	20.5	21.0	16.8	18.2	15.2	19.0	23.2	22.9	16.4
M	<u>16.0</u>	<u>26.0</u>	19.4	15.2	<u>12.4</u>	15.6	<u>25.3</u>	18.3	<u>13.0</u>
H	16.9	20.9	16.1	15.6	<u>36.2</u>	18.3	19.3	16.4	20.7
		C-5-27			C-6-7			C-6-25	
L	23.2	20.2	17.2	28.1	21.4	20.7	17.3	18.3	14.7
M	16.6	<u>36.6</u>	18.4	<u>36.5</u>	17.3	15.2	24.3	16.0	<u>13.9</u>
H	<u>16.1</u>	17.1	20.9	16.9	18.3	<u>13.4</u>	<u>31.0</u>	21.4	21.2

Table A-6 (*Continued*)

	L	M	H	L	M	H	L	M	H
		C-5-30			C-6-12			C-6-24	
L	20.2	14.1	17.3	19.5	18.1	14.5	16.8	13.4	10.7
M	15.7	16.8	18.6	20.2	16.3	18.5	20.6	18.2	19.5
H	15.4	25.7	18.5	24.3	21.5	17.7	31.9	26.7	34.4
		C-5-31			C-6-13			C-7-8	
L	25.0	36.6	19.4	18.5	18.9	15.7	20.9	13.0	11.1
M	16.6	20.2	28.1	28.8	18.3	25.5	20.8	15.8	16.1
H	18.2	15.6	16.8	20.6	24.6	14.7	20.9	22.1	20.2
		C-5-32			C-6-14			C-7-9	
L	29.5	21.1	17.7	18.2	22.2	14.1	21.2	15.2	15.2
M	17.1	23.5	22.0	25.0	15.7	16.6	20.9	17.3	20.2
H	16.2	20.2	16.1	20.9	19.4	16.9	24.6	36.5	16.1
		C-7-10			C-7-23			C-7-31	
L	20.8	19.6	17.8	16.6	33.8	16.1	20.1	38.1	24.3
M	20.9	17.3	28.0	20.7	16.7	18.3	25.7	18.2	14.2
H	0	36.5	14.3	21.4	17.1	16.1	21.4	16.4	13.8
		C-7-18			C-7-25			C-7-32	
L	24.6	17.7	11.5	17.7	18.7	16.2	23.6	17.1	13.7
M	20.9	14.1	10.0	18.2	15.8	14.2	22.5	36.5	18.8
H	18.9	18.2	17.2	21.4	26.7	31.0	18.2	22.1	16.1
		C-7-19			C-7-26			C-7-36	
L	25.0	17.6	20.9	21.4	15.8	10.6	20.9	18.0	19.3
M	20.0	25.9	15.5	15.7	19.4	18.8	15.1	13.3	16.1
H	16.8	16.8	20.5	20.9	35.7	16.5	27.5	31.9	14.1
		C-7-20			C-7-27			C-8-9	
L	24.6	13.0	12.0	30.4	20.6	17.8	9.9	15.9	27.2
M	16.3	21.5	16.1	21.4	18.2	18.3	13.4	16.4	21.8
H	21.4	17.7	11.8	20.7	35.7	12.2	16.6	26.6	19.7

Table A-6 (*Continued*)

	L	M	H	L	M	H	L	M	H
		C-7-22			C-7-30			C-8-10	
L	18.4	37.2	25.0	16.3	19.8	16.2	20.9	17.7	27.2
M	25.7	25.8	14.2	20.5	19.4	14.3	13.8	16.4	21.5
H	21.4	16.4	16.1	26.5	15.0	22.3	10.9	16.1	20.0
		C-8-18			C-8-25			C-8-32	
L	24.6	14.3	29.9	10.7	16.1	20.6	13.7	16.4	21.2
M	10.7	16.1	17.8	11.8	16.0	16.3	18.2	26.0	40.4
H	16.1	0	19.9	21.2	30.4	29.1	13.0	18.1	21.2
		C-8-19			C-8-26			C-8-36	
L	16.6	20.3	26.7	15.1	16.8	21.2	7.5	16.8	20.2
M	12.5	17.9	20.2	13.0	15.7	25.4	12.9	14.7	25.2
H	15.6	16.6	20.9	14.8	22.2	22.1	16.9	22.3	19.0
		C-8-20			C-8-27			C-9-18	
L	13.0	14.5	14.7	16.2	16.8	22.1	17.7	16.5	19.2
M	19.8	16.0	21.8	14.0	15.7	20.4	18.5	13.0	12.4
H	11.8	16.2	20.2	12.2	18.1	23.8	14.3	23.3	17.3
		C-8-22			C-8-30			C-9-19	
L	14.6	24.3	27.2	12.5	16.4	19.4	25.7	22.6	18.3
M	13.4	14.7	22.4	13.4	16.1	20.9	15.5	19.4	19.7
H	15.6	16.8	20.2	14.1	21.4	27.2	16.5	16.4	27.5
		C-8-23			C-8-31			C-9-23	
L	10.7	16.1	23.7	18.6	24.3	26.0	15.0	24.3	18.3
M	13.2	25.3	23.7	15.0	15.5	29.1	20.6	18.8	30.4
H	16.2	16.6	20.9	9.9	16.8	19.4	17.4	16.4	16.2
		C-9-25			C-9-32			C-12-31	
L	16.5	20.2	16.6	16.8	18.5	24.6	25.2	27.1	20.9
M	14.3	14.5	18.1	26.2	18.8	26.6	16.1	17.4	29.2
H	21.4	21.4	36.7	16.1	20.2	16.9	14.5	18.5	17.7

Table A-6 (*Continued*)

	L	M	H	L	M	H	L	M	H
		C-9-26			C-9-36			C-12-32	
L	16.8	15.8	18.3	16.8	18.2	0	16.4	18.5	19.4
M	15.7	18.5	22.2	14.3	15.1	13.5	15.9	18.2	36.5
H	16.1	20.9	18.5	0	13.4	22.2	18.3	16.2	20.1
		C-9-27			C-10-22			C-13-30	
L	16.1	21.2	27.2	20.1	24.6	26.6	15.2	18.3	16.2
M	21.4	16.7	16.9	23.1	31.0	14.2	18.1	16.9	16.1
H	15.2	16.7	20.1	21.4	17.4	16.1	14.6	25.7	36.6
		C-9-30			C-10-25			C-13-31	
L	16.8	17.3	16.3	16.2	41.3	16.1	23.3	21.7	25.5
M	16.1	21.4	20.1	22.4	16.0	14.0	16.1	23.6	11.8
H	23.6	18.5	19.7	21.5	21.2	41.9	14.3	17.7	16.5
		C-9-31			C-12-30			C-13-32	
L	36.6	24.3	20.1	16.4	12.5	20.5	18.5	21.5	16.2
M	21.5	13.9	16.9	15.9	15.0	19.4	12.0	18.2	25.6
H	13.2	17.5	27.5	14.7	20.2	33.8	16.2	25.2	15.4
		C-18-19			C-18-27			C-19-22	
L	17.2	14.3	18.2	17.7	15.8	23.6	24.7	20.1	19.0
M	10.0	18.2	22.7	16.6	14.1	18.3	16.5	15.2	28.1
H	18.5	10.0	18.8	9.2	15.4	12.1	0	23.7	16.8
		C-18-22			C-18-30			C-19-23	
L	0	13.0	16.3	7.8	15.7	18.2	24.7	18.2	22.1
M	25.7	15.2	18.3	17.7	14.7	16.1	31.1	18.8	10.6
H	14.7	21.2	18.8	18.5	15.2	31.0	15.0	21.5	18.5
		C-18-23			C-18-31			C-19-25	
L	0	15.4	15.3	0	14.7	18.3	16.2	19.7	16.8
M	9.2	11.9	18.3	29.6	15.2	24.6	25.0	15.7	15.1
H	17.7	21.2	21.4	14.3	20.9	15.2	33.0	27.2	20.7

Table A-6 (*Continued*)

	L	M	H	L	M	H	L	M	H
		C-18-25			C-18-32			C-19-26	
L	14.7	19.9	<u>14.1</u>	18.1	20.9	<u>26.2</u>	21.0	18.7	17.3
M	18.5	15.2	16.3	14.7	<u>10.4</u>	18.3	<u>17.2</u>	19.7	18.5
H	17.9	<u>21.4</u>	19.8	0	14.7	16.1	<u>24.7</u>	18.2	18.1
		C-18-26			C-18-36			C-19-27	
L	21.2	18.1	<u>21.4</u>	17.7	20.9	<u>24.6</u>	25.0	20.0	16.8
M	16.6	<u>11.9</u>	18.3	14.7	13.1	15.2	17.6	<u>25.9</u>	16.8
H	13.8	15.4	16.1	19.2	<u>13.0</u>	18.3	20.9	<u>15.5</u>	20.5
		C-19-30			C-20-25			C-22-26	
L	16.0	17.0	16.1	<u>13.0</u>	16.1	14.7	16.6	15.2	19.1
M	16.5	21.5	<u>13.4</u>	15.2	16.3	18.5	16.0	19.6	18.5
H	<u>25.2</u>	19.8	18.5	<u>26.9</u>	21.5	20.2	<u>25.0</u>	<u>13.9</u>	20.2
		C-19-31			C-20-26			C-22-27	
L	26.6	20.1	22.0	15.2	<u>21.5</u>	20.9	24.6	19.7	17.2
M	15.2	17.4	<u>28.1</u>	<u>11.8</u>	18.3	16.6	<u>26.6</u>	17.6	19.0
H	<u>13.8</u>	24.2	16.4	14.2	16.2	16.1	20.4	<u>14.3</u>	20.5
		C-19-32			C-20-27			C-22-30	
L	23.3	<u>23.7</u>	17.7	<u>13.8</u>	<u>26.2</u>	16.1	16.3	18.3	<u>14.2</u>
M	21.7	18.8	<u>15.1</u>	14.1	18.2	19.0	18.1	<u>14.2</u>	18.6
H	21.1	19.7	22.1	14.7	14.3	20.9	<u>27.2</u>	18.8	18.5
		C-19-36			C-22-23			C-22-31	
L	0	19.9	17.3	20.8	15.2	24.0	23.0	18.9	<u>36.2</u>
M	16.2	<u>10.5</u>	15.1	20.9	18.3	<u>12.0</u>	16.2	17.6	20.5
H	15.6	19.7	<u>27.5</u>	20.7	<u>28.1</u>	18.1	0	<u>14.1</u>	16.8
		C-20-22			C-22-25			C-22-32	
L	<u>13.0</u>	16.2	0	18.4	16.5	17.2	24.6	20.5	18.5
M	15.2	<u>18.3</u>	0	20.1	<u>14.0</u>	16.4	<u>26.6</u>	18.9	15.1
H	15.4	15.4	18.1	28.7	<u>29.6</u>	20.7	20.1	<u>14.3</u>	20.2

Table A-6 (*Continued*)

	L	M	H		L	M	H		L	M	H
	C-22-36				C-23-31				C-25-30		
L	0	18.2	17.7		25.2	20.5	20.7		18.9	16.3	18.2
M	21.4	13.1	14.9		16.4	16.7	28.1		15.4	17.9	20.9
H	35.1	16.9	27.2		22.1	12.0	16.6		19.7	15.1	28.8
	C-23-25				C-23-32				C-25-31		
L	18.3	13.0	16.8		29.5	20.5	17.7		19.4	24.8	36.6
M	19.4	13.4	15.8		22.5	20.2	24.6		16.5	13.9	26.5
H	32.5	27.2	21.4		18.3	16.8	16.1		14.7	15.8	20.9
	C-23-26				C-23-36				C-25-32		
L	21.3	20.5	17.3		0	15.2	18.5		16.2	16.4	21.4
M	19.7	18.2	22.0		15.2	10.5	15.6		18.3	19.1	30.4
H	22.1	20.9	15.0		16.9	24.4	19.2		18.3	14.3	29.6
	C-23-27				C-25-26				C-25-36		
L	24.3	20.2	16.6		16.2	15.2	21.4		16.8	15.2	21.2
M	16.9	18.3	18.5		19.4	15.7	25.2		15.4	14.7	13.1
H	16.4	13.4	20.9		16.9	20.1	32.0		16.9	14.1	36.9
	C-23-30				C-25-27				C-26-27		
L	22.5	13.9	16.2		17.2	24.4	30.7		16.4	24.6	23.2
M	15.7	20.1	17.7		17.6	15.4	21.4		18.3	18.2	25.2
H	18.3	20.2	18.5		15.4	13.4	20.9		20.7	14.1	16.1
	C-26-30				C-27-31				C-30-36		
L	16.2	18.3	22.3		24.3	31.6	20.7		17.3	17.7	18.5
M	17.7	16.0	16.1		21.5	15.2	20.5		16.2	16.1	14.7
H	18.3	19.1	22.3		16.6	19.0	12.1		18.3	14.2	16.9
	C-26-31				C-27-32				C-31-32		
L	20.7	28.6	25.1		16.4	20.4	23.3		26.2	23.6	17.7
M	16.6	18.2	16.5		27.5	18.3	20.9		31.6	17.0	18.8
H	17.3	18.5	15.2		22.1	15.3	15.4		24.7	16.1	15.2

Table A-6 (*Continued*)

	L	M	H	L	M	H	L	M	H
		C-26-32			C-27-36			C-31-36	
L	17.3	19.4	0	17.3	18.4	13.6	0	19.7	17.3
M	15.1	18.3	26.6	13.5	20.3	12.5	20.7	13.4	14.5
H	0	17.0	16.9	30.4	14.2	13.4	18.3	15.6	27.3
		C-26-36			C-30-31			C-32-36	
L	16.8	18.5	0	19.4	22.7	36.6	18.1	12.3	0
M	13.0	14.7	16.1	12.5	15.0	19.7	10.9	15.1	15.2
H	36.2	19.7	13.9	14.2	16.8	16.8	0	27.4	14.2
		C-27-30			C-30-32			C-38-2	
L	16.4	22.1	11.1	16.4	18.6	18.5	17.7	16.1	15.2
M	17.3	17.6	14.7	18.3	16.0	30.4	20.1	20.6	11.8
H	24.3	16.9	18.2	16.3	15.4	18.3	20.9	18.2	15.9
		C-38-3			C-38-9			C-38-31	
L	17.7	17.2	12.5	17.3	27.2	12.1	36.5	19.4	25.9
M	21.7	24.3	23.9	21.4	18.8	14.7	20.5	20.2	16.1
H	30.7	19.7	22.0	36.5	18.0	16.9	19.4	13.2	14.1
		C-38-4			C-38-22			C-38-36	
L	25.8	25.0	18.3	28.3	16.3	28.4	18.5	18.2	6.9
M	20.1	16.0	16.1	25.8	19.7	14.2	13.0	16.1	14.7
H	21.4	15.4	14.3	20.2	18.3	11.1	36.2	24.6	14.1
		C-38-5			C-38-23				
L	22.1	20.1	15.2	24.0	19.7	16.9			
M	20.5	17.2	25.7	26.0	19.4	15.9			
H	21.2	17.8	12.5	19.4	18.4	14.3			
		C-38-7			C-38-25				
L	21.4	20.5	22.5	17.7	16.2	16.5			
M	19.0	18.2	35.7	17.5	24.3	13.9			
H	31.0	19.8	14.2	21.5	23.9	28.0			
		C-38-8			C-38-26				
L	15.1	17.2	11.8	20.9	13.3	13.9			
M	17.3	24.3	14.7	19.4	18.8	18.3			
H	22.1	19.7	25.2	29.3	24.3	16.1			

INDEX

Individual countries are covered in the items referred to.

181